SYRIA

through writers' eyes

SYRIA
through writers' eyes

Written and edited by Marius Kociejowski
With linocuts by Mungo McCosh

ELAND
LONDON

First published by Eland Publishing Ltd
61 Exmouth Market, London EC1R 4QL in 2006
This revised, enlarged edition published 2010

ISBN 978 0 907871 84 2

Cover design and typesetting by Rose Baring & Katy Kedward
Front cover image: The Picturesque Entrance of the Aleppo Citadel
by Vartan Derounian © Nareg Publications
Back cover image: Arab peasant drinking coffee
by Vartan Derounian © Nareg Publications
Linocuts © Mungo McCosh
Map © Reginald Piggott

Contents

Maps & Illustrations

Acknowledgements

W E WOULD LIKE to thank all of the authors for making this collection possible by allowing us to use their material, and gratefully acknowledge permission to reprint copyright material as follows:

Ross Burns; Colin Thubron for the extract from *Mirror to Damascus*; Laurence Deonna for the extract from *Syrians: A Travelogue* (1992-94) translated by Christopher Snow; Brigid Keenan; Sarah Maguire; Kegan Paul for the extract from *The Black Tents of Arabia* by Carl R Raswan; Jacques Réda and his translator Jennie Feldman; the Special Collections Library, Robinson Library, University of Newcastle upon Tyne for permission to use Gertrude Bell's letter to Charles Doughty-Wylie; Nigel Wheale and Walid Abdul-Hamid for their translation of Al-Mutanabbi; Mark Hudson; Eric Ormsby; Harper Collins for the extract from *From The Holy Mountain* by William Dalrymple; Frances and Katharine Fedden for the extracts from *Syria and Lebanon* by Robin Fedden; Peter McDonald; Barnaby Rogerson; John R Murray for permission to publish a letter from *Letters from Syria* by Freya Stark; Josceline Dimbleby for memories of her Damascus childhood; Gerald Maclean; Philippa Scott and Peter Clark. And thanks to Mungo McCosh for his linocuts. 'The Master Calligrapher of Aleppo' first appeared in the online magazine *The Bow-Wow Shop*.

All the extracts have been reprinted as they originally appeared in English, which accounts for any apparent discrepancies in spelling.

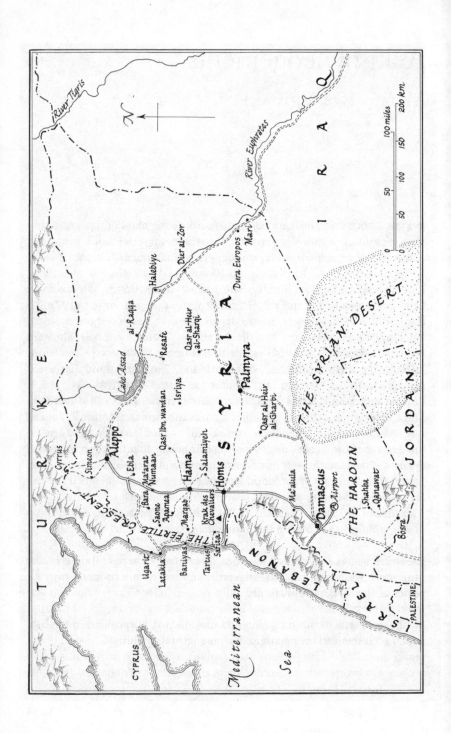

Preface

Marius Kociejowski

THIS BOOK comprises, for the greater part, the writings of foreign visitors to Syria. It is a view of the country as seen not just by English people but also by those of other nationalities – American, French, German, Italian, Portuguese, Swiss and early Arab and Persian travellers. Their writings span roughly six centuries. The book is characterised both by the sins of omission – there are some notable absences – and the virtues of commission; it is to be hoped there will be a few surprises. Its structure is based on the most likely itinerary of a traveller going to Syria for the first time. It will take him from Damascus, through the Syrian Desert to Palmyra and from there to Aleppo, with a swing north-west to Saint Simeon and the Dead Cities, and then south through the fertile crescent which includes Hama and Homs and the Crusader Castles, and, finally, south from there into the Jebel Druze and onwards to Bosra. Afterwards, the reader will have to make his own way home. The aim is that he be given some additional historical and literary weight to what he sees. The most abstract section, in a sense, because there is so little for an untrained eye, is that devoted to the Syrian Desert. It is, in some respects, the most vital: the desert was not just the conduit for trade over many centuries but also the area that helped define the personality of the Syrian people.

Syria, for all its woes, has been blessed with a sympathetic literature.

C F Volney, in the preface to his *Voyage en Egypte et en Syrie* (1787), states, 'I have endeavoured to maintain the spirit with which I conducted my researches into facts; that is, an impartial love of truth. I have restrained myself from indulging any sallies of the imagination, though I am no stranger to the power of such illusion over the generality of readers; but I am of opinion that travels belong to the department of history, and not that of romance. I have not therefore described countries as more beautiful than they appeared to me. I have not represented their inhabitants more virtuous, not more wicked than I found them, and I have perhaps been enabled to see them such as they really are, since I have never received from them either benefits or injuries.' The same holds true for all the writers presented here. They would appear to be innocent

1

of the charges of Orientalism that are so often levelled at anyone writing from a foreign perspective. Those who make the accusations are, by and large, those who are paid to do so. Academe is its own life support system. It is to be wondered if Orientalism is not the province of a small handful of people, artists in particular, who, within a very short historical period, sought not the Orient of reality but the Orient inside themselves. At least some of them ought to be treated with indulgence. The truly pernicious tends to come under smarter guises. I have been impressed in my readings by the spirit of enquiry that typifies even the most obscure writers. A number of these lesser works are appalling, true, but they are so mainly out of blighted innocence or, in some instances, because the writers themselves would have been just as appalling at home. Occidentalism is just as much their problem. Others I simply chose to ignore. They have been mostly ignored in any case, and to set them up in order to knock them down again, as being characteristic of the worst in human nature, or as supporting some thesis on people's inability to step outside their own culture, arguments which, after all, could be turned against the Arabs themselves, seems to me to serve but little purpose.

'Syria *is* history,' a Phoenician from Aleppo tells me, adding that this is where my focus should be, and while I could not agree with him more there comes a point when an undertaking such as this would burst at the seams if one were to include more than even a fraction of that country's history. What, for example, would one do with the Crusades alone? What could one say about them that would not make my Syrian acquaintance wince? There is no area of the country that has not been steeped in blood, and in this respect it is always worth recalling the words of the poet al-Ma'arri: 'Take care where you walk because you walk upon the dead.' There are several excellent histories of Syria, whereas this is the first collection of its kind. It is, as the title says, a perspective of the country as seen *through writers' eyes*. This said, the majority of the pieces at the very least reflect history and do so without losing the immediacy that comes of direct experience. After all, when considering the observations of Volney or della Valle or Raswan, are we not looking at history as it is being made? My choices are, to an extent, random: I have sought to cater to various interests and tastes – the shopper is invited to share the carpet with the musicologist, the versifier and the lover of antiquities. Also important to me have been writers' imaginative responses, which bespeak a truth beyond brute facts, although, sadly, the fiction and poetry inspired by Syria have been a bit on the lean side. Another criterion, almost too obvious to mention, is that the works chosen be pleasurable to read.

I am grateful to the following who have assisted me in my researches: Brigid Keenan, Gabriel Levin, Philip Mansel, Christopher Middleton, Alain Richert, Yasser Sagherie, Philippa Scott, Zahed Tajeddin and my publishers, Barnaby Rogerson and Rose Baring.

Editorial Note

So that the reader may be kept in the proper time frame most of the pieces have been dated with the year of composition whenever possible, otherwise with the year of first publication. No attempt has been made to regularise the spelling of names and places, which vary from author to author and from century to century.

Introduction:
Time Travelling in Syria

Ross Burns

IN THE FIRST EDITION of *Monuments of Syria*, which was completed in 1991, I opened the foreword with the rash remark: 'The exploration of Syria is one of the most satisfying pleasures that remain in the field of travel.' Such assertions are often destined to have a limited shelf life, so quickly can undiscovered gems in the world of travel become over-exploited by mass tourism. Some, like Egypt, manage to survive the onslaught through the sheer scale and splendour of their ruins. (An amazing number of coach- and boat-loads of tourists can be crammed into the huge Karnak Temple complex without too much pain.) Syria, however, remains a largely undiscovered destination, which reveals itself to fairly select and dedicated groups of travellers or enterprising individuals. The present book is a wonderful initiative by its publishers to remind modern readers that Syria has long attracted in some of the most astute and adventurous travellers of recent centuries reactions that still await the visitor who is willing to put aside the preconceptions fed by the mass media.

The reasons for these preconceptions, of course, are largely political and related to wider Middle East issues. They have little to do with the situation a traveller meets on the ground in Syria where hospitality towards foreigners is unreserved and genuine. In fact, Syria is one of the safest travel destinations and the contrast between uninformed supposition and reality could not be starker. If the traveller lets the imagination wander freely through the wonderful panorama of the past that Syria presents, there are few readily accessible destinations that present the same stimulus and satisfaction. What is the essence of this experience, an experience that strikes the traveller in so many different ways?

As part of my informal continuing 'market research' to check how *Monuments* is meeting the demands of travellers who want to get the most out of their time in Syria, I make a point of asking recent visitors which site struck them as the most singular and striking experience. I get a fair proportion of 'Palmyras' and a number of 'Aleppos' but on the whole most of those whom I interrogate find it difficult to choose. Much depends on passing factors of mood, weather, the light at a certain time of day.

I must admit I have the same problem, even after twenty years or more of living in and visiting the country. It is simply impossible to nominate one site in Syria and stick to it in the same way that one might nominate a standout choice like the Karnak Temple or the Pyramids in Egypt or Petra in Jordan. One week I might choose the Krak des Chevaliers, another the remote fortress at Halebiye, that massive but forlorn Byzantine outpost along the mid-Euphrates. I have had the odd day of intense absorption re-creating the last days of Dura Europos or a wonderful insight into the Bronze Age splendours of Ebla. The Roman theatre at Bosra never fails to take the breath away when I emerge from its internal passages into the blinding light of day in the theatre's *cavea*, the monument almost as intact as it was one thousand eight hundred years ago. The simple symmetry of much Ayyubid architecture strikes me often as the embodiment of perfection. I cannot enter the Fardous Madrasa in Aleppo without realising that my eye has found a sublimity that could never be described. The courtyard of the Umayyad Mosque in Damascus numbs the senses with its brilliant pastiche of the history that has flowed through it.

There is an explanation for the visitor's surfeit of choice. It reflects the extraordinary diversity of historical and archaeological material that Syria presents. The range and coverage of historical periods outclasses even Egypt where the spectacular ruins concentrate around two main periods – the high Pharaonic and the Islamic Middle Ages. Only Turkey (with its much greater geographical area) rivals Syria's coverage of most historical eras and there the sites are often difficult of access or poorly documented.

The fact is that there are only a few centuries here and there where Syria's record of the past is not incomparably more complete that most of its neighbours. It would be nice to have a bit more evidence of the Hellenistic period (the Romans did such a good job of developing *Provincia Syria* that they obliterated the more modest achievements of their Greek predecessors) and almost nothing has survived of the Abbasids. On the whole, however, Syria is an incomparable haven for researchers in practically all periods from the Neolithic to the Ottoman.

One hundred years ago, this rich cavalcade of historical material was explored for the first time on a major scale by a series of American expeditions, largely raised through Princeton University. The expeditions were led by Howard Crosby Butler, who in turn had been inspired by the French traveller, the Marquis de Vôgué, whose brilliant illustrations of some of the more spectacular sites had first aroused European interest in the richness of Syria's historical material. Butler and his team, which included experts in both Semitic and classical inscriptions, criss-crossed northern and southern Syria (including parts of present-day northern Jordan) and recorded literally hundreds of previously unknown sites. Even then they were hardly doing more than skimming over Syria's past although the numerous volumes Crosby and his experts published have formed an incomparable knowledge base to which all future researchers are still indebted. And we are not talking here of 'sites' comprising a few stray stones or fallen column drums. These are substantive settlements with recognisable buildings – usually churches or houses but including many tombs and even inns – often simply lacking a roof to serve equally well the purpose for which they were built one thousand five hundred years ago.

In the northern zone explored by Butler, the area of hill country between Aleppo and Antioch, there are some six hundred or more settlements with such substantive remains. Butler documented only a fraction of them and a few more have been surveyed in the superb study of the Frenchman, George Tchalenko, and in the works of a team of Franciscan researchers. Few locations have been subject to excavation, perhaps because the range from which to choose is simply so bewildering. But thanks to Butler and his successors what we have in this one corner of Syria is perhaps the fullest record anywhere of the late classical world – a world largely undisturbed until the repopulation of the area in recent times. If you want a glimpse of what late antiquity was like, there is no better way to experience it than driving around this hill country east and south of Aleppo, occasionally stopping off at one of the larger villages or scrambling a few hundred metres from the road to walk through a still deserted settlement that was last populated one thousand two hundred years ago. There is simply no part of the Mediterranean world which presents this experience in such a formidable concentration.

There is a counterpart region in southern Syria, which also presents the transition from Roman to Byzantine in wonderful detail. The basalt-built towns of the Hauran south of Damascus reveal a prosperous series of communities well integrated into the economy of Roman-Byzantine Syria. Even the dense volcanic stone yielded to the skills of the local craftsmen who shaped from it decorative and sculptural elements which still grace their buildings as elegantly as Roman marble. Even small towns like Qanawat (ancient Canatha) offered a standard of living and of civic amenities that rivalled Italy. The beautiful civic complex at Qanawat, later adapted to provide two churches clustered around an atrium, survives to this day as a witness to this lifestyle.

The late classical world is only a part of the whole range of any Syrian experience. The high classical era is equally well represented particularly through sites like Palmyra and Apamea, ruins again largely undisturbed by later occupation and which still yield their secrets to the excavators and the restorers. The Bronze Age record includes a number of sites that are of great historic importance and help fill the significant gaps in the scientific record left by a pattern of research which, since the nineteenth century, had heavily emphasized areas of Biblical or Mesopotamian civilization and forgot about the bits in between. While Bronze Age sites elsewhere often provide little stimulus to a visitor who can recognize them as little more than holes in the ground, Syrian sites including Ebla, Ugarit and Mari retain significant architectural features, which illustrate graphically the achievements of Bronze Age civilization.

One of the most fascinating periods in the Syrian cavalcade is the transition from late Antiquity to Islam. The first Arab dynasty, the Umayyads, chose Damascus as their capital but particularly in the second half-century of their one-hundred-year rule, they were a peripatetic elite. They built a series of 'desert palaces' along the cultivated fringes of modern Syria and Jordan. The word 'palaces' is somewhat misleading since the complexes served a variety of practical purposes and were not simply centres of sybaritic indulgence. Both countries are doing a great deal to present the palaces to visitors. The results in many cases, especially at Qasr al-Hayr East, one hundred kilometres north-east of Palmyra, are a spectacular tribute to the inventiveness and boldness of the Umayyad vision, which so successfully integrated many classical elements into their Semitic world. To see the extraordinary success of this Umayyad synthesis, the visitor need go no further than the main doorway to the National Museum in Damascus where the gateway to the western Qasr al-Hayr shows what can happen when a fresh Arab decorative vision is applied to a form basically native to the more mundane purposes of a Roman fortress entrance.

It is the later Islamic centuries which fittingly provide Damascus and Aleppo with the status of 'living museums' – functioning Arab cities, which still retain much of the economic and social environment in which the monuments of the past retain their roles. There is no better record of the architectural achievements of the Zengid-Ayyubid rulers than the surviving mosques and *madrasas* of Aleppo and Damascus. The tomb of Nur al-Din remains modestly tucked in among the bazaars of the commercial heart of Damascus. Above his cenotaph, though, is poised one of the most sublime realizations of the use of *muqarnas* (small triangular segments of a sphere), the basic shape of a dome rising effortlessly from a square. Twelfth-century Islamic architecture excelled in its use of sparsely decorated basic shapes with a harmony and sense of proportion rarely matched. Yet it remains one of the most neglected fields of world architecture. If you type 'Ayyubid architecture' into any search engine, you will find only one book on the subject in print (Yasser Tabbaa's study of Ayyubid Aleppo). There is no general survey except for the excellent work by Terry Allen, which had to find a publisher on the internet where thankfully it can still be accessed with all its illustrations.

Syria, much more so than Cairo or Jerusalem, remains the heartland of this sober architectural achievement.

The Zengids and Ayyubids could only devote a proportion of their resources to piety and the consolidation of Islam in the face of the Crusades. Much of their resources had to be devoted to military architecture, a field barely exploited in the earlier Islamic centuries when siege warfare was rare. Yet almost from a zero base, the Zengids and Ayyubids also developed a spectacular range of fortresses, many of which share the common feature of a huge conical mound with its top cut off to provide a fortified *enceinte*. The sides were then clad with smooth limestone blocks to form a *glacis*. Examples of this form are still found at Aleppo and Harim as well as at Qalaat Najm, Qalaat Jaber and Qalaat Rahba along the Euphrates. The wonderful gems of Crusader military architecture in Syria, the great fortresses of the Krak des Chevaliers, Marqab and the 'Castle of Saladin', have been celebrated in several accounts and surveys. Much has been heard about them. Extraordinarily, there have been no counterpart studies of the Zengid-Ayyubid fortresses which matched them on the eastern side of the Orontes and which showed equal innovation in adapting to the new military environment the Crusader confrontation brought to the region.

The next Islamic empire, that of the Mamluks, moved the centre of gravity to Cairo where the scale of their building achievements simply outweighs all the other monuments in the secondary cities of the Empire such as Aleppo, Damascus, Jerusalem and Tripoli. Yet Syria has some wonderful gems of Mamluk architecture, particularly important for their illustration of the extent to which the Cairo Mamluks borrowed many of their ideas from Ayyubid Aleppo and Damascus. Ottoman architecture, too, avoided the gigantism of the capital (in this case, Istanbul), but its debt to the Syrian repertoire is also well illustrated in such local projects as the Tekkiye built by Sultan Suleiman II ('the Magnificent') in recognition of the growing importance of Damascus as a key stop on the Hajj route to Mecca.

The sheer range and number of Syrian monuments and sites explains why the amount of research now pouring out of Syria in the archaeological and historical fields is expanding so vigorously. When I wrote the first edition of *Monuments* it took a solid three years of reading and writing, admittedly building on earlier years of weekend visits to sites. To revise the work now will require at least another three years. In fifteen years the amount of research published has simply doubled the volume of written material that has to be combed through.

A final reason why the experience of Syria is more deeply satisfying than even the most sybaritic Nile Cruise is that the visitor is largely left to form his or her own impressions of how the past unfolds. Many other countries of the eastern Mediterranean world try to impose a specific interpretation on the visitor whereas Syria and Jordan largely present the story as it comes. There may be the occasional effort to highlight the achievements of a particular era but that is often to correct a record, which has for many centuries been badly skewed by prejudice and an unwillingness to attribute to Arab and Islamic civilisations their due.

Perhaps *the* most important reason why a visit to Syria is more than a routine travel experience is that the rich tapestry of the past is experienced in a society which is still largely influenced by the traditions of that past. The customs of Arab hospitality live on in Syria in a way which is remarkable even by the standard of the rest of the Arab world. As a result, though the environment is strange, even exotic at times, the visitor feels entirely at home, part of a continuum which connects the present to the rich traditions of the country. Stand for a minute in the Aleppo souq and watch the faces and style of dress of the passing crowd. There is something from almost all of the past ten centuries of the city's history – the tea-seller in his Ottoman garb; the Kurdish women from the hills north of Aleppo; the inevitable boy on a donkey weaving a perilous path through the crowds; the Bedouin in his traditional clothes topped with a smart pinstriped jacket. There's no 'have a good day!' effusion and Syrians can often be reserved or cautious on first meeting but they respond well to a genuine interest in their country. You need no phoney folkloric experience to bring Syria's past alive. It's there all the time before your eyes in the unstinting welcome of its people.

I: Damascus

THE SYRIAN NOVELIST Rafik Schami writes: 'They say when a city has been lived in continuously for over a thousand years, its citizens inherit the accumulated eccentricities of ages past.' Damascus is its people. One Damascene I know, speaking of his home, describes it thus: 'There are treasures within the walls of this city. And not only physical ones. I know people who always dream of finding treasure, and who dig for jars of old coins, but there are far more obvious treasures one finds here. There are the people within these city walls (*sur*), whom you'd never meet on the outside.' What he says is reason enough to go there. If one travels *through people*, Damascus is one of the greatest cities in the world in which to confabulate.

As to the actual cityscape, travellers' accounts differ wildly over the ages, their impressions being of a place one either loves or hates. The city as it is today swings between the dour and the sublime – concrete vies with stone. That most highly esteemed of travellers, the Prophet Muhammad, seeing Damascus for the first time from the mountain above, declined to enter the city, saying it is not for anyone to enter Paradise twice in a lifetime. An irony, often lost on Damascenes, is that the city he saw would have been Christian in character – a church stood where the Umayyad mosque now is, and before that there was a Roman temple. There seems to be no getting to the bottom of the many layers in Syrian history. Nowadays, when one stands on the slopes of Mount Qasiyun, the pollution can be so bad one sees nothing of the old historical centre, just a thick yellow haze. The surrounding grey modernity is all too visible. And still my informant speaks of there being 'these reservoirs of energy, this holy ozone' – certain mosques, for example, inside of which he tells me, 'one feels one's soul is swimming.' There is more than enough in Damascus to satisfy an appetite for the azure.

Mukadassi, describing Damascus in 985, writes: 'The city is in itself a very pleasant place, but of its disadvantages are, that the climate is scorching and the inhabitants are turbulent. Fruit here is insipid, and meat hard; also the houses are small, and the streets sombre. Finally, the bread there is bad, and a livelihood is difficult to make.' The geographer Idrisi, writing in 1154, says, 'Damascus is the most beautiful city of Syria, the finest in situation, the most temperate in climate, the most humid in soil, having the greatest variety of fruits, and the utmost abundance of vegetables.' All very nice, but then he appears never to have visited there: Arab writers, however, were not adverse to hearsay. Yakut, writing in 1225, describes Damascus as 'the Garden of the Earth'. Arabs tend to praise, Europeans criticise: I have chosen those writers who allow the city the greatest latitude.

Where to begin other than with the Holy Bible, *The King James Version*. This is not to push Islam into second place, but merely to acknowledge that for many westerners their first idea of Damascus will be as the scene of the greatest turning point in the spread of Christianity, when Saul, soon to be Paul, walked through the Roman gate (*Bab Sharqi*), which still stands at one end of the street called Straight. Without so much as a single descriptive note, those passages from *Acts* provide the reader with a powerful sense of place, the drama enacted there so potent one may easily conjure one's own stage. What is the primary role of any author but to make his reader *see*? Whatever its dimensions, the imagined is bound to be a more accurate depiction of the area than what one sees today. The street called Straight was twice the width once; it must have been prettier too. At the far end of one of the lanes running off the street is the house of Ananias, where Saul took shelter, and whose original cellar survives. Mark Twain who visited Damascus writes: 'The street called Straight *is* straighter than a corkscrew, but not as straight as a rainbow. St Luke is careful not to commit himself; he does not say it is the street which is straight, but the "street which is *called* Straight." It is a fine piece of irony; it is the only facetious remark in the Bible.' Although the book containing this passage is almost *wholly* facetious in tone, *The Innocents Abroad* (1869) is entertaining nevertheless and to be relished for all the wrong reasons. The present reader will have to satisfy himself with the foregoing passage.

Another inhabitant I spoke to, when asked what he loved best about Damascus, answered immediately – *its stone*. The greatest bulk of stone is that which forms the Umayyad Mosque, also known as the Jami'a al-Umawi. In July 1184, the Spanish Arab Ibn Jubayr (1145-1317) visited Damascus. A man given to rhetorical flourishes, he devotes much space in his diary to a description of the city and, in particular, the mosque. A somewhat bridled version of what he wrote is included here, its opening passages containing a description, much of it derived from earlier writers such as Ja'kubi and Ibn al Fakid, of one of the most climatic moments in Damascene history, when in 635 (the year 14 in the Muslim calendar) the church was turned into a mosque.

The greatest Arab traveller of all, Ibn Battutah (1304-c.1369), left his native Tangiers in 1325 on a pilgrimage to Mecca and stayed away for almost three decades. His journeys, which took him as far as China, covered almost fifty thousand miles and he made a point of never going over any one road twice. In the spring of that first year he came to Damascus, but prior to reaching the city he visited, near Beirut, the tomb of Abu Ya'qub Yusuf, a native of Damascus once, and relates his story, which, with its blend of legend and moralistic purpose, demonstrates why the work from which it comes is the most famous travel narrative in mediaeval Arabic literature. Most recently Ibn Buttatah's reputation has been newly revived in the writings of Tim Mackintosh-Smith who has been travelling in his footsteps, one leap at a time.

Arguably the first 'modern' account of Damascus is that provided by the Italian, Ludovico di Varthema, or Vertomannus (c.1465-1517). His *Itinerario* was first published in Italian at Rome in 1510 and an English translation by Richard Eden appeared in 1576. A native of Bologna, he set sail from Venice in 1502 and his object seemed to be one of adventure for adventure's sake. After adopting Islam, or else pretending to, he enrolled in the Mameluke garrison in Damascus and from there he made his way to Mecca, the first Christian to have made that dangerous pilgrimage. Later, when he was arrested as a Christian spy, one of the sultanas of Yemen secured his release, which suggests he had a certain panache. Richard Burton writes: 'For correctness of observation and readiness of wit [he] stands in the foremost rank of the old Oriental travellers.'

The French poet, historian and statesman, Alphonse Lamartine (1790-1869), describes his journey into Damascus and although he has been criticised for not being wholly accurate in his depiction of the Orient, there is little cause to argue with the passages reproduced here. Poor Lamartine, his reputation as a poet was on the wane as early as 1911 when his biographer in the *Encyclopaedia Britannica* wrote, 'Lamartine's chief misfortune in poetry was not only that his note was a somewhat weak one, but that he could strike but one.' His *Voyage en Orient* was published in 1835.

Writing to Frank Savery in July 1913, James Elroy Flecker (1884-1915) says of *Gates of Damascus*: 'I consider this to be my greatest poem – and I am glad you seem to agree. It was inspired by Damascus itself by the way. I loathe the East and the Easterns and spent all my time there dreaming of Oxford. Yet it seems – even to hardened Orientalists – that I understand.' Surely this is a curious instance of a negative producing a positive, but then worse things have come of love. Flecker, who, in 1911, was vice-consul in Beirut, albeit a not terribly effective one, spent only three days in Damascus and the topography of his poem is doubtful at times, but it is fascinating to observe how for one who professed to dislike the Orient, it was the Orient that informs the best of his verse. A self-confessed Parnassian whose goal it was 'to create beauty, a beauty somewhat statuesque, dramatic, and objective, rather than intimate', Flecker was removed from the public eye by both Modernism and tuberculosis.

The problem of finding 'real' antiquities in the souq was as true in Isabel Burton's day as it is now. A chapter from her two-volume *The Inner Life of Syria* (1872) takes her imagined addressee on a shopping spree through the souqs of Damascus, and pauses at some length at a nargileh shop. She dwells on the pleasures of the weed. What she is too polite to mention is that when passing the mouthpiece of the *nargileh* to your neighbour be sure to bend the mouthpiece towards yourself unless, that is, the intention really is to make a sexual advance. Isabel (1831-1896) was Richard Burton's wife, and although she speaks of her relationship to him as being 'the mere bellows player to the organist', her writings are full of splendid insight and compare favourably to his writings on Syria. Many harsh words have been said against her for having committed, after her husband's death, the bulk of his private papers to the flames, but, in her defence, it has to be remembered she was instructed to do so by his apparition. Clearly she loved Damascus, describing it as 'my beautiful white City with her swelling domes and tapering minarets, her glittering old crescents set in the green of every shade, sparkling with her fountains and streams.' She kept there a menagerie, so varied its species it was all she could do to keep them from devouring each other. A hyena and a panther were among their number.

Damascus is one of the most religious of cities. The area of Salihiyya, on the slope of Mount Qasiyun, has been long associated with holy figures, chief among them the saint and mystic, Ibn al-'Arabi, the greatest of all Sufi teachers. There you will find his tomb, which is a place of pilgrimage. Silence is requested. Colin Thubron, in this excerpt from *A Mirror to Damascus*, describes this little-visited area.

Much of Damascus is under threat, and the sense is of the new continually encroaching upon the old, especially in the dilapidated area of Saruja, just outside the city walls, where each year more and more buildings fall to the wrecker's ball. The Swiss journalist Laurence Deonna has written extensively on Syria. In her essay, she meets Nadia Khost, 'the *pasionaria* of old Damascus', whose efforts to preserve the old city have brought her into dangerous conflict with the developers and, by implication, with those who have allowed them free rein to do as they like. It is because of people like her that significant progress has already been made. There are many other people who have done much to preserve, and to draw attention to, the city's heritage, and nowhere has this been more sumptuously illustrated than in Brigid Keenan's *Damascus: Hidden Treasures of the Old City* (Thames & Hudson, 2000). She writes not as a mere visitor but as one who has lived in old Damascus and who has restored one of the old houses. In the present essay she goes beneath surfaces to consider the magnetic effect the city has had on women travellers over the ages. Another woman the city has put its stakes into is the poet Sarah Maguire who has the distinction of being the only contemporary English-language poet with a book in print in Arabic. Her selected poems, *Spilt Milk (Haleeb Muraq)*, was translated by the distinguished Iraqi poet, Saadi Yousef, and published by Al-Mada House in Damascus, in August 2003. She demonstrates, poetically, Keenan's argument that the sexual is ingrained in the city's very architecture.

Damascus is still a stopover for people making the Hajj, the pilgrimage to Mecca, although, with the advent of modern travel, there is nothing left of its former epic grandeur and, by extension, the exalted style that informs C M Doughty's masterpiece. As his very name suggests, he was quite prepared to endure the hardships of the road. The opening lines of his *Arabia Deserta* are here used to cap the wonderfully vivid description buried beneath Andrew Archibald Paton's rather pedestrian title, *The Modern Syrians; or, Native Society in Damascus, Aleppo and the mountains of the Druses, from notes made in those parts during the years 1841, 2, 3 by an Oriental student*, which was published anonymously in 1844. Paton (1811-1874) was a diplomat and author of considerable insight and also wrote on Egypt and Bosnia, and on the writer Stendhal whose *coloratura* would seem to have made a positive impact on his own prose style.

The spices that perfumed Josceline Dimbleby's Damascus childhood were doubtless a contributory factor to her later becoming a cookery author of worldwide reputation. She is also the author of *A Profound Secret* which recounts her great-grandmother's secret relationship with the Pre-Raphaelite artist Edward Burne-Jones. Dimbleby grew up in Damascus when one could still walk from one end of the city to the other in a few minutes.

From *Acts of the Apostles (c. 70-90AD)*

And Saul, yet breathing out threatenings and slaughter against the disciples of the Lord, went unto the high priest, and desired of him letters to Damascus to the synagogues, that if he found any of this way, whether they were men or women, he might bring them bound unto Jerusalem.

And as he journeyed, he came near Damascus: and suddenly there shined round about him a light from heaven: and he fell to the earth, and heard a voice saying unto him, Saul, Saul, why persecutest thou me?

And he said, Who art thou, Lord?

And the Lord said, I am Jesus whom thou persecutest: it is hard for thee to kick against the pricks.

And he trembling and astonished said, Lord, what wilt thou have me to do?

And the Lord said unto him, Arise, and go into the city, and it shall be told thee what thou must do.

And the men which journeyed with him stood speechless, hearing a voice, but seeing no man. And Saul arose from the earth; and when his eyes were opened, he saw him and brought no man: but they led him by the hand, into Damascus. And he was three days without sight, and neither did eat nor drink.

And there was a certain disciple at Damascus, named Ananias; and to him said the Lord in vision, Ananias.

And he said, Behold, I am here, Lord.

And the Lord said unto him, Arise, and go into the street which is called Straight, and enquire in the house of Judas for one called Saul, of Tarsus: for, behold, he prayeth, and hath seen in a vision a man named Ananias coming in, and putting his hand on him, that he might receive his sight.

Then Ananias answered, Lord, I have heard by many of this man, how much evil he hath done to thy saints at Jerusalem: and here he hath authority from the chief priests to bind all that call on thy name.

But the Lord said unto him, Go thy way: for he is a chosen vessel unto me, to bear my name before the Gentiles, and kings, and the children of Israel: for I will shew him how great things he must suffer for my name's sake,

And Ananias went his way, and entered into the house; and putting his hands on him said, Brother Saul, the Lord, even Jesus, that appeared unto thee in the way as thou camest, hath sent me, that thou mightest receive thy sight, and be filled with the Holy Ghost.

And immediately there fell from his eyes as it had been scales: and he received sight forthwith, and arose, and was baptized. And when he had received meat, he was strengthened.

Ibn Jubayr
From *The Travels of Ibn Jubayr (1184)*

The Great Umayyad Mosque

Of the wonders of the Jami' Mosque of Damascus is that no spider spins his web there, and no bird of the swallow-kind (Khuttaf) alights thereon. The Khalif al Walîd was he who began to build the Mosque. He applied to the King of the Greeks at Constantinople to send him twelve thousand men of the artificers of his country, at the same time threatening him with chastisement if he delayed. But the King of the Greeks did as he was commanded with all docility, and many embassies went from the one Sovereign to the other, even as is related in the books of history. Then the Khalif began, and brought to a close, the building of the Mosque. And all its walls were overlaid with the mosaic work called Al Fusaifusa. With this ornamentation they depicted in varied colours all manner of objects, such as trees, making the semblance of their branches hanging down, all worked into a pattern. Also there were interlaced scrolls of mosaic, whereon were depicted various novel and wonderful subjects most astounding to behold; so that, on account of the brilliancy and splendour, those who came were fain to cover their eyes. The sum expended on the building of the Mosque – according to the authority of Ibn al Mughlî al Asadî, in his work descriptive of the building – was four hundred chests, each chest containing twenty-eight thousand Dînars, the sum total coming to 11,200,000 Dînars.

It was the Khalif al Walîd who took possession of that half of the Mosque which was still in the hands of the Christians, and threw the two portions into one. For in early days the building was divided into two portions – one half – and it was the eastern – belonged to the Muslims, and the other half – namely, the western – to the Christians. And this by reason that Abu ʻUbaidah ibn al Jarrah had (during the siege) entered the city on the west quarter, and had reached the western side of the church, and here had made a capitulation with the Christians; while, in the meantime, Khalid ibn al Walîd had taken the eastern part of the city by assault, and had from this side arrived at the eastern wall of the church. The eastern portion (of the Church of St. John) thus came by conquest into the hands of the Muslims, and they had made of it a mosque; but the western half, where the treaty of capitulation had been granted, had remained to the Christians, and was their church until the time when Al Walîd took it from them. He would have given them another church in exchange; but the Christians would not agree, and they made objection to the act of the Khalif, and forced him to take their church from them by force, and he himself began the work of demolishing the building. Now, it had been said that he who should pull down this church would become mad; but, none the less, Al Walîd made haste to begin, crying out, 'Let me be mad; yea, mad in the work of God!' and so began to pull down the walls with his own hands. Then the Muslims hastened to his aid, and very soon the whole was demolished. Afterwards, during the days of the Khalif ʻOmar ibn ʻAbd al ʻAzîz, the Christians laid a petition before the Khalif on this matter, and they brought forth the treaty which was in their hands, in which the Companions (of the Prophet who were present at the siege) had agreed to leave the western portion to them entirely. ʻOmar would fain have given the Mosque back to the Christians, but the Muslims were of a mind to prevent him. So the Khalif gave the Christians in exchange for their consent to its remaining to the Muslims a great sum, and with this they went away content. It is said that the first who raised the Kiblah wall at this spot was the Prophet Hûd – peace be on him! –

so, at least, says Ibn al Mughlî. According to the authority of the traditionist Sufiyan ath Thûri, one prayer said in this Mosque is equivalent to thirty thousand prayers said elsewhere.

Abu Ya'qub Yusuf
From *The Travels of Ibn Battutah (1325)*

We made an excursion from Bairut to visit the tomb of Abu Ya'qub Yusuf, who, they say, was one of the kings of the Maghrib. The tomb is at a place called Karak Nuh in the Biqa al-Aziz, and by it is a religious house at which food is provided for all who come and go. It is said that the Sultan Salah al-Din [Saladin] assigned the religious endowments for its upkeep, but some say it was the Sultan Nur al-Din, who was a man of saintly life and of whom it is told that he used to weave mats and live on the proceeds of their sale.

It is related that after coming to the city of Damascus he [Abu Ya'qub] fell ill there of a grievous malady and remained for some time lying on the ground in the bazaars. When he recovered from his illness, he went out to the outskirts of Damascus to seek some orchard for which he might serve as keeper. He was engaged to keep an orchard belonging to the king Nur al-Din and continued to tend it for six months. When the fruit was due to ripen the sultan came to that garden, and the superintendent of the garden bade Abu Ya'qub fetch some pomegranates for the sultan to partake of. He brought him some pomegranates accordingly, but the superintendent, finding them sour, bade him fetch some others. He did so, and the superintendent, finding them sour also, said to him, 'Have you been looking after this orchard for six months and cannot tell the sweet from the sour?' He replied, 'It was for keeping that you hired me, not for eating,' whereupon the superintendent came to the King and told him the whole story. The King sent for him, for he had seen in a dream that he should meet with Abu Ya'qub and that some advantage would accrue to himself from him, and he had an intuition that this was he. So he said to him, 'You are Abu Ya'qub?' and on receiving his answer, 'Yes,' he rose to welcome him, embraced him, and bade him sit beside him. After that he took him in his cortège to his own residence, where he entertained him. Abu Ya'qub stayed with him for some time, but subsequently left Damascus in solitary flight during the season of severe cold, and came to one of the villages in the district. There was in this place a man of humble station, who invited him to stay in his house and, on his consenting, prepared soup for him and killed a chicken and brought it to him with barley bread. Having partaken of this, Abu Ya'qub prayed for a blessing upon his host. Now the man had several children, one of them being a girl who was shortly to be conducted to her husband. It is one of their customs in that country that the girl receives an 'outfit' from her father, the greater part of which consists of copper utensils. These are regarded by them with much pride and are made the subject of special stipulations in the marriage contract. So Abu Ya'qub said to the man, 'Have you any copper in your house?' 'Yes,' he replied, 'I have just bought some in order to give this girl her outfit.' 'Fetch it to me,' he said, and when the man had brought it added, 'Now borrow all the copper that you can from your neighbours.' So he did so and laid all the vessels out before him. Then Abu Ya'qub lit fires around them, and taking out a purse which he had containing the elixir, he threw some of it upon the copper and the whole collection turned into gold. After putting these into a locked chamber, Abu Ya'qub wrote a letter to Nur al-Din, the King of Damascus, telling him about them and exhorting him to build a hospital for sick strangers and to constitute endowments for it. He bade him also build religious houses on the highways, satisfy the owners of the copper vessels and provide for the maintenance of the owner of the house, and concluded his letter with these words: 'If Ibrahim Ad'ham renounced the kingdom of Khurasan as he did, I too have renounced the kingdom of the Maghrib, and now renounce also this art. Farewell.' He at once took to flight, and the owner of the house brought the letter to the King Nur al-Din, who came to that village and carried off the gold, after satisfying the owners of the copper vessels and the man himself. He made search for Abu Ya'qub, but failing to find any trace or light upon any news of him, returned to Damascus, where he built the hospital which is known by his name and which has not its equal in the inhabited world.

Ludovico Di Varthema
From *The Navigation and Voyages of Wertomanus (1502)*

Of the Citie of Damasco

It is in maner incredible, and passeth all beleefe to thinke howe fayre the citie of Damasco is, and how fertile is the soyle. And therefore allured by the marueilous beautie of the citie, I remayned there many dayes, that learnyng theyr language, I might knowe the maners of the people. The inhabitants are

* Principate or government

Mahumetans and Mamalukes, with also many Christians, lyuyng after the maner of the Greekes. By the way, it shall not be from my purpose to speake of theyr Hexarchatus*: the whiche (as we haue sayde) is subiect to the Lieuetenaunt, viceroye or gouernourne of Syria, whiche some call Sorya. There is a very strong fortresse or Castell, which a certayne Ethruscan, borne in the citie of Florence, buylded at his owne charges, while he was there ye chiefe Hexarchatus or gouernour, as appeareth by the flower of a Lilie there grauen in marble beyng the armes of the citie of Florence. The citie is compassed with a deep fosse or diche, with foure goodly high towres. They passe the dyche with a hangyng brydge, which is lifted vp or lette downe at theyr pleasure. There is all kynde of great artillerie and munition, with also a garde of fyftie Mamalukes, whiche dayly assyste the gouernoure or captayne of the castell, and receyue theyr stipende of the gouernoure or viceroye of Syria. Fortune seemed to giue the Hexarchatus or principate to the sayde Florentine, whiche we wyll declare as we haue haarde of the inhabitauntes. They say that poyson was once geuen to the Soltan of Syria: and when he sought for remedie, he chaunced to be healed by the sayde Florentine, which was one of the companye of the Mamalukes. After whiche good fortune, he grewe dayely in fauoure with the sayde Prince, who for rewarde gaue hym that citie: where also the sayde Florentine buylded a Castel, and dyed: whom to this daye the Citisens honour for a sainte, for sauyng the lyfe of theyr prince: after whose death, the gouernment returned to the Syrians. They say furthermore that the Soltan is well beloued of his lordes and princes, for that he easely graunteth them principates and gouernementes: yet with condition to paye yeerely many thousandes of those peeces of gold which they call Saraphos. They that denye to paye the summe agreed of, are in daunger of imminent death. Of the chiefe noble men or gouernoures ten or twelue euer assiste the Prince. And when it pleaseth hym to extorte a certayne summe of golde of his noble men or merchauntes (for they vse great tyrannye and oppression by the iniuries and thefte of the Mamalukes agaynst the Mahumetans) the Prince geueth two letters to the captaine of the Castell. In the one is contayned, that with an oration he inuite to the Castell suche as pleaseth hym. In the other is declared the mynde of the Prynce, what he demaundeth of his subiects. When the letters be read, withal expedition they accomplishe his commaundement, be it ryght or wrong, without respecte. This meanes the Prynce inuented to extorte mony. Yet sometymes it commeth to passe, that the noble men are of suche strength, that they wyll not come when they are commaunded, knowyng that the tyrant wyll offer them violence. And therefore oftentymes when they knowe that the captayne of the Castell wyll call them, they flee into the dominions of the Turke. This haue we geathered as touchyng theyr maners, we haue also obserued, that the watchemen in towres, do not geue warning to the garde with lyuely voyce, but with drommes, the one answearyng the other by course. But if any of the watchemen be so sleepye, that in the moment of an houre he aunsweare not to the sounde of the watche, he is immediately committed to prison for one whole yeere.

Of such thynges as are seene in the citie of Damasco

After that I haue declared the maners of the Princes of Damasco, it seemeth agreeable to speak of some suche thynges as I haue seene there. And therefore to speake fyrst of the excellencie and beautie of the citie, it is certaynely marueylously wel peopled, and greatly frequented, and also marueylous ryche. It is of goodly buildyng, and exceedeth in abundance and fruitfulnesse of all thynges, and especiallye of all kynde of victuales, flesh, corne and fruites, as freshe damesenne grapes all the whole yeere: also Pomegranets, Oranges, Lymons, and excellent Olyve trees. Lykewyse Roses, both white and red, the fayrest that euer I sawe: and all kyndes of sweete apples, yet peares and peaches were vnsauery. The cause whereof, they say to be to much moysture. A goodly and clear ryuer runneth about the citie: and therefore in maner in euery house are seene fountaynes of curious worke embossed and grauen. Theyr houses outwardly are not very beautyfull, but inwardly marueylously adourned with variable woorkes of the stone called Ophis, or serpentine Marble. Within the towne are many temples or churches, which they call Moscheas. But that which is most beautyfull of all other, is buylded after the maner of Sainct Peters church in Rome, if you respect the greatnesse, exceptyng this, that in the myddle is no roofe or couerture, but is all open: but about the rest of the temple, it is altogeather vaulted. There they obserue religiously the bodye of the holy Prophet Zacharie. The temple hath also foure great double gates of metal, very fayre, and many goodly fountaynes within it. There are yet seene the ruins of many decayed houses, which were once inhabited by the Christians. Those houses they cal Canonicas, and are of woorke both carued and imbossed.

There is also to be seene the place where (as they say) our sauiour Christ spake to Sainct Paule these woordes, Paule, Paule, why doest thou persecute me, etc. This place is without the citie about a myle.

There are buried the Christians that die in the citie. There is seen also the Tower in which Sainct Paule was committed to pryson, and ioyneth to the wall of the citie. But that place of the Tower where Paule was brought foorth by the Angell, the Mahumetans do not attempt to close vp: Saying, that yf it be closed ouer nyght, they fynde it open agayne in the morning. I saw also there, those houses in the whiche (as they say) Cain slue his brother Abell. These are on the other part of the citie a myle of, in a certayne valley, yet on the syde of a hyll.

Alphonse de Lamartine
From *A Pilgrimage to the Holy Land (1833)*

No man's education and views can be enlarged unless he has travelled much; unless he has changed twenty times his modes of thinking and the habits of his life. The conventional and uniform customs adopted by the man who leads a regular and monotonous life in his own country, are moulds which give a diminished impress to everything. Taste, philosophy, religion, character, all are more enlarged, more just and accurate in the man who has seen nature and society under various points of view. Travelling supplies an optic for the material and intellectual universe. To travel in search of wisdom, was a sort of proverb among the ancients; but it is not understood among us. They travelled not merely in search of unknown dogmas and lessons of philosophy, but to see and to judge everything. For my part I am constantly struck with the narrow and petty view we take of the institutions and customs of foreign nations; and if my mind has been enlarged, if my views have been extended, if I have learned to tolerate things by understanding them, I owe all these advantages to my frequent changes of scene and points of view. To study past ages in history, men by travelling, and God in nature, that is the grand school. We study everything in our miserable books, and compare everything with our petty local habits. And who have made our habits and our books? Men who knew as little as ourselves. Let us open the Book of books! Let us live, see, and travel! The world is a book of which we turn a page at every step. How little must he know who has turned but one page!

We put on our Turkish dresses, that we might not be known for Franks in the environs of Damascus. My wife wore the costume of the Arab women. She was covered from head to foot with a long white veil. Our Arabs arranged their dress with great care, and pointing towards the mountains which we had yet to cross, exclaimed 'Scham! Scham!' This is the Arabic name for Damascus ...

At nine in the morning we passed along the side of a mountain covered with country-houses and gardens, belonging to the inhabitants of Damascus. A fine bridge is thrown across a torrent at the foot of a mountain. We saw numerous strings of camels laden with stones for new buildings, and everything indicated that we were approaching a great capital. After another hour's journey, we perceived, on the summit of an eminence, a little insulated mosque, the dwelling of a solitary Mahometan. A fountain flows near the mosque, and copper cups, chained to the basin, enable the traveller to slake his thirst. We halted for a short time in this spot, beneath the shade of a sycamore. The road was now thronged with travellers, peasants, and Arab soldiers. We again mounted our horses, and after proceeding along an ascent of a few hundred paces, we entered a deep defile, bounded on the left by a mountain of schistus, rising perpendicularly above our heads; and on the right by a ridge of rock thirty or forty feet high. The descent was rapid, and fragments of loose stone rolled under our horses' feet. I rode at the head of the caravan, at a few paces behind the Arabs of Zebdani. They suddenly stopped short, and uttering exclamations of joy, pointed to an opening in the rock on our right; I approached, and looking through the cleft, I beheld the grandest and most singular prospect that ever presented itself to the eye of man. It was Damascus and its boundless desert, lying at the depth of a few hundred feet below us. The city, surrounded by its ramparts of black and yellow marble, flanked by its innumerable square towers, crowned by sculptured crannies, commanded by its forest of minarets of every form, and intersected by the seven branches of its river and its numberless streams, extended as far as the eye could reach. It was a labyrinth of gardens and flowers, thrusting its suburbs here and there in the vast plain, encircled by its forest of ten leagues in circumference, and everywhere shaded by groves of sycamores, and trees of every form and hue. From time to time, the city seemed lost beneath the umbrageous canopies of these trees, and then again reappeared, spreading into broad lakes of houses, suburbs, and villages, interspersed with labyrinths of orchards, palaces, and streamlets. Our eyes were bewildered, and only turned from one enchantment to fix upon another. We stopped simultaneously. All thronged round the little aperture in the rock which was pierced like a window, and we contemplated sometimes with exclamations, and sometimes in silence, the magic spectacle which had suddenly opened beneath our eyes at the close of a journey through so many barren solitudes, and at the commencement of another desert, which has no bounds but Bagdad and Bassora, and which it requires forty days to traverse. At length we pursued our course. The parapet of rock which concealed from us the plain and the city, lowered insensibly, and soon afforded us an uninterrupted view of the whole horizon. We were now not more than five hundred paces from the walls of the suburbs. These walls, which are surrounded by charming kiosks and country-houses in various styles of oriental architecture, glitter round Damascus like a circlet of gold. The square towers, which flank them and which surmount their line, are encrusted with arabesques pierced in ogive, with columns as slender as reeds, and edged with crannies surmounted by turbans. The walls are covered with stone, or slabs of yellow and black marble, arranged alternately with elegant symmetry. The tops of the cypresses and other large trees in the gardens in the interior of the city rise above the walls and towers, and crown them with sombre verdure. The innumerable cupolas of the mosques and palaces of a city containing four hundred thousand inhabitants, now reflected the rays of the setting sun, and the blue and brilliant waters of the seven rivers sparkled and disappeared amidst the streets and gardens. The horizon was boundless as the ocean, and blended itself with the purple of a fiery sky inflamed by the reverberation of the sands of the great desert. On the right the broad sides of the Anti-Libanus receded one behind the other, like immense waves of shadow; sometimes advancing like promontories into the plain, and sometimes opening like deep gulfs in which the plain embedded itself with its forests and large villages: several of the latter contain as many as thirty thousand inhabitants. Some branches of the river and two large lakes were here visible, shining in the obscurity of the general tint of verdure in which Damascus seems to be veiled. On our left, the plain was more open, and it was only at the distance of twelve or fifteen leagues that we again saw the summits of mountains, blanched with snow, shining in the blue sky like clouds on the ocean. The city is entirely surrounded by orchards, or rather by forests of fruit trees, in which the vines are entwined, as at Naples, and hang in festoons among fig, apricot, pear, and cherry trees. Under these trees, the earth, which is rich, fertile, and always well watered, is carpeted with barley, corn, maize, and all the leguminous plants which this soil produces. Little white houses peep out here and there, from amidst the verdure of the forests: they are either a lodging for the gardener, or summer retreats belonging to the family who own the ground. These cultivated enclosures are peopled with horses, sheep, camels, and doves, and everything that can impart animation to nature; they are on the average two or three acres in extent, and are separated one from another by mud walls baked in the sun, and by fine green hedges. Numerous shady paths, refreshed by fountains, intersect these gardens, leading from one suburb to another, or to the different gates of the city. The gardens form a boundary of twenty or thirty leagues in circumference round Damascus.

We had advanced for some time in silence through the first labyrinths of trees, somewhat uneasy at not seeing the guide we expected. We halted; and he at length made his appearance ...

James Elroy Flecker
Gates of Damascus (1911)

> Four great gates has the·city of Damascus,
>   And four Grand Wardens, on their spears reclining,
> All day long stand like tall stone men
>   And sleep on the towers when the moon is shining.

This is the song of the East Gate Warden
When he locks the great gate and smokes in his garden.

Postern of Fate, the Desert Gate, Disaster's Cavern, Fort of Fear,
The Portal of Bagdad am I, the Doorway of Diarbekir.

The Persian Dawn that flaunts and flows may tinge and touch the mountain
      snows:
But my gaunt buttress still rejects the least light shadow or her rose.

Pass out, pass out, O Caravan! This road may reach the World's frontier:
Knowst thou that River and that Town who dost call black Diarbekir?

Pass out, pass out! Bagdad ye cry, and down the billows of blue sky
Ye beat the bell that beats in hell, and who shall thrust ye back? Not I.

The Sun who flashes through the head and paints the shadows green and
      red, –
The Sun shall eat thy fleshless dead, O Caravan, O Caravan!

And one who licks his lips for thirst with fevered eyes shall face in fear
The palms that wave, the streams that burst, his last mirage, O Caravan!

And one – the bird-voiced Singing-man – shall fall behind thee, Caravan!
And God shall meet him in the night, and he shall sing as best he can.

And one the Bedouin shall slay, and one, sand-stricken on the way
Go dark and blind; and one shall say – 'How lonely is the Caravan!'

Pass out beneath, O Caravan, Doom's Caravan, Death's Caravan!
I had not told ye, fools, so much, save that I heard your Singing-man.

This was sung by the West Gate's keeper
When heaven's hollow dome grew deeper.

I am the gate toward the sea: O sailor men, pass out from me!
I hear you high on Lebanon, singing the marvels of the sea.

The dragon-green, the luminous, the dark, the serpent-haunted sea,
The snow-besprinkled wine of earth, the white-and-blue-flower foaming sea.

Beyond the sea are towns with towers, carved with lions and lily flowers,
And not a soul in all those lonely streets to while away the hours.

Beyond the towns, an isle where, bound, a naked giant bites the ground:
The shadow of a monstrous wing looms on his back: and still no sound.

Beyond the isle a rock that screams like madmen shouting in their dreams,

From whose dark issues night and day blood crashes in a thousand streams.

Beyond the rock is Restful Bay, where no wind breathes or ripple stirs,
And there on Roman ships, they say, stand rows of metal mariners.

Beyond the bay in utmost West old Solomon the Jewish King
Sits with his beard upon his breast, and grips and guards his magic ring:

And when that ring is stolen, he will rise in outraged majesty,
And take the World upon his back, and fling the World beyond the sea.

> *This is the song of the North Gate's master,*
> *Who singeth fast, but drinketh faster.*

I am the gay Aleppo Gate: a dawn, a dawn and thou art there:
Eat not thy heart with fear and care, O brother of the beast we hate!

Thou hast not many miles to tread, nor other foes than fleas to dread;
Homs shall behold thy morning meal and Hama see thee safe in bed.

Take to Aleppo filigrane, and take them paste of apricots,
And coffee tables botched with pearl, and little beaten brassware pots:

And thou shalt sell thy wares for thrice the Damascene retailers' price,
And buy a fat Armenian slave who smelleth odorous and nice.

Some men of noble stock were made: some glory in the murder-blade:
Some praise a Science or an Art, but I like honorable Trade!

Sell them the rotten, buy the ripe! Their heads are weak; their pockets burn.
Aleppo men are mighty fools. Salaam Aleikum! Safe return!

> *This is the song of the South Gate Holder,*
> *A silver man, but his song is older.*

I am the Gate that fears no fall: the Mihrab of Damascus wall,
The bridge of booming Sinai: the Arch of Allah all in all.

O spiritual pilgrim rise: the night has grown her single horn:
The voices of the souls unborn are half adream with Paradise.

To Meccah thou hast turned in prayer with aching heart and eyes that burn:
Ah Hajji, whither wilt thou turn when thou art there, when thou art there?

God be thy guide from camp to camp: God be thy shade from well to well;
God grant beneath the desert stars thou hear the Prophet's camel bell.

And God shall make thy body pure, and give thee knowledge to endure
This ghost-life's piercing phantom-pain, and bring thee out to Life again.

28

And God shall make thy soul a Glass where eighteen thousand Aeons pass,
And thou shalt see the gleaming Worlds as men see dew upon the grass.

And son of Islam, it may be that thou shalt learn at journey's end
Who walks thy garden eve on eve, and bows his head, and calls thee Friend.

Isabel Burton
From *The Inner Life of Syria* (c. 1870)

A Day's Shopping in the Bazars

After a long residence in Damascus, I always say to my friends, if you have two
or three days to spare, follow the guide books; but if you are pressed for time
come with me, and you shall see what you will best like to remember, and you
shall buy the things that are the most curious. We will make our purchases first,
visiting on the way everything of interest. We will ride our white donkeys with
their gaudy trappings, firstly, because the horses slip over the stones, and
secondly, because, just as you are examining an *abba* or an *izar*, my horses will
probably lash their heels into the middle of the stall, and playfully send
everything flying; perhaps they may pick up a child in their mouths, and give
it a shake for pure fun, or, as we move along in the crowd, devour an old man's
tray of cabbages from the top of his head. It is a state of funny familiarity into
which all my animals grow in a very short time – amusing, but sometimes
tiresome. Whilst our donkeys are preparing, let us go and sit for a little while
in a myrtle wood in Abu Dib's garden, next to my house, and which is just as
open to me as if it were my own. It gives a delightful shade, and will be a refuge
from the heat and sun until we are obliged to face them. The cool stream is very
pleasant as it gurgles by.

Do you hear that strange noise like a rustling in the air, and the shouts of
the people? And do you see how darkness comes on? Do not be frightened, it
is a flight of locusts coming. In ten minutes they will be here. Down they fall
like a hail storm. It is very unpleasant to be covered with them; they will not
bite us, but they will strip every garden in an hour. If you do not fear a few
nestling in your hair and hat, and running about your throat, you may watch
that tree covered with blossom; it is already alive with locusts, and you will see
them strip branch after branch, as if somebody were using a knife. Poor people!
No wonder they shout. These dreadful insects will destroy all their crops,
produce a kind of famine by raising the price of provisions, and often in the
hot season announce cholera.

Before we enter the bazars, look at that Afghan sitting under yonder tree. If you like to invest in a little brass or silver seal, he will, for a few piastres, engrave your name upon it in Arabic. We will then enter the sadlery bazar, where you can buy magnificent trappings for a pony or donkey for the children at home. This is a pretty *suk*. There are saddle-cloths of every colour in cloth, embossed with gold, holsters, bridles of scarlet silk, with a silken cord – a single rein, which makes you look as if you were managing a fiery horse by a thread, and the bridle is effectively covered with dangling silver and ivory ornaments. There are mule and donkey trappings of every colour in the rainbow, mounted with little shells. As we leave this bazar I must call your attention to a venerable plane tree; its girth is forty feet.

We should do wisely to go into the shoemakers' bazar. You see how gaudy the stalls look. I want you to buy a pair of lemon-coloured slippers, pointed at the toe, and as soft as a kid glove. The stiff red slippers and shoes are not so nice, and the red boots with tops and tassals and hangings, are part of the Bedawi dress, and that of the Shaykhs generally. Why must you buy a pair of slippers? Because you must never forget at Damascus that you are only a 'dog of a Christian,' that your unclean boots must not tread upon sacred ground, and that if you wish to see anything you must be prepared at any moment to take off the impure Giaour things, put on these slippers, and enter reverently; all around you will do the same for that matter. Here we cover our heads and bare our feet to show respect; you Franks cover your feet and uncover your heads. Do not forget always to have your slippers in your pocket, as naturally as your handkerchief and your purse, until you return to the other side of Lebanon, or you will often be hindered by the want of them.

We will now inspect the marqueterie bazar, where we shall find several pretty things inlaid with choice woods, mother-of-pearl, or steel; the former are the best, if finely worked. These are the large chests which form part of the bride's trousseau. Those ready made are generally coarse, but you can order a beautifully fine and very large one for about five napoleons. There are tables, and the clogs used by the *harim* in marble courts. You will likewise find toilette hand-glasses, but they are far better at Jerusalem or Bethlehem. Now we will go to the smithy-like gold and silver bazar, where they sit round in little pens, hammering at their anvils. Each seems to have a strong-box for his treasures. All this is the greatest possible rubbish for a European to wear, but you will pick up many barbarous and antique ornaments, real gold and real stones, though unattractive. You may buy all sorts of spangling things as ornaments for your horse; you will find very beautiful *zarfs*, or filigree coffee-cup-holders; you may order, on seeing the pattern, some very pretty *raki* cups of silver, inlaid with gold, very minute, with a gold or silver fish trembling on a spring, as if swimming in the liqueur.

Whilst we are here, I will take you up a ladder on to the roof, not to lose time. The men will give me the key of the door for a little *bakshish*. By this way we shall reach the southern side of the great mosque, and after scrambling over several roofs, and venturing a few awkward jumps, we shall arrive at the top of a richly ornamented triple gateway; it is outside the mosque, and hardly peers above the mud and débris and bazar roofs, which cover up what is not already buried. Over the central arch is a cross, and Greek inscription: 'Thy kingdom, O Christ! is an everlasting kingdom, and thy dominion endureth throughout all generations.' It is a serious reflection that this bit of truth should have remained upon a mosque, perhaps for 1762 years. It doubtless belonged to the stupendous Temple of the Sun, befitting the capital. After the birth of our Saviour it became a Christian Cathedral, dedicated to St. John the Baptist, whose head is said to lie under a little railed off cupola'd tomb, and is still venerated by the Moslems. The Christian Cathedral was divided at the conquest between Christians and Moslems, but it has long since become wholly and exclusively Moslem. Yet this inscription testifying to the truth has lived down every change of masters.

We will now pass down a narrow lane joining two bazars. A wretched wooden stall with shelves, filled with dirty bottles, and odds and ends of old china, here attracts your eye, and squatting on the counter a shrivelled little old man sits under his turban, with his palsied chin shaking like the aspen leaves. You see how smilingly he salutes me: out of those unwashed bottles he is looking for his finest atr(ottar) and his best sandalwood-oil. Being fond of ladies' society, he will saturate our handkerchiefs and clothes with his perfumes, and we shall be traceable for a week to come – it is not easy to divest yourself of ottar when it has once touched clothes. He has long ago given me all his confidence. He is not so poor as he looks. He has sold ottar and sandalwood-oil all his life, some ninety-five years; he has fifteen wives and one hundred and two children, and he would still like, he says, to marry again. I reprove him for having married eleven more than allowed by the Korán.

Now we will repair to another bazar, and likewise to a *khan*. You must see both before choosing an *abba* – a large, loose, square robe worn by Shaykhs, of the richest silk, powdered with gold. The ground may be black, scarlet, sky-blue, rose-coloured, or what you please. It will make a fine smoking dress for your husband, or a *sortie de bal* for yourself. The other articles are Damascus silks, and carpets – a *kufiyeh*, which is a large coloured and tasselled handkerchief of pure silk, or more generally of mixed silk and cotton, also gold-powdered. The Bedawin wears it on his head, falling about the shoulders, and fastened by a fillet (*aghal*) of camel's hair. How anybody can travel in any other head-dress I don't know. It keeps the sun off the head and the nape of the neck, which are the dangerous places – it takes the place of umbrella, hat, pagri, veil, and spectacles; in one word, you have not to make a 'guy' of yourself, nor encumber yourself with what you would like to throw away on a restive horse. It keeps out wind, cold, and rain. I used to wonder how I should be able to bear Europe without one. The best are those from Mecca or Baghdad, sold at Damascus, and the usual *aghal* is chocolate dyed, with gold knobs and tassels.

You can also buy an *izar*, to walk about the bazars incognita like a native. It covers all, except your face, from head to foot, like a shroud. It is pure silk, and you can choose your own colours; they are mostly brilliant, but I care only for black. Some are worked beautifully in gold. If you wish to pass for a Christian, you may expose your face, or wear an apology for a covering; but as Moslemahs we must buy *mandils*, white handkerchiefs, or coloured, with flowers and figures so thickly laid on that no one can recognize our features. If you have one of the black and gold or coloured *izars*, you will be a great personage. If you want to pass unobtrusively, you must wear a plain white linen sheet, with a thick *mandil*, and in that costume you might walk all day with your own father and not be known except by the voice.

We will now have our donkeys saddled with ordinary native saddles and trappings, and ride. You need not be ashamed of appearing *en cavalier*, for the Syrian women know no other way of riding. There are only three of us here who really do ride, and we attract immense attention by our funny seats. The people gape, and wonder how we manage 'to hang on that peg,' and they are satisfied, until our horses have done something unusual, that we shall fall off. Think that nobody knows you are a European in this dress. I remind you of this, because I remember how ashamed and miserable I felt the first time I dressed and rode like a native, forgetting that I looked like the myriads of white, ghost-like looking women who passed us.

I will also recommend you to invest in an embroidered jacket (*damr*), of gold-embroidered cloth, with long flying open sleeves, to be worn over a white muslin bodice; it will be very effective in red, blue, or black. You must not forget to buy a few pure silk towels; they are very pleasant – likewise an embroidered towel or two, worked with gold. The latter is slung over the shoulder of the servant who hands you the sherbet, and you wipe your mouth with it.

In a broad street outside the saddlers' bazar are all the brass carvers. You will see in most shops, plates, pans, chargers, and basins covered with Arabesque ornaments, and carved with ancient inscriptions. Some are seven or eight hundred years old, and bear the names of kings or famous personages. Figures, such as the lion and the sun, or the spies of the Promised Land bearing on a pole bunches of grapes – the grapes of Eshcol – bigger than themselves, are the commonest kind. We will try to pick up a handsomely carved brass basin and ewer of antique shape, which are here used for washing the fingers before and after meals. Incense-burners, carved trays for cigarette ashes, large carved coffee-trays, both of Arab and Persian work, the former with far broader and grander lines, the latter incomparably more delicate, seduce almost every traveller. I never see them out of Damascus, and some are real antiques. Is it not strange that we English are the only people who have no original idea of form. If I were to visit the commonest potteries above our house – mere holes in the mountain side – every lad would say, 'May I make you a vase, lady?' He will then twirl a bit of soft, muddy clay upon a common wheel with his finger and thumb, and from his own device in five minutes he turns me out something exquisitely graceful.

You want a divan. Now, as I know that the European houses will not admit of seats all round the room, I will recommend you to have two in each chamber. Order your carpenter to make two common deal settles, ten feet long, four broad, and one high. On them put comfortable mattresses, and six long narrow cushions or pillows upon each. At the Greek bazar (Súk el Arwám) we can buy divan covers, which you will take to England. The Damascenes of the higher classes use gay silks, stiff with cotton backs, for this purpose. I greatly prefer the peasants' woollen stuff with a black or dark-blue ground, and a thunder-and-lightning pattern, or the ordinary blue and white prayer-carpet. Here you can also purchase gaudy Persian rugs. No traveller should miss the Súk el Arwám: it is full of curiosities. You ask what is that Moslem eating for supper? That is *leben*, and the other dish is a peculiar salad – two of the most delicious things that he knows. *Leben* is soured goats' milk, an admirable drink when you halt after a long, scorching ride, dying of thirst, and almost afraid of water. You will call to the first goat-herd, 'Have you *leben*?' and he will hand you an earthenware basin, something like the saucer of a large flower-pot. I have drunk three bowls, almost without drawing breath, when entering the tent. This is how it is made: take the milk and boil it, let it become lukewarm, and then add a handful of sour yeast, or leaven. A little of the boiling milk must be mixed till it becomes a thin gruel, then strain it into the rest, and throw away the dregs. Cover up your bowl with flannel or blanket, in a warm place, and leave it to stand all night; next morning it will be cold, thick, and sour. To continue it, you must take a cup full of it, boil some milk, and when lukewarm mix the old *leben* with a little milk, pour it in and stir it, and leave it to stand as usual; do this every day. In England I should use rennet instead of leaven. You may not succeed in getting *leben* the first four or five times, but when you do you can always make the new with a cup-full of the sour. The other dish, the salad, is made by chopping garlic, thyme, mint, water-cress, sage, or any other sweet herbs, putting in a piece of salt about the size of a nut, mixing it all, and then burying the whole in leben, sprinkling the top with chopped herbs; then dip your bread in it, and eat.

What is that brown powder?

No; it is not snuff. That is henna; it is mixed with lime-juice, spices, burnt nuts, and other things, and it stains the hands, feet, and finger nails. Brides, and especially Moslem brides, are ornamented with moons, and all sorts of devices in henna. They will dye a pet lamb. My servants stain, for ornament, my white donkey and my white Persian cat, but it is mostly used for the human hair. Mix about two teaspoonfuls with half a small tea-cup-full of water, boil it till it bubbles, and take it off once or twice as soon as ebullition begins; strain it through a coarse muslin, and drop it into the water with which you wash your hair; or you may comb it through your hair: it cleans and strengthens it, and makes it glossy and bright. There is black henna from Baghdad, and red from Mecca. The former is the powdered leaf of indigo.

That dish of what you think are lumps of mud or clay is incense. You see it is arranged in heaps and in various sections. There are many different qualities. That black-looking stuff is very dear – a sovereign would not buy you much. It has a delicious aroma, and realizes the idea of 'all the perfumes of Araby the blest.' That small, gummy looking quality is cheap enough – you can buy a great deal for a few piastres. The best comes from Somali-land, and all the country round about Guardafui; it is imported by the Arabs to Jeddah, thence to Mecca, and the Haj, or Meccan pilgrimage caravan, brings it here.

This reminds me that I have not yet taken you to the pipe and *narghileh* bazar. The incense is somewhat connected with them. The usual use, however, is to take your brass incense-burner, put into it a little live braise, and drop a lump or two of this incense upon it. When you receive a visitor in Oriental fashion, a servant precedes her into the house, so that coming out of the fresh air she may find nothing but what is agreeable. But by no means the worst use is to take a small speck of the very best incense, and place it on your *narghileh*, or *chibouque*; it would not answer with a cigar, this sprinkling meat with sugar or eau de cologne. All my European visitors wonder why my *narghilehs* are so much better than others, and I feel sure that the reason is a little trick of this kind. I am very fond of Oriental luxury. Most people leave it behind, but as far as *narghilehs*, coffee, incense, and divan goes, I shall always take mine with me.

Now we come to the pipe and *narghileh* bazar. Firstly, we will look for some amber mouthpieces. We shall see thousands of fantastic shapes and different sorts, and if we do not suit ourselves in the bazar, we shall at Shaykh Bandar's. This worthy will try to sell his worst at his best price, but let me choose for you. We will make one up. Firstly, I will take the stick of the mouthpiece, and will choose three or four fantastic-shaped lumps and knobs of the purest lemon-coloured gum, without streaks or flaws. I will then separate the first and second pieces by a gaudily enamelled Persian ring – if you were a Rothschild I should prefer a hoop of diamonds. The third and fourth pieces we will divide by a cylinder of black amber, two inches long, with inlaid gold figures. When we have fastened these all upon this little stick, you will have a mouthpiece twelve inches long, and fit for Harún el Rashid, had he smoked. The next thing is to look for a good straight pipe-stick, about two yards long. Jessamine and myrtle are the best, cherry is the common use, and the green stick of the rose is not in the market. A good Moslem will not smoke the latter, because it is one of the trees of Paradise. Moreover, it is troublesome, and you must have fresh ones – the old are fit only for burning. You can have an assortment of earthenware bowls, adorned with gilt figures. I will also have some fancy things made for you in the potteries above our house. My husband's held nearly an ounce of tobacco, to the wonder and astonishment of the natives, who suggested small flower-pots.

Now we reach the *narghileh* stalls. Firstly we choose a *shishah*, a prettily carved and fanciful looking water-bottle, of graceful shape, and a saucer or tray of the same material for it to stand on. In another stall we find the *ras*, or head: you may be as fanciful or as simple as you please in your *narghilehs*. You may have one for 15 francs, or one for 50 pounds sterling. The *ras* – supposing it to be of brass and pink china – looks almost like a little Chinese pagoda, or a series of cups and balls, terminating in a metal cup, to hold the *tombak*; it is hung also with bells and dangling things, in fact, with any fantasia you may choose. In another part of the bazar you choose the *narbish*, or tube made of kid-skin, and twined around with gilt wire. One end of this snake fastens into the side of the *ras*, and the other is a wooden mouthpiece, through which you draw as if you were discussing a sherry cobbler. I always use wooden mouthpieces, as they retain a single drop of otar, or any other perfume, and they are always clean; many, however, prefer metal. If you are going to travel, I recommend to you the short, common, strong, plain red *narbish*. For the house and for guests, you must have the gaudiest, several yards in length: the longer the *narbish* the higher your rank, and the greater compliment you pay your guest. I always order mine to be of dark chocolate colour and gold, and measuring from four to six yards. It is not safe to have less than twelve *narghilehs* in your house. Preserve one for your own smoking, and a silver mouthpiece in your pocket for visiting. Keep a dozen for guests, and a servant on purpose to look after them, and to clean them every day. Constantly change your *narbishes*, and also have two or three in the kitchen for your servants, and your servants' friends, to save your own.

I must explain to you how to use these things, or you will buy them to no purpose. Firstly, you wash out your glass with a brush like that used to clean lamp chimneys, and fill your bottle three-quarters full of either plain water, or you may drop some perfume (rose-water, for instance) into the water. For fantasia a red berry or two, or a flower, may be placed to dance and bubble on the surface. Then you take a handful of *tombak* (not tobacco), break it into small pieces, and wash it, squeezing it in a bag to lessen its strength. Some require it to be wetted seven times; if this be not properly done, the nicotine will affect the strongest head. Then ball it in the hand and put it in the *ras*; inhale for a moment through the hole into which you are going to put the *narbish*; if the water rise up too high pour a little out, if it only bubbles all is right, and you may put on the *ras*. Then take a *k'ras*, or lump of prepared charcoal, with a hole in the middle; it is shaped like a little pincushion, almost the size of a halfpenny, and sold in strings about the market. Make it red-hot, and with the pincers set it on the top of the *tombak*, screw on your *narbish*, and draw. You may also put flowers in the saucer, or stick them in the little dangling chains. It is very amusing to see people smoking a *narghileh* for the first time. Firstly, they blow down instead of up, and puff the *k'ras* and the *tombak* over the carpet, and there is a scrambling of servants to pick it up. They are afraid to inhale too hard, for fear tobacco water should rise to their mouths, and they look very red and foolish because they can't make the water bubble. Then they use so much exertion that the smoke goes the 'wrong way,' they swell their cheeks, and they get purple and exhausted, till you are obliged to stop them, for fear of apoplexy. All the early struggles would cease if young smokers would only remember the sherry cobbler and the straw, and work away calmly without fear. Some gain a violent headache or dizziness by their exertions, and never touch a *narghileh* again.

There is also a *narghileh* pipe much used among the peasants – a cocoanut, which is often encased or ornamented with brass or silver, for a bowl, and two tubes protruding from it, forming a triangular-shaped pipe. It is picturesque and pleasant to smoke, but you must be sitting low and balance it on your knee. The best of these pipes are the *kalyuns* sold in the Persian bazar. *Tombak* is a peculiar growth of tobacco that comes in large dried leaves, and is bought by the bag, as big as a coal sack. It reaches us with the *Haj*, and we can get excellent qualities at Damascus at 25 piastres (50 pence) the oke (two lbs).

To make your *chibouque* pleasant, invest in some Jebayl tobacco. It is Syrian, and the best and most delicate. Always blow through your pipe stick, in case anything might have got into it; the servant fills your bowl and puts, with the pincers, a bit of braise in the middle. A little carved Persian brass tray on the ground holds the bowl, and catches the fire if it falls.

I must tell you – and try not to conceive an insular prejudice against me for saying so – that you had better learn to smoke if you can. You will find yourself rather an alien in the *harims* without it, and be a wet blanket to other women. They will always be flattered at your visit, and like to receive you as a visitor, but *en intime* never. They will respect your prejudice if you tell them that it is not the custom of your country, but they cannot feel that you wish to be as one of them, unless you adopt theirs. They would suffer greatly if they had to pass a whole day without *tombak* or tobacco. Besides, to confess the truth, do you not think there is something vulgar in attaching any idea of respectability to not smoking? Of course, if the fumes really hurt you it is quite another thing, but as to holding smoking 'fast,' when it depends solely on country and climate, it is no more so than siesta or snowshoes. I am glad to see that some of the *haute volée* of England are throwing off that insular prejudice, and I hope soon that it need not be done *en cachette*. I cannot conceive why this idea should exist only in England, where I am told that the middle classes imagine that if a woman smokes she must have all the other vices. This is certainly not so. In Russia, Spain, South America, Austria, nay, in almost every country, the best of society smoke. In many lands where I have lived and travelled, all our festivities have ended in a supper and cigarettes. In Brazil we used to have them handed round between the courses. I confess I do not think that a big cigar looks pretty in a woman's mouth, nor would a short *meerschaum*, but what can be more graceful than a cigarette. Still more so the *narghileh*, or even the *chibouque*, which is, however, quite a man's pipe.

At the same time I sympathize with those who have small rooms, stuffy with curtains and carpets, where the smell of stale smoke would be intolerable. I speak to those who can have a proper smoking divan in the house.

Women who dislike, or affect to dislike, smoke, because they think it is the correct thing, can have no idea how they drive their husbands away from home. If a man may not smoke in his own house he will smoke in some other house, in preference to a lonely puff in the street: and that is worth a thought.

Allow me to end this long tirade about smoking with the charming old French sonnet:

> Doux charme de ma solitude,
>   Fumante pipe, ardente fourneau,
>   Qui purge d'humeur mon cerveau,
> Et mon esprit d'inquiétude.
>
> Tabac dont mon âme est ravie,
>   Lorsque je te vois perdre en l'air,
>   Aussi promptement qu'un éclair,
> Je vois l'image de ma vie.
>
> Je remets dans mon souvenir,
> Ce qu'un jour je dois devenir,
>   N'étant qu'une cendre animée.
>
> Et tout d'un coup je m'aperçois,
>   Que courant après ta fumée,
> Je me perds aussi bien que toi.

I think you would regret missing the roof of the book bazar, which leads to the west gate of the Mosque. On its left is a curious flight of steps through private houses. Arriving at the head of these stairs you can see four massive columns in a line, and at each end a square pier of masonry with a semi-column on the inner side. The shafts alone are visible from the bazar, as the capitals rise over the domed roof. The people will not mind our scrambling over their roofs, as we are '*harim*,' and then we can examine both capitals and superstructure. These pillars formerly formed part of the magnificent pagan temple, which must have extended some six hundred yards square, for there are columns here and there in situ, all in four straight lines. They are unnoticed, because the bazars, houses, and mud walls cling to them like wasps' nests. They support a rich and beautiful arch, of which only a fragment remains above the roofs; but if you examine this remnant you will say that it is one of the finest of ancient art in Syria. This noble gateway must have been at least eighty feet long and seventy feet high.

Now we will come down, and in the first friend's house I pass we will borrow *izars* and veils, so as not to be known, and get a Moslem woman to accompany us, and to speak for us. I want to show you something to amuse you, and if they know what we are we shall see nothing. We will go to an old Shaykh who sells charms, spells, and potions. You see his reception place is full of women with their faces well veiled. I will not speak to anyone but our Moslem friend, and that in a whisper. Not long ago a native said to me, 'Would you like A to hate B?' speaking of a bad man who had a very evil influence over a good, honest man. Without thinking, I replied, 'Yes; it would be the best thing that ever happened.' He only answered me by a gesture of the hand, which literally means, 'leave it to me.' The next day he secured a bit of the bad man's hair, and sewed it into the coat of the good man. Strange enough, as chance fell out, that day an event happened which opened the eyes of the latter to his friend's character, and they parted company; of course nothing would persuade the native that it was not the effect of his charm. The ingredients they use are wonderful. The hair of a pig, the tooth of a monkey, the poison of a snake, and goodness only knows what else. That young-looking woman, and I know her by her voice, is asking for a drug to make her husband love her. That other, with the dark *mandil*, wants something to make her spouse hate all his other wives. That client, who is aged enough to be our grandmother, pays the Shaykh to write her a paper that she may become the happy mother of a son. You cannot imagine the intrigues which are hatched here, and the extraordinary charms and spells that are manufactured and given, the honest faith which the people have in them, and how readily they pay. I must pretend to want a charm, or else we have no business here, and may be suspected of being spies. I will therefore ask for a paper, through the interpreter, to make my husband put away his fourth wife, of whom I will feign to be jealous. My case is to be dealt with by an old crone who is partially mad. She makes me put money in a basin of water, and predicts. She can only hear when spoken to in a whisper. This corresponds with fortune telling at home.

Let us retire now – a little of this goes a very long way, and I never come except to amuse English friends – to the sweetmeat bazar. Some of the 'goodies' are not bad, and here we can hand over the *izars* and veils to our Moslem friend. We will finish our afternoon at Shaykh Bandar's, the venerable, white-bearded Abu Antika (father of antiquities), as he is nicknamed. We must ride, for it is far away from the bazars.

That hole in the wall is his door, opening upon a poor courtyard. He is a venerable, white-bearded, turbaned Turk, with an eye full of cunning, the manners of a gentleman: at least so you think. Wait a little, until I excite him by bargaining over his prices; you shall see him tear off his turban, rend his beard, and fling a few solid brass and head-breaking pots across the room. The blood will rush to his face, as if he were going to have a fit; he will disappear, and after a short absence he will come back and beg pardon most humbly. He is the only Oriental I ever saw so moved about money. It makes me suspect Jewish blood somewhere, or else it is a splendid piece of acting to frighten women – he never does it when the *Kawwasses* are there. I always tell him he will play this trick once too often, and some day he will end in an apoplectic accident – an unpleasant bourne to all his pecuniary prospects. He smiles grimly when told where his faith consigns the usurer and the miser; it is a long way off; but when I add that another will have all his goods and money, the smile vanishes with an expression of ghastly dismay. One day, the first time, I was frightened and sorry, and followed him to see if anything did happen to him, and found behind all this apparent poverty that the old Harpagon had a magnificent court-yard, marble fountains and gold fish, orange and lemon trees, a very fair *harim*, and a house full of riches; splendid old china, too, of which I bought a quantity for my friends. We will go in there as soon as we have finished our greetings.

'Good evening, O Shaykh! Peace be with thee.'

'Good evening, O lady! And blessed with good luck. May Allah be praised for the sunshine of thy honourable visit!'

He unlocks a mysterious door, and introduces us into a small temple of treasures. Yes! You may well ask where you are to sit down. There are specimens of every curiosity and antiquity on the face of the Syrian earth, in incongruous piles and heaps on the floor, the divan, and the tables, hung to the ceiling and to the walls, and crowding all the shelves. The next difficulty after sitting is to find anything you want, or to distinguish one article from another. He will clear a space on the divan, where we may sit and rest. We shall have a cup of coffee in five minutes, and meanwhile we will chat with the old man and look about us. Presently he will offer us some sweetmeat, which he fancies, poor soul, is slightly intoxicating. It is not so in the least, but it is delicious, and he always imagines that people buy more after eating it. So I favour the delusion, and in order to extract it I bid low till he produces it, and rise a few piastres with every mouthful.

As you justly observe, divans and *narghilehs* require Turkish coffee, and whilst the old man is looking for his sweetmeat I will explain to you how coffee is made. The little gold or silver thing (*zarf*) which you hold in one hand guards a china egg-cup (*finjan*), and the latter contains the coffee. You can buy both here, but antiques chiefly. I have a very handsome silver-gilt set, studded with turquoise – coffee-pot, sugar-basin, and rose-water stoup to match – from this collection. The coffee is delicious, thick, and oily, with a sort of bubbly cream (*kaymak*) at the top. Pick your beans, carefully clean, roast on an iron plate until brown – not black, as in England – grind them, have a small pot of boiling water, put in two tablespoonfuls of coffee, stir it, and hold it on the fire a second or two till it is ready to bubble over. Take it off, and repeat this, say, three times. Set your cups in a row – first put in your sugar, if you mean to have sweet coffee – fill up, disperse the bubbly cream equally into all the cups with a small teaspoon, and serve it hot. Your cup must not be bigger than a doll's, because you are obliged to take it perhaps fifteen times a day – you must drink coffee with every visitor – and it is as strong and refreshing as champagne. Many eat the dregs with a spoon! When I first came I brought English coffee-cups with me, which greatly amazed the servants. I had also a stable-mill to grind Indian corn, as that was what our horses lived upon in Brazil. The groom came to me one day, and asked if that was an English coffee mill.

'No,' I said; 'why do you ask?'

'Because I thought, O lady, that if those were the cups, this must be the coffee-grinder to fit them.'

As coffee was made an unkind use of in our nursery, I grew up to the age of twenty-two without tasting it, and did not even know what it was like, unadulterated. I was once twenty-four hours on a journey without even a crumb of bread or a drop of water, and at the end of that time a kind soul brought me a cup, with a little cognac in it. I thought it was the most delicious thing I had ever tasted: it broke the ice, and I have liked it ever since. I could not, however, drink English coffee which is bought ready ground, and mixed with all sorts of things, and kept perhaps a week in a paper; two teaspoonfuls to a pint of water finally boiled, instead of a tablespoonful to six doll's cups!

I see the sweetmeat coming, and I am going to bid low. When I have collected upon the floor a heap of things you want to buy, I will say, 'How much for that heap, O Shaykh?' He will ask a fabulous price, and swear that under Allah's protection he is losing an enormous sum to gain my friendship, and the patronage of my friends. That suit of armour he recently refused to my cousin Lord B— for 100 pounds sterling; he repented when it was too late, and has never had a higher bid than 30 pounds. Don't fancy that those are Damascus blades, or that that one belonged to Harún el Rashid; there is not a Damascus blade left in the city, at least for sale. They come from Sheffield, Doncaster, Berlin, and Munich, and are set up in antique handles and sheaths.

You see there is every kind of bric-à-brac. Persian enamel, coffee-cups, jewellery, bits of jade, eastern inkstands, incense burners, rose-water stoups, brass trays, china, and what not. Those little bottles of silver, with crescents and chains, contain the *kohl* for the toilette. It is finely powdered antimony, and is put into these little bottles. They take a long pin, bodkin, or stick of silver or ivory, wet it if much is to be put on, dip into this powder, close the eyelids upon it, and draw it through from end to end. For an instant the eye is filled with the powder, smarts and waters. They then wipe away the superfluous black under the lids. Men use it as well as women; the latter prefer a mixture of the mineral with lamp-black, oil, and spices, and men prefer simple powder, without any addition. It is a pity European oculists do not order it to their patients. The object is to strengthen and cool the organ, and to keep off ophthalmia. With the eye well *kohl'd*, you can bear the reflection of heat from the desert, and look at objects without being affected by that wavy, quivering glare so painful to the sight. Thus I would undertake to stare without blinking at an English sun, and perhaps for this reason I never had ophthalmia, and scarcely ever wore spectacles in our long desert rides. In Europe it seems out of place, and would be considered as painting; here, also, the chief drawback is writing and studying so many hours under gas, in which case it is not so beneficial. The *harims* apply it for ornament, but it is openly and coarsely put on. If they would learn to use it as English and French actresses apply their paint, it would be very effective; but they smear it like an unwashed sweep, and only partly wipe away the surplus.

Now I see you have chosen your things, a Persian brass tray, an incense burner, a rose-water stoup, an inkstand for the belt, some ash-trays, a little amber and gold cigarette mouthpiece, a brass saucer for chibouque bowl, a gold inlaid dagger, a silver-backed hand mirror for toilette, a brass-carved drinking cup, coffee-cups and holders, coffee-pot, brass jug and basin for washing the hands, and a silver-mounted *narghileh*.

'Now, O Shaykh! what do you want for all this?'

'O lady! Allah knows that if his servant gives them to thee for 1,000 francs it will be like a gift, and may they bring thee a blessing!'

'Thou art mad, O Shaykh! I will give thee one hundred francs.' (I know they are worth between three and four hundred.)

The blood is rising in his face, but he struggles to keep it down, and to cool his temper walks away for a little, as if it were not worth his while to do any business with me. Whilst he again fetches the sweetmeat, I will tell you a story about him. The Comte de B— , an Italian, who was travelling for pleasure and adventure, paid a visit to Abú Antíká, and on seeing the treasures he went quite beside himself. He suddenly looked up from choosing items, and asked how much he would take for the whole room full, offering at the same time 15,000 francs. The Shaykh was struck almost dumb with joy; but seeing the Italian so excited, he was 'too clever by half' as they say, and thought that he could get more; so showing no emotion, he replied,

'Not so, *khawaja* (mister); but I will take 20,000.'

So they parted. The Italian come to the hotel, and raved up and down the room, saying to a friend, 'Do you think the Shaykh will relent and take my offer?' and he was very nearly running back to offer the 20,000. 'Yes,' said his friend, who had lived at Damascus for some time; 'he will come, but not till he has removed all the most valuable things into the *harim*, which you will never miss nor remember.' The Italian was cured, and thanked his friend. Abú Antíká went to his *harim*, and raved as the Count had done, occasionally lifting up his turban to cool his head, and exclaiming,

'15,000 francs! Why I could start doubly and trebly again with that. What a fool I have been! I wonder if I am too late, if that mad Frank will be gone. If Allah only protects me through this act of avarice, I will be an honester man for the future.' Accordingly, Abú Antíká appeared and said, 'O Dowlatak (your Highness), I have been considering the matter, and in my anxiety that your Highness should go away satisfied from Esh Sham, and pleased with your humble servant, I have resolved to forego the 5,000 francs, and to content myself with the poor little sum of 15,000 francs, though the goods are worth double the money, and I must begin life all over again.' The Count replied, 'I am very sorry, O Shaykh, that thou hast had this trouble. The sight of the things drove me mad, but the fever that I had to possess them when I offered thee the 15,000 francs has passed away, and I now see how rash I was to do so. I would rather have my money, were they worth double the sum.' Abú Antíká has been mentally tearing – not his hair, because he is shaved, but his beard, ever since that affair, still it has not cured him.

Now you see he has returned quite coolly, and offers us more sweetmeat as a peace offering. We will now go up 50 francs at every mouthful, because it is near sunset; we have three quarters of an hour's ride to Salahíyyeh, and the gates will be shut. If you give me *carte blanche*, I will stop at 500 francs. I have made a mental calculation whilst I have been talking. They will be well paid for at 460 francs, and 500 will give him something over. He will have every reason to be satisfied, and so will you, for they are really worth the money, and in Europe they would fetch a much higher price – at the same time, none but English would give him that sum here, and their travelling dragoman would cheat him of half of it. So now I have told him, and also that we wish him a cordial good day, and blessings upon his house. We will mount our donkeys, leaving a *Kawwass* to pick up the goods and load a boy with them; the Shaykh attends us to his gate, swearing that we have ruined his prospects forever.

You ask me if it is always necessary to go out with so much state, with one or more *Kawwasses*, and I must answer this – it is necessary, unless you go out in native dress, veiled. I mean, of course, at this side of the Lebanon. I thought the honours of my position, never being allowed out without an escort, a very great bore at first. It used to distress me to be made so much fuss with, and to have the road cleared for me as if I were a sacred object. I used to beg of the *Kawwasses* not to show their zeal by doing more than was needful for the customs of the country and the honour of the Consulate; but after I saw one group get a pail of dirty water thrown over them with insolent gestures, after hearing of a minister's wife being kissed in the bazar, and a clergyman's wife being struck by a soldier because her dress touched him *en passant*, rendering him unclean, I learnt that my meekness was quite misplaced, and that it takes some time to know how to behave in a manner which will gain respect in the East, which is the very opposite of that in the West. What would be considered conciliating, high-minded, delicate, and well-bred in certain cases, would here be only mistaken for cowardice, meanness, and half-wittedness. The person who is most loved and respected *per se* in the East, man or woman, is who is most brave, most just, most strict with them, most generous with money, and whom they cannot deceive with little intrigues. To punish an Eastern you have but two holds over him: to hurt his person or his pocket; but he much prefers the former. Hence it is that frequently an official sent out from England, without any previous knowledge of the East, a gentlemanly, quiet man, who would have been a great success in Paris or Berlin, is despised beyond measure in the East.

I dare say you feel quite tired. We will go home, and you shall go to your room and wash your hands for dinner at once; I will go round to the stables and see that the animals are all right, and be with you in ten minutes.

Colin Thubron
From *Mirror to Damascus (1967)*

A brown mountain rimmed with white mosques and schools, a refuge of piety and peace; such was the Kassioun mountain after the Jerusalem refugees had built Salihiye against its side. Under Saladin's dynasty, the Ayyoubid, men came to think of it as holy and eternal, and the bones of many hundred prophets speckled the land between the city wall and its lower slopes.

Today Salihiye is linked to the walled city by the boulevards of the modern one. Often a haze blurs its houses into the mountain rocks, so that the black doorways and windows resemble clean-cut caves. Its southern outskirts are very quiet, the houses and apartments shuttered. Lines of plane trees slope up the streets, and myrtle saplings drowse over the Barada. Beyond the canal of Yezid, the modern houses fall away and the main street of Salihiye traverses the mountainside.

I remember many broken cupolas with cockleshell window-lets, and the façades of anonymous tombs. Golden-stoned walls clasped each side of the road. Above them rose a stunted minaret the colour of evening sunlight, and opposite stood the mausoleum of a thirteenth-century vizier, decorated inside by an Andalucian sculptor, like some dark room of the Alhambra.

A few yards beyond I came to a mosque with cracked walls where a dome had once shielded the grave of a princess of Mosul. In a nearby street stood an Ayyoubid mosque, whose timbered ceiling poured down a mélange of fans and chandeliers. A pair of grey-flecked Crusader columns flanked the *mihrab*, and a grandfather clock had decided on an eternal ten minutes to three. Every religious building in Damascus is filled with European clocks, but the Moslems have thwarted them by refusing to wind them up or by twiddling their hands round into fanciful hours.

The clock in the Ayyoubid mosque had been still for years, and the prayer-hall was empty, but a mausoleum stood at the end of the court. Its white plaque declared: 'Tomb of the Lady Ismat, wife of the Sultan Nureddine the Martyr.' I grated open the door.

'Come on in,' said a voice.

A man in a fez was sitting in the gloom. I was bewildered to see that the room was full of chairs and tables, and that he had installed his medicine-chest against the wall. He pointed out the stained-glass windows, and told me which of the plaster mouldings were new and which old. After a while I asked what had happened to the wife of Nureddine, now that he was living in her tomb.

'She is under our feet,' he said, stamping. 'The dome fell in some years ago and smashed the sarcophagus. It is all sealed up under the floor now and they have built a new dome, praised be God. I am caretaker here. My house is next door, but there is not room for all my furniture there. So God sent me this place...'

On the far side of the road lay an exposed grave. It belonged to Mitqal, an officer of Saladin, and its casket was banded with inscriptions: 'May God have pity on one who implores His mercy in favour of Saladin, conqueror of

Jerusalem. I was in his service ... the day of Hattin, and at the capture of Saint Jean d'Acre and Ascalon ...' And on its west side, the broken words: 'Whosoever ... this tomb, alters, modifies or diminishes it, or effaces one of these inscriptions, or tries to steal a part of it, or executes a work which reduces it, or tries to ... this tomb, either in words, or in acts, may God ... may God hound him, may God exterminate him, may God bring him to justice on the day when neither riches nor family protect a man if he comes not to God with a pure heart, and thereafter may he be cursed of God and angels and all men.' But it is the wind and the sun which scratch at the grave of Saladin's general. Men ignore it.

The streets were full of fruit-sellers with boxes of tomatoes and aubergines and water-melons ribbed like Turks' turbans. Boys from restaurants were carrying plates of soup and peppers to mysterious customers in the lanes, and children were playing brick-bat against a canteen which was once a food-dole for the poor, built by the Ottoman Sultan Suleiman.

Opposite, through a handsome doorway, spread the empty, whitewashed courtyard of the derelict Qaymari hospital. In mediaeval times it had been filled with doctors and nurses, a chemist and an occulist. A patriarchal fig-tree now reached out over the courtyard pool, its branches shedding big leaves into the water. Four tall arches flanked the court. Under one glowed plasterwork rosettes like pale suns, and beneath them ran a band of script, worked round with flowers.

'Beautiful,' I said to an old man, who had appeared at my elbow. 'Do you know anything about them?'

'How should I? They were done long ago. You could never do such work now. Djinns' work. They did such things'.

I stared at him, thinking that perhaps he was laughing at me; but his face was serious and rather sad. His mouth was swathed in a *keffieh*, so that only the smudge of his moustache quivered when he spoke.

I told him I thought the djinns had emigrated to the mountains long ago; but he only peered at me, as if puzzled by my ignorance, and stubbornly muttered 'Djinns' again, this time to himself. He sat down on a bench facing the fig-tree, pulled his *keffieh* over his forehead and fell asleep. I looked at his bundled figure in its crumpled jacket and *cheroual*. It was the first time I had heard a Damascene express his belief in djinns.

His ancestors had told tales of crabs as huge as hills; of a serpent which drops from the clouds when they pour rain, and devours everything in its path until it dies; of valleys of diamonds and mountains of precious stones, and of the demon voices in a djinns' market in Kashmir. If he dreamt of a line of camels, might he believe, as his fathers had, that angels were descending to inspire his children? If he woke with a bleeding nose, he could think himself freed from the witch who tries to part Syrians from their mothers.

I remembered a village schoolteacher telling me that if a man is murdered his head flits away in the form of an owl – he cupped his hands round his mouth: '*Ihteres!* Woooh-ooh-ohoooh!' In past times, if a man's death were unavenged, the owl would shriek out 'Give me to drink!' And if somebody sees what he imagines to be a dog at dusk, it may be 'a certain small animal that has no good in it', which makes a special point of lifting its leg in the direction of Mecca.

Djinns picked their curved teeth in rooftops at daytime and flapped out at midnight in horrid shapes. *Afrits* fell in love with women who wore anklets and followed them wherever they went. Frogs had wonderful properties: they would stop the boiling of cooking-pots, draw confessions from sleeping people, delay the growth of hair and fill women with a madness for love. To spit three times down a frog's mouth was an infallible contraceptive, and if you sat in bat's gravy you would be healed of paralysis.

But the old man was still sleeping when I left the Qaymari, and I never discovered what more he knew. Next door glowed the rose-coloured courtyard of the Mohiy ad-Din Mosque. From a grove of pillars in the prayer-room I looked out over vines and roof-tops and saw Damascus: a view which had touched even the heart of Tamerlane. Down the courtyard stairway, the tints of the stone deepened, until they reached a sanctuary decorated in Turkish faience, higher than a man's reach. In the centre of the room stood the sepulchre of Ibn el-Arabi, the most famous mystic in Islam, surrounded by a silver and brass grille. By his side lay a heavily inscribed sarcophagus from Tunis, the grave of the Algerian warrior Abd el-Kader.

Two men were never coupled more strangely in one tomb. On one side rests the soldier who resisted the French in Algeria for seventeen years and found honourable exile in Damascus; on the other lies the prophet who taught the divinity of all existence, and declared that he had learnt the secrets of alchemy, treading a delicate course between heresy and sainthood:

> My heart is capable of every form
> A cloister for the monk, a fane for idols,
> A pasture for gazelles ...
> Love is the faith I hold: wherever turn
> His camels, still the one true faith is mine.

El-Arabi had a dangerous breadth of outlook in a society blinkered by tradition. His position became so difficult when he wrote a volume of erotic verse to a lady of Mecca, that he had to append footnotes, imbuing the poems with a purely mystical meaning. Now the family and friends of the heretic-saint are buried near him in the mausoleum, and the grille of his tomb has been smoothed fine by the kisses of women.

The grave of Abd el-Kader, the hero of Algeria's struggle against France, is remembered but not worshipped. Standing in the quietness of the Mohiy ad-Din, I could not think of his wars, only of his incongruous imprisonment on the Loire, and of his release by Louis Napoleon; of the emperor and the emir squatting down to eat cous-cous on the floor of the Château d'Amboise; of Abd el-Kader kneeling to afternoon prayer in the vestibule of St Cloud, and of his accidentally seeing the standards of his warriors among the captive banners hanging in the Hôtel des Invalides – 'Those times are past. I wish to forget them. Let us always endeavour to live in the present.'

It was growing late. The sun had lost its heat and lay across the lanes in flaccid streaks. Every afternoon Damascus seemed to be caught too early in this ambush of light, and to trifle with it a long time before darkness. It was the hour when men start to walk about in pyjamas and sandals.

I reached the outskirts of the old town – a dribble of *madrasas* among the flats – and saw the Omariya school, the oldest building on the mountain, its ruined arches festooned with washing; and the big, white courtyard of the Mozaffari Mosque, with ancient columns and a prayer-hall rich in carved wood, where people stared at me and kissed their Korans. I passed the Madrasa Sâhibiya, charged with the treble roar of school-children, and the lanes slanted to a mosque whose walls were stippled in shrubbery – the last building of Saladin's city. Beyond it, only modern houses trampled downhill along the neck of the orchards.

The Kassioun Mountain had grown tawny as a camel in the dusk, its arteries darker. I leant against the wall of a house, and looked down into the plain between the hill and the main city, where autumn poplars stood among a tangle of orchards which looked as if they would never bear fruit again. Inside the house a woman was singing a popular song:

> My eyes, pour out your tears now all you will,
> Tears are not saved ...

The clop of horses' hoofs over the cobbles filled the lane with their sound, and died away.

> I am an unlit star which falls through the long night,
> A cloud without rain ...

Below, flights of pigeons flickered white in a snare of sunlight, like scraps of paper tossed through the trees. And twilight came rolling in from the desert.

Laurence Deonna
Memory Versus Money (1992)

Giving a sharp turn of the wheel, Nadia managed to avoid a reckless driver. 'The bastard!' she exclaimed. 'It reminds me of them – wait till you hear what they did to me!' Nadia Khost is a writer, a woman with a mission, and the people she was referring to are the speculators who are destroying old Damascus – or what is left of it. She is doing her best to take the bread out of the mouths of 'those vultures,' as she calls them, 'who buy old houses and dismember them.' Columns, painted ceilings, inlaid works of wood and mother-of-pearl, the city's architectural heritage is being desecrated and carted away ... What remains of the shattered interiors can later be found in antique stores, in Damascus or elsewhere. 'And when they have stripped these old houses bare,' she said, 'they tear them down and build over them.'

At just over fifty, Nadia, slim and plainly attired in a somewhat old-fashioned dress, had kept her girlish good looks. With her blond hair and large glasses, she still resembled the student she had once been in Moscow, immersed in Chekhov and his moods (she had written her doctoral thesis on Chekhov after studying philosophy and aesthetics in Damascus). 'I am not aware of everything that goes on,' she said, 'yet every day I have the feeling that something beautiful, somewhere, is passing out of our lives forever ... It hurts me to think of it.'

The light turned green and Nadia drove on. 'Have you ever heard of the Ecochard plan?' she asked. 'It dates back to 1936, when the country was under French administration, but that doesn't prevent our plunderers from referring to it today. It's so convenient. Ecochard wanted to 'modernize' Damascus, claiming his purpose was to improve living conditions. And he was all the more eager to do so as dark alleyways and hidden recesses are dangerous places for the occupying forces of any city! Ecochard's plan was a crime. If he had suggested a similar one for Paris he would have been hanged. And the crime was aggravated by the fact that the people of Damascus have almost no idea of the wealth their city contains. Damascus was never turned into a museum: people lived there, that's all. As the oldest city in the world, it has thousands of unknown treasures, but so far only two hundred and fifty palaces and monuments have been inventoried. Countless generations of artists have made Damascus what it is. The city wasn't built by engineers, whose imagination is as dull as their flat walls!'

Pitting memory against money, defying bulldozers with a pen: Nadia's is surely a noble cause, but was it worth risking her life? 'They began by threatening me – using others to convey the message, of course, while they bravely stood in the background. "My dear lady", I was told, "traffic being what it is these days an accident could so easily happen." '

Nadia stood firm and went on with her crusade. 'Then they became bolder,' she said. 'The first time I was able to avoid them, but not the second. They rammed my car when I was driving over a bridge on the freeway. The impact sent me hurtling over the railing.' Nadia suffered a serious head injury and had to remain lying down for three months without moving. Today she still complains of migraines and dizzy spells.

The world is sadly lacking in heroes, and no one will be surprised to learn that Nadia often feels very lonely... On the other hand, she no longer fears a thing. At a lethargic meeting of 'urban experts' she once attended at the air-conditioned Cham Hotel, one of the most luxurious in the capital, she had the nerve to provoke them with these words: 'The more I listen to you, gentlemen,' she said, 'the more certain I am that if any Arab city survives into the future with its architecture intact it will be in Israel.'

It was a nice stab but I fear Nadia is deluding herself. The biblical landscape is rapidly disappearing, whichever way you look. And whatever war has not destroyed will soon be finished off by human hands. The dusty olive trees, the grazing sheep, the villages that blend so naturally into the chalky hills, the slow, harmonious pace of life, all that is passing away and soon no trace of it will be left... Acting in collusion, Arab and Israeli developers will have no rest until they have built a new Singapore in Palestine, a new Miami Beach on the Red Sea, until Coca Cola reigns supreme on the banks of the River Jordan... The scene is set for peace, and prefabricated ugliness is lurking in the wings.

Nadia used to be a member of the Damascus city council. 'After a while I was thrown out of office – or rather, I was kicked out the door! The press never dropped me, though, nor did the intellectuals and artists, all those who are determined to preserve the city's soul. Our petitions have forced the politicians to give in, at least a bit. The part of Damascus that lies inside the ancient city walls can no longer be touched. But the old city that lies outside the walls is even more beautiful, for over the centuries its inhabitants have kept adorning it and setting off its charm, and it will be much more difficult to protect.' Nadia sighed. 'The city council can pass all the laws it wants, it cannot stop people with money from doing whatever they please.'

Nadia Khost grew up in Saruja, a neighborhood 'as old as history itself.' Situated in the very heart of the capital, where the price of land is spiralling, it is slowly being strangled and swallowed up by the modern buildings whose ugliness befouls the sky. After Nadia had taken me to Saruja I could understand why she dies a bit more every time she goes there.

Saruja profaned. Gutted. Pitted with giant craters like the one we stood in front of and which looked as if it had been blasted out by a bomb. A bomb? Why not? The destruction was on the scale of a holocaust. 'The most exquisite palace used to stand here, the Sabah palace, but it was torn down in the 1960s. Why? What for? For no reason at all. The first president of Syria, who was elected in 1946, used to live here and...' Nadia paused. A crowd of students had invaded the alley. 'A friend of mine – a professor – it killed him...' What did? I asked. 'There. That is where he used to live. His house looked out on the palace. When they destroyed it they destroyed him too – they destroyed the man whose window looked out on the palace. He gazed at that gaping hole for so long that it ended up by breaking his heart.'

In one of Nadia's short stories, *The House of Yussuf al-Azmi*, the main character, a national hero of the 1920s and a symbol of Syrian resistance to French rule, returns to earth and can no longer find his house, his street, or anything at all. Nothing is left of the city he once knew, which is now in the hands of new rulers called speculators. On the cheeks of the city's inhabitants, who have called on him for help, Yussuf al-Azmi sees tears 'that go ding, ding, ding when they fall' – bitter coins, bitter small change.

While Nadia was telling me about Damascus, I thought briefly of Homs, whose old districts had been systematically torn down. I had gone back to Homs in 1992, years after the destruction. The ruins were still there, whiter and dustier than before: the only relic left standing was the 'Mosque of the Forty,' a heart-rending sight amid the rubble. Consigned to the edge of the disaster area and enjoying an unobstructed view of a wasteland that used to be throbbing with life – the life they once enjoyed there – the storekeepers were as suspicious as ever: no smile, no cup of coffee for me. Inquisitive visitors, especially foreigners, were clearly not welcome.

Accompanying Nadia to Saruja was a moving experience. People called out to her from the dark shops, engaging her in long, worried conversations: 'Anything new? No? Are you sure?' These simple words concealed a message: 'Talk to those people on top, tell them about my door and its hand – shaped knocker, the balconies overlooking the courtyard, the coolness of the basin, the fragrance of the jasmine and the orange tree, tell them that my house is also theirs since it is Syria itself. We have lived here for centuries.'

During those centuries Saruja had amassed its share of hidden treasures. The neighbourhood was a multilayered slice of history. At first glance the cobbler's shop seemed perfectly ordinary, but its leathers, hides and tools concealed a monumental painted column and a splendid coffered ceiling. The back courtyard opened onto an abandoned lot, overgrown with wild grasses and shaded by an ancient fig tree. Nadia's face lit up: 'Imagine this courtyard alive with music, people, voices, laughter... You see, this is not just any old place: it used to be a political cabaret, the famous Café Karagueuz.' How many ministers, how many officers had tried to muzzle the writers, poets and actors who gathered here, and who continued to make fun of them until the 1950s when democracy lay dying. When it was finally crushed, so was the Café Karagueuz.

Nadia brushed the dust from her skirt and when we were both out in the street again she raised her head towards what had once been a *musharabieh*, a balcony from which one can see without being seen. Its exquisitely carved woodwork, as fine as lace, was now in shreds. 'Look,' she said, 'another casualty.' As we walked on she added, 'You know, I often tell myself that protecting the past and teaching our children to see its beauty forges a link between generations. It makes children see the genius in man, and shows them why life is so precious. It also gives them a sense of dignity – it's a political act, if you like.'

With their crooked lines that deflect the path of the sun, their corbelled façades and their bulging, lopsided walls, ancient cities, where everything is asymmetrical, remind us poor human beings of ourselves. Is that why we feel so at home in them? For we also have our locked doors, our inner courtyards and our hidden staircases, and our souls are in disarray. Modern cities are obsessed with perfect symmetry, and their orderly architecture reflects the philosophy of a world where everything is logical – as simple as a straight line! A world where everything can be proved, demonstrated and explained, but which is as cold as metal and as indiscreet as a pane of glass.

Nadia quickened her pace. People were expecting us. A moment later, in a district of old Damascus that lay within the city walls, a small, ordinary-looking door opened up for us, letting us into a veritable gem of a house. But why was everything so overdone? Colored lights had been strung over the patio, making it look like a fair-ground. Under the archway, in the depths of a large alcove lined with divans, the walls were overladen with a jumble of old sabers and swords, clocks, verses from the Koran and portraits of ancestors in tarbooshes. Ali, the prophet of Shiite Muslims, kept a watchful eye above it all. Dare I say what I thought? He looked like Jesus.

Looking quite as theatrical as the décor, the potbellied owner was wearing a white robe and cap; his eyes were so black they seemed made up and his thick moustache looked fake.

In the living room of this house from days gone by, a Swiss clock had stopped running at midnight. Midnight: as in a fairy-tale ball? Unfortunately, custom prohibited my host from taking me by the waist and we were not to waltz together under the high inlaid ceilings. But there was nothing to prevent us from standing by the gramophone, a mammoth dating from the 1940s, and singing along with Jacqueline François as she belted out *Mademoiselle de Paris* on an old seventy-eight-rpm record.

Translated by Christopher Snow

Brigid Keenan
Lady Damascus (2006)

I can pinpoint the exact moment that I fell in love with Damascus – it was the first time I went inside one of the great courtyard houses of the Old City. It was a palace called Beit Mujallid: I was quite unprepared for what I was going to see, and overwhelmed by its glittering beauty. Then, when I realised what a poor state the building was in, I was filled with concern and rushed back to try and persuade my husband that we should sell our home in England and rescue a Damascene palace instead. Luckily our marriage was preserved when someone else stepped in to save Beit Mujallid – this was Nora Jumblatt, the Damascene wife of Druze leader Walid Jumblatt, who bought it and restored it exquisitely. So there was a happy ending for the palace, but my own newfound passion for the Old City was still unfulfilled: I had no place there, I was an outsider – I felt a bit like a frustrated lover, only able to visit the object of my desire in daytime, never staying the night.

How can you fall in love with a whole city because of one house, you might wonder? The simple answer is because it opened my eyes. Until I was taken to see it I was simply a foreign tourist shopping in Straight Street or in the spice souk, not suspecting that behind the facades of the houses surrounding me lay so much beauty and hidden treasure. Being shown Beit Mujallid was like being let into a wonderful secret. I spent the next months desperately searching for a house in the Old City cheap enough for me to buy, so that I could belong to this fascinating place, become a real part of it.

Then the strangest thing happened, the sort of uncanny miraculous event which seems to happen in Damascus: a relative whom I had never met, an architect it turned out, died and left me enough money to buy a little house that I had found in the Muslim area behind the great mosque. I bought it and restored it over the next couple of years, and lived there with my husband for the short time we had left in Syria, between the house being finished and our posting to that country coming to an end.

I was not the first Western woman to fall in love with Damascus. It is said (I don't know by whom, but it is quoted in Marie Fadel's charming little book, *Damascus, Taste of a City*) that 'when a man has lived for seven years in Damascus, Damascus lives in him.' In fact, I didn't notice this happening to the *men* around me in Syria so much, but the city certainly had a magnetic attraction for the other foreign women I knew there – as it has to many women in the past.

Isabel Burton, wife of Richard, the famous writer and explorer who was the

British Consul in Syria in 1869, lived there for much less long but fell under its spell. Mrs Burton should have been in Damascus for many more years, but her husband was abruptly recalled to London because he had upset too many powerful factions in the city (including the British missionaries). Isabel wrote that the afternoon before she heard the news that they were obliged to leave was her 'last happy day'. And long afterwards when people asked her if she had liked Damascus, her response was: '*Like* it! My eyes fill and my heart throbs even at the question...' Like me, Mrs Burton couldn't exactly explain her passion for the city. When friends asked her why she had become so fond of it, she had to reply that she didn't know. They would go through lists of possible reasons: The climate? The luxuries? The house she had lived in? The society? the power which her husband's position gave her? In the end she would simply say 'I can't tell you – if you had lived there you would know...' *Indeed.*

Seventy-odd years later, the archaeologist Freya Stark found herself equally enchanted by Damascus and just as lost for the reason why. 'In spite of dust, noise, tawdriness, ugliness of detail, there is a magic, not to be understood in a day or even two! ... I am in love with the enchanted city ... there seems to be something peculiarly luminous in the air of Damascus – as if the atmosphere were thinner than elsewhere and the light could shine through more easily.'

By far the best known of Damascus's western female admirers was Jane Digby, the English aristocrat and beauty, who went there in 1853, fell in love with an Arab Sheikh twenty years younger than herself, and never left. (She is buried in the Protestant cemetery there.) Of course, in her case it is hard to separate her love for the Sheikh and her love for the city, but she lavished attention on the two homes she built there which were greatly admired by Western visitors. The Prince of Wales, who called on her in 1862, wrote that her rooms were 'charmingly arranged' and that her garden was full of roses. Jane Digby became a great friend of Richard and Isabel Burton during their brief posting to Damascus and later wrote nostalgically about the evenings they spent on the roof of the Burtons' residence on the edge of Damascus – together with another exile, 'Abd al-Qadir, the Algerian leader whose country had been conquered by the French. 'It was all wild, romantic and solemn: and sometimes we would pause in our conversation to listen to the sounds around us: the last call to prayer on the minaret-top, the soughing of wind through the mountain gorges and the noise of the water-wheel in the neighbouring orchards.'

Jane Digby's biographer, Mary S Lovell, went to Damascus in 1992 to research her book, *A Scandalous Life*, and, like her subject, found herself instantly smitten; she has been back many times since. 'It exerted a very powerful pull on me from the first ... somehow I have always felt at home in Damascus. Initially, I suppose, I noted only the lift of spirit caused by the dry desert air and the radiant light so peculiar to this enchanting and enchanted place ... then there was the tug of history; of Jane Digby's history in particular, but a much wider history ... here is the home of Ananias who took in the blinded St Paul ... here is the tomb of Saladin, the arch-foe of Richard the Lionheart ...'

Only one woman seems to have remained impervious to the charm of Damascus – Lady Hester Stanhope, another British aristocrat, who visited in 1812. After a bad start in a house in the Christian area, where she refused to stay 'surrounded by Greeks and Armenians' because she wanted to experience the *real* Orient, the Governor of Damascus allocated her a magnificent mansion in the Muslim quarter where she held court for a while, but then moved on to Palmyra where, later, the locals crowned her queen. Perhaps Lady Hester had too big an ego to be happy in Damascus. Mark Twain wrote that this city 'measures time not by days, months and years, but by the empires she has seen rise and prosper and crumble to ruin', and it seems to me that such a place does not have much patience with people who show off or give themselves airs. To be accepted there, you must surrender to Damascus and live on her terms, rather than trying to impose your own.

I don't know who worked out that Damascus's horoscope sign is Leo, but I am sure they are wrong. It *must* be Scorpio. Damascus is an extraordinarily sensual – you could even say sexual – city, and *that*, I have come to the conclusion, is the reason why we western women are so drawn to it. Of course this has something to do with Syrian men who are attractive, and seem to like women – not just young and pretty ones, but all sorts – and who are courteous and flatter them in a way that no one does anywhere else, but it is much more than that. This is a city that delights in the difference between the sexes, where there is a gentle game going on between men and women – a kind of flirtatious conspiracy. There is nothing overt or unpleasant, nothing that hassles or frightens – it is a question of an exchange of glances as you buy your vegetables in the market, a second of eye contact in a restaurant, a light hand that hardly brushes a shoulder or elbow to guide you across the street. It's innocent and even humorous, but it gives the atmosphere a sexual charge, a frisson of excitement. And there is no denying that it is very pleasant to be in a place where you are made to feel good.

Damascus is a city where women walk with a jauntier step – but it is also a city all about women, and full of women. Its icons and saints are women: Mohammed's granddaughter Zainab, and Ruqayya, his great-granddaughter, are buried in Damascus and every year up to two hundred thousand Iranian pilgrims, most of them women, come to pray at their shrines. The streets teem with them in their flapping black *chadors*, brushing shoulders with other women out shopping in mini skirts, Mother Theresa nuns going about their good works, women up from the Haroun with tired tattooed faces, young women with big hair, women whose hair is covered by the modest Muslim scarf or *hijab*. Down in the Christian area is a young woman, Myrna, who has had visions of the Virgin Mary and whose house is crowded with yet more women pilgrims, some from as far away as Australia. And in the secular world, it is not surprising to me that the owner and creator of the first tourist hotel in Old Damascus is a woman. Only a woman who loved the city would have been able to overcome as many man-made obstacles as Maya Mamarbachi has done, to fulfil her dream.

I lived in Damascus for nearly six years and it was there that I learned how Arab women enjoy each other's company. *Really* enjoy it, I mean, and not just while they are waiting for the men to arrive – for at the women's parties thrown to celebrate weddings and other joyful family occasions (occasionally in a *hammam* or bath house where everyone ends up wrapped in towels and smoking hubble-bubble pipes) the men never will arrive. They are not invited. The women are happy together, eating, gossiping, singing karaoke, dancing sexily with and for each other, and generally letting their hair down, like girls on some sort of unlikely non-alcoholic hen night. There is camaraderie and fun and bonding among these women that I have never come across outside the Arab world. And here is another women's secret – in the souk in Damascus you can buy the most erotic underwear I have ever seen. Slowly it occurs to you that the veiled, nun-like women who pass you in the street, so modestly clothed, are the customers for the open-nipple bras and crotchless, musical knickers and such. (I bought a couple of pairs of the musical knickers to put in my daughters' stockings one Christmas as a joke. The man who sold them to me called me back as I walked away with my tiny parcel. 'What is it?' I asked, 'Extra batteries for you', he said, pressing them into my hand and looking into my eyes with a huge smile.)

To my mind, Damascus itself is female. The Old City is perfumed with the aroma of spices and fresh-ground coffee from the souk, and its architecture is curvy and sensuous. In Aleppo – a masculine city – the houses are built in cut stone, but in Damascus they are stone only on the ground floor; the rest of the house is made of mud-brick coated with mud 'plaster' which has been smoothed onto the building with human hands; all is rounded and tactile. It is a cliché to talk about the Damascus house being like a veiled woman who reveals nothing of herself on the outside and keeps all her beauty for those privileged to be close to her (like the modest women in the saucy underwear) but it is true in a way. The city has a very female mysteriousness – you know there are architectural glories – courtyards, fountains, and exquisite decoration – but they will not be revealed to you unless you have access. You cannot walk from a dark alley into a dazzling sunlit courtyard unless invited. (The entrances to most of the grand houses are built with a bend so as to prevent anyone on the street from seeing inside.) And women are the gatekeepers in Damascus: I could never have written my book on the houses of the Old City had I been a man because no woman would ever have opened the door to me.

But the city is as flirtatious as its inhabitants – not all the houses have angled entrances and as you pass through the streets you occasionally catch glimpses of their courtyards - a spray of jasmine here, a fountain there, a patch of exquisite paving at the bottom of some steps somewhere else. These are the city's equivalent of glimpsing an ankle under a long dress or a lock of hair escaped from a veil. Of course I am being wildly romantic in describing it this way; the sensuous mud plaster has fallen off half the buildings, and as for 'behind the veil', there are museums and houses open to the public, which you may easily enter and explore – but nonetheless, sensuality, secrecy and mystery are the overwhelming sensations I have in Damascus.

The political regime and the predominant religion of Syria play no mean part in creating the exotic mood of Damascus. I cannot imagine that the place would hold quite the same allure if it was the capital of a modern, non-religious, Western-type country, with its streets lined with chain stores, and not a veil or *chador* to be seen. And there is something relaxing about a city where you can be certain you will never see a drunk. Another vital part of its charm is that the Old City is living in a different time frame from most of the rest of the world, one in which men are shaved with cut-throat razors, medicine shops sell dried baby crocodiles to improve men's fertility, and the heating oil is delivered in a cart drawn by a horse with ostrich feathers and pompoms on its head. As Ross Burns writes in his book *Damascus: A History,* 'Traditional life continues in the old city with a matter-of-fact air that makes light of the centuries. While Damascus has had to face more tumultuous challenges than most historic cities... it has done so with an inner strength...'

I remember thinking when I lived in the Old City and friends used to ask nervously 'What will you do there if there is a revolution?', how easy it would be to disguise oneself in Damascus in a time of turmoil or trouble: whatever sex you were, you could just put on a *chador* and literally disappear into the streets unnoticed. On the other hand, it would be very difficult to have an illicit affair in the Old City – neighbours are ever-watchful and prying, noting everyone who goes into and out of your house, how long they stay there, and what they have with them.

When Tim Beddow, the photographer, and I were working together on *Damascus: Hidden Treasures of the Old City* it was obvious that we should base ourselves in my little house in the Old City so that rather than driving in from the suburbs each day we could walk to the places we wanted to photograph. But I was warned by Syrian friends, 'Pretend he is your brother or people will be shocked'. One evening, after a day spent photographing houses in the Christian quarter, I came back to the house, ahead of Tim, exhausted. As I put my key in the lock of my door, my neighbour stepped out of his house – he had obviously been waiting – and asked me 'How is your brother?' 'My brother?' I said unthinkingly, 'I haven't seen my brother for months.' 'But he is staying with you, is he not?' came the reply. 'Oh no,' I said, quick as a flash, 'that's my *half*-brother who is staying with me...'

I am perfectly sure that my neighbour knew the truth, but honour was satisfied. That is the way in Damascus, city of secrets and hidden glances, where things are not always what they seem but where everyone respects the outward proprieties, and where, despite the neighbourhood watch, everyone keeps his own council. Damascenes have a saying, which perhaps explains why they are such an enigmatic people: 'A secret must be kept only between two' – meaning your own two lips.

Sarah Maguire
Damascene (2005)

Centuries of barefoot pilgrims have walked
his white marble to the stuff of glass –

billowing, doubled in *hijab*, I look down
into the heavens' absolute descent.

Swarming aloft from the rink of the Umayyad Mosque
a dark crowd of pigeons rips

open the golden fabric of dusk –
figures scaling the last slow heat of September,

a heat heavy with the end of a summer's summer –
its dust now settling onto cupolas and pantiles,

onto the balconied, octagonal minaret
where Jesus, one day, will alight to bring Judgement.

In the greenish, underwater gloom of the Prayer Hall
the head of John the Baptist waits behind bars.

*

How strange I am to myself here –
out of bounds, unknown.

Lost in the night streets of Damascus
I am a figment of shadows

cast by yellowing lamps
down pleated corridors of overlapping homes;

their whitewashed flanks are still warm from the sun –
breathing, intricate, woven from wattle and thatch.

*

In a room walled with carpets,
a room warm with the smell of shorn wool

and the mineral tincture of dyes –
he laid me on a *kilim*, and I bled.

Andrew Archibald Paton
From *The Modern Syrians (1841)*

Departure of the Mecca Caravan

To Europeans Damascus is the Pearl of the East, begirt with emeralds, – the city
of gilded saloons and bubbling fountains, environed with flowing rivers and
cool shady retreats. How oft have the songs of the birds, in the soothing twilight
of its umbrageous woods, produced in me oblivion of the fierce passions of the
people, and the base artifices of the rulers recalling the lines of Tieck, –

> Waldeinsamkeit du bist mir lieb,
> Und Oh wie lieb waldeinsamkeit.

But to the Moslem Damascus is the Holy City, the point at which the progress
to the Caaba of Mecca assumes a more sacred character. Notwithstanding the
revolutions of which Syria has been the theatre, nothing has ever occurred to
disturb the thoroughly Oriental and orthodox features of Damascus. A *firman*
of the Sultan Caliph opens all the mosques of Constantinople, the tolerance of
Mehemet Ali allows the astonished Anglo-Indian to gaze at the grand lines of
the four Lewaween in the mosque of Sultan Hassan, at Cairo; but no Frank ever
entered, in his own costume, the mosque of Beni Omeia at Damascus. Mr Rich,
when he visited it, was disguised as a Georgian Turk; and Ali Bey must be
classed as a Moslem. The departure of the Mecca caravan is the greatest day in
the calendar of the Damascenes. It is, however, a very singular fact, that while

the people of Cairo (in other respects disciplined to tolerance) used to maltreat the Christians and Franks who dared to look at the departure of the African pilgrims, the Damascenes, on the contrary, gave every encouragement to Christian spectators, in the hope that the pomp and solemnity of the scene might induce them to embrace Islamism. In the first year of Ibrahim Pasha's occupation of Syria the more fanatical of the Egyptians maltreated several Christian spectators; but, in the following year, Shereef Pasha issued orders which insured the continuance of the ancient milder usage.

For a month before the departure the streets of Damascus are crowded with wanderers from the Black, the Caspian, and the Aral Seas – from the bracing breezes of the Caucasus, the pestilential vapours of the Oxus, and the still remoter regions of Samarcand. Religious motives weigh with many, but not with all. Commerce, with its excitements and advantages, gives an impetus to the Hadge, but for which it might, long ere this, have fallen into partial desuetude, and been placed in the category of duties as being inconsistent with the extension of Islamism to new climes, and places unknown to the Prophet, even by name. The daggers of Khorassan are exchanged for the silks of Damascus. The camel that carries to Mecca the rice for the southward journey returns with the coffee of Mocha. In the Hedjas horses are scarce and dear, camels are plentiful and cheap. The humbler Hadgi rides to Mecca a horse, which he sells for the double of its purchase-money, and returns back on a camel, which he has bought for three hundred piastres, and sells in the Meidan for a thousand. In Damascus such was the traffic that it put one in mind of a Leipsic fair. The gold gazzi, the legal value of which is twenty-one piastres, rose to twenty-five, but, when the Hadge had gone, rapidly fell again. The duties of hospitality to the Hadgis are incumbent on the Damascenes, without being grievous or burdensome, for the host has a right to two and a half percent on all that the pilgrim, his guest, buys or sells. The wealthier merchants are usually the Persians.

The first proceeding after the arrival of the Aleppo caravan is to hold a divan, which is attended by the Pasha, the Emir-el-Hadge, the Sur Emini, or Treasurer of the Porte, the Cadi, the Mufti, and the Ayan of the town, for the purpose of hiring camels. This is no trifling affair, for, besides four thousand horses, the Hadge requires upwards of eight thousand camels. The usual hire of a camel from here to Mecca is three thousand piastres; but this year, in consequence of the cheapness of provisions, the price was fixed at two thousand five hundred piastres. The four *mokaymeen*, or camel-contractors, begin by asking three thousand five hundred piastres, on which the Ayan take a piece of paper, and putting down all the items of the camel's expense – barley, water, drivers, attendants, &c. – point out the fall of prices, and after a full hearing of arguments on both sides the bargain is concluded.

The ceremonies previous to the departure of the Hadge commenced on a Wednesday. At the *Asr*, or hour of afternoon prayer, the green banner of the Prophet was conveyed from the old castle to the mosque of the Sangiacdar, and thence after prayer to the seraglio. As I followed with my eyes this curious procession, and gazed first at the tenement the banner had left, and then on its ultimate receptacle, my mind involuntarily reverted to the 'Turk's progress.' The Castle of Damascus, from which the emblem was brought, recalled, with its massive masonry and frowning battlements, the days when the Selims and Soleymans fortified the strongholds of the early Arab conquerors, – while paint and varnish, covering the flimsy wooden seraglio, erected in the last bastard style of Stamboul, which a mere spark, fanned by the first breeze, may devote to destruction, reminded me of the present fabric of Ottoman power.

Ahmed Pasha, on the approach of the banner, descended the steps, divested himself of his shoes, and, advancing, received from the Sangiacdar the sacred emblem, for which he gave a formal receipt. Having kissed the banner, he carried it on his shoulder up the steps, while the cannon roared a salute.

On the following day the Hadge took its departure with great pomp, the sight of which, in the magniloquent language of the country, was enough to burst the gall-bladder of a lion. Sooth to say, the interest of the scene was derived from its thoroughly Oriental character, and the absence of any object that could remind one of the West, except the surtouts and trousers of the Emir-el-Hadge and his attendants. The town was astir by daybreak. The Durweesheey, the Tarik-el-Mustakeem (the straight street), and other thoroughfares leading to the Meidan, were thronged with spectators in their holiday-clothes, and encumbered with camels receiving their loads of provender, or gay litters and their tenants. Some pilgrims wept a farewell, but the loud exclamations of others showed that the religious end of their journey was forgotten in the bustle and impatience of its commencement.

Mr. Wood having procured the use of a terrace on the line of procession, I accepted his invitation to join his party, and make a day of amusement. At eight o'clock we left the Consulate for our destination, preceded by eight cavasses, which was a mere form, for Mr Wood's presence was a sufficient protection; for by his personal qualities, aided by his Oriental scholarship, he has completely conquered the good opinion of the Damascenes.

From this hour until eleven o'clock the street presented one unbroken line of loaded camels and irregular cavalry, which with difficulty threaded its way, the roofs of the houses and numerous mosques being as crowded as the pavement below; in fact, never did I see the sombre features of a Damascene street so gaily relaxed. Water is the *summum bonum* in the East. Ever and anon came a group of water-carriers, on the shoulders of whom stood a sheikh, supporting himself by leaning on long poles held up to his service. Artillery, drawn by camels in pairs, unused to any exertion but that of bearing heavy burdens, and as impatient of draught as of working in pairs, alternately amused and terrified the spectators with their uncouth restiveness and fearful zigzag motions, so different from their accustomed stately measured pace. Troops of Kurds (the Cossacks of Turkey), with their long formidable lances, barbarous but picturesque accoutrements and caparisons, followed the artillery.

A gap intervened in the procession: the atmosphere was beautifully clear; and I turned round to survey the barren, fawn-coloured line of Anti-Lebanon, cut in twain by the dark green bronze-like minaret of the Djama-el-Sannaneey, when the guns of the Castle announced the departure of the Emir-el-Hadge and the sacred emblems. Preceded by a regiment of Spahis, an immense and singular object slowly approached: this was the *mahmel*. Conceive a camel of the most gigantic stature to be found in the East saddled with a crate-frame, covered with a cloth of green silk, embroidered in gold and silver, reaching almost to the feet of the animal. This covering was made in Cairo during the first year of the Egyptian invasion, to replace the former one, which had disappeared after the revolt against Mohammed Selim Pasha. It cost six hundred purses, or something less than three thousand pounds; and the weight of the whole *mahmel* is six hundred and sixty pounds. Next followed the *sangiac*, or banner, and after it the Ayan of the town; and the procession was closed by the Sur Emini and the Emir-el-Hadge Cara Ali Pasha.

By ancient usage only three individuals can employ mules to carry their litter, or *takterwan*, as it is called – the Emir el Hadge, his *kiahia*, and the Sur Emini, who is the bearer of the ten thousand purses which the Sultan expends on the pilgrims: the other litters are suspended between two camels. The third Sultana performed the pilgrimage in a European carriage, as the road from here to Mecca is perfectly level. It was certainly the first carriage that ever went to Mecca, and the third ever seen in Damascus; the two first having been those of Shereef Pasha, and Mr Consul-General Farren. The Sultana did not appear in the procession I have described.

Five hundred camels are assigned for the personal service of the Emir-el-Hadge, which, by a legal fiction, in order to keep their number complete, are supposed never to die, and are fed from the proceeds of property entailed for this purpose. Every two camels have an *akkam*, or leader, who receives five hundred piastres from the contractor for his trouble in going to Mecca; and every ten camels have a feeder, who receives a hundred. The *djammal*, or camel-driver, and the tent-men, receive a hundred piastres from the Hadgi for the journey; then come the backshishes, likewise fixed by ancient usages. The journey to Mecca lasts forty days, at the end of every fifth day of which pilgrims and beasts of burden have a complete rest of twenty-four hours: there are thus seven rests, at each of which the Hadgi gives to the *akkam* and the other

61

attendants twenty piastres or more, generally a gold gazzi: he supplies the *akkam* with a certain amount of food, but not the others. The cloth which covers the litter is the perquisite of the *akkam*.

The first complete resting-place of the caravan is Mezareib, where the compacts are concluded with the Arabs for protection and immunity from subsequent exactions. The rest of the journey is made in the winter without difficulty. But when the revolution of the Moslem cycle brings the month of Shawal to midsummer the fatigue is dreadful. In the day some die of strokes of the sun; in the night others, in a state of somnolence, produced by the peculiar motion of the camel, imagine themselves in the bath, and strip themselves of their clothes, which are picked up in the night by the Arabs. Three days before arrival at Medina they are met by the caravan of succour. It is beyond my province to describe the ceremonies at Mecca; suffice it to say, that the Pasha, before entering that city, takes off his Frank clothes, and dresses in the Oriental costume.

C M Doughty
From *Arabia Deserta (1876)*

A new voice hailed me of an old friend when, first returned from the Peninsula, I paced again in that long street of Damascus which is called Straight; and suddenly taking me wondering by the hand 'Tell me (said he), since thou art here again in the peace and assurance of Ullah, and whilst we walk, as in the former years, toward the new blossoming orchards, full of the sweet spring as the garden of God, what moved thee, or how couldst thou take such journeys into the fanatic Arabia?'

Josceline Dimbleby
A Child in Damascus

In the early summer of 1950, aged seven, I arrived in Beirut after a rough sea voyage from England on a small cargo ship, the *Henzee*. I was on my way to Damascus to join my mother and my stepfather, who had just been posted as Minister to the British Legation in Syria. Accompanying me was a formidable woman with a large beak of a nose and grey hair cropped like a man; Mrs Rydon was to be my governess as there was no English school in Damascus. I was clutching Alice, my yellow-haired rag doll, and Little Mut, a miniature bear with an endearing expression who I had picked up on the street outside Harrods in London; I could not have gone anywhere without these two. My mother, Barbara, and my stepfather Bill, had travelled ahead by the much talked about new aeroplane, the Pan American Airways 'Constellation', a great lion of the sky which conveniently flew from England via Rome to Damascus. My mother was surprised that it was warm enough in the plane not to have to wear an overcoat. Travelling with them were Dudley, my stepfather's adored Siamese cat, and Eustace, a Maltese terrier who was soon to expire in the Damascus heat.

I could see my mother and Bill waiting on the quay. I was introduced to the Legation chauffeur Shafiq, a slim, handsome young man with green eyes, dressed in a khaki uniform and driver's cap. In the official diplomatic car, a black Humber Hawk, Shafiq drove us out of Beirut and up over the stony Anti-Lebanon mountains into a beautiful and verdant valley, the Bekaa, rich with crops and fruit trees. After the frontier the country became barren once more, dotted with craggy rocks and a few cattle. As we came down a steep slope we passed one of the large American cars used as shared taxis, crammed with passengers, at a standstill on the way up; its engine was boiling and the driver had cut a water melon in half and put it on the radiator to cool it down.

At the frontier Bill expected to be waved through in his official diplomat's car which flew the Union Jack on its bonnet, but clearly the border guard that day was suspicious. Sharply, he asked Bill to produce his papers, and, frowning, took them into his hut. A few minutes later he emerged with another guard. They both smiled broadly as the first guard returned Bill's papers. 'Drive on Sir Wizir Bollock' the second guard said, with a theatrical sweeping gesture. Bill's double-barrelled surname, Montagu-Pollock, was funny enough; we used to tease him that it sounded just like Carlton-Browne of the FO.

A stream which had started up in the bare mountains became fringed with green and when the road entered a dramatic gorge I realised that what had been a stream was now a river, flowing swiftly beside us on our right. This was the Barada, known as 'the lifeblood of Damascus', the creator of the oasis the city was built within. We emerged from the gorge and drove to a high point where we got out of the hot car to a wonderfully cooling wind. A magical sight greeted us in the sun-bleached desert below; here was Damascus, famously known as the oldest continuously inhabited city on earth. The Prophet Muhammad, seeing it as I was from the desert, found it so beautiful that he would not visit it because he felt it would be wrong to anticipate the joys of Paradise, even though it was a Christian city at that time. Now I was going to live in this paradise. With its story book domes and minarets Damascus nestled in its famous oasis, known as the Ghouta, where I could see waving poplars and sycamores, shimmering as their leaves moved in the sunlight. Narrow sparkling streams appeared to run everywhere, criss-crossing countless fruit orchards. This unexpected greenery was encircled completely by the yellow desert hills.

As the car descended from the hills we entered the most foreign-looking place I'd ever seen. For the first time I heard the muezzin's cry from the minarets. There was no electrical amplification then and the beautiful, haunting sound captivated me. We drove into the city along a wide street. We seemed to be almost the only car, but there were trams and horse-drawn vehicles – an incongruous mix. There were hardly any women around and the few I noticed hurried along, mostly with veiled faces, black waist length capes over their heads and long black skirts. Plenty of men stood in the street talking or sat in cafés smoking hubble-bubble pipes; they wore Turkish style red fezes with black tassels, and extraordinary dark blue or black trousers, baggy and capacious, but tight around the ankles. When I asked my mother about these she smiled and said they were called *cheroual*, explaining to my great surprise that they were baggy because it was thought that the second Messiah would be born to a man, so the men wanted to be ready for childbirth.

At the start of the 1950s, with the Syrian people experiencing independence for the first time, there was a feeling of excitement and tentative hope but also, as ever, uncertainty. The last of the French troops had been forced to move out of Damascus by Syrian nationalists aided by British pressure in April 1946. But after centuries of colonisation independence did not come easily. The republican government formed under the French Mandate was overthrown in 1949 by Colonel Adib Shishakli who had been an officer under the French; a series of military coups and the assassinations of three successive presidents followed. A few months after our arrival Shishakli seized total power that lasted, tenuously, during our years there, creating a comparatively more stable period when ordinary people got on with their daily lives.

As a seven-year-old, apart from becoming quite used to hearing distant gunfire, I knew nothing of the political situation. To me the excitement of being in Syria was that this was the Holy Land. Although I grew up to be what my children jokingly called 'a heathen' I loved Bible stories as a young child and always did well in Divinity lessons. And Damascus did not only bring those stories to life; it also had an Arabian Nights magic about it; you could see it in the covered alleyways of the market, the great al-Hamadiye souk, where gold jewellery and silk brocade shimmered in the half-light, in the elegant minarets of the mosques, in the trickling fountains, mosaic floors and graceful arches of courtyards in the old houses, in the ancient Umayyad mosque and in the clear night sky of the desert, like midnight-blue enamel decorated with a silver crescent moon and flashing stars. Damascus had exotic beauty, drama, danger and mystery. At that time it still looked like a place of great antiquity; you could see signs of its complex, turbulent history all around you. It seemed like a city that the modern world had not yet discovered.

I was entranced by my new life in this very different place and years later I understood the saying that once you have lived in Damascus, it lives in you. Those early days in Syria became the most vivid and surviving memories of my childhood. Recently I re-met, after more than fifty years, an old man, near to death, who we had known in Damascus at the start of the 1950s. He had lived in many other countries since but he told me he had never felt the same about anywhere else; his pale eyes moistened and he sighed: 'Damascus catches your heart'.

The British Legation residence was a lovely house, dating back to the Turkish era of the late 19th century. It was on University Street, which ran from the Hijaz railway station to the university, in the Halbouny area of the city, which had been developed as a smart residential area at the beginning of the 20th Century. The streets here were paved evenly with new cobbles, unlike the timeworn cobbles in the old city, which tripped you up. The residence looked spacious, light and welcoming, even though I was at first alarmed by the shouts of a mad woman by the gates, who was surrounded by a group of women beggars and several ragged children. These women and children were always there, including the harmless mad woman, sitting against the wall, and with time I almost felt they were part of our household. Next to the beggars was a wooden sentry-box where one of our armed night guards used to sit; on a moonless night a few months later one guard mistook the other for an intruder, and shot him dead, but nobody treated the incident as very important. I was always in bed by the time the guards arrived and was surprised to learn there were any.

The house was wide and two storied, topped by an ornamental balustrade. The walls had been painted white, and the windows had dark turquoise blue shutters. Set a little above the street, tall metal gates followed by a steep stone stairway led up to a central front door. On the street side the windows looked onto the perfect little domes of an old Turkish mosque, Tekkiye Suleymaniye, with the Barada River, the verdant orchards of the Ghouta, and the bleached desert mountains beyond.

The first thing you noticed as you stepped inside the house was how cool it was; in fact a very thick roof was the reason that even in mid-summer the rooms never got hot. In characteristically Arab style the ground and first floors were mainly taken up by a ballroom-sized reception room stretching from front to back, with smaller rooms on both sides. The floors of the reception rooms were marble; wooden pillars on the ground floor supported the floor above, which trembled as you walked across it. Bill was told that it was dangerous to have more than twenty people at one time on this upper floor but as he was what must have been one of the least conformist of English diplomats, with natural urges to be disobedient and foolhardy, he continued to hold large parties up there. At the back of the house two pairs of double doors opened onto a wide terrace and, I soon discovered, a large garden full of delights.

There were paved paths and lawns, and an orchard at the far end with olive, lemon and little mulberry trees. Criss-crossing the whole of the garden were narrow irrigation streams, so that everything was a fresh green and the famous scented Damas roses continued to flower despite the dry summer heat. In the middle of a main lawn was a statuesque old walnut tree; as the sun shone fiercely down the contorted branches made dramatic shadows on the velvety carpet of green beneath. Steps from the terrace led up to a long arched tunnel with vines and flowering creepers climbing over it, creating a shady walkway to a wider area where the grownups would sit under a pergola. At the far end of the garden, in a small mud building, the gardener lived with his wife, eight children and a sheep. Two of the children were to become my constant playmates when I was in the garden; Nowall, who was my age, and her younger brother Farouk, who was dressed in skirts as was still the custom for little Arab boys.

Outside my ground floor bedroom on one side of the house was a fountain surrounded by a circular pool. After our hot journey from Beirut on my first day I stripped down to my underpants and sat in it to cool down; the water reached my shoulders and the fountain spattered over me. Wide leaves of a large mulberry tree partly shaded the pool and later that summer when the fruit dropped the water turned a clear blood red. In the street below the garden wall I could hear the clip-clop of horse's hooves on the cobbles pulling the gharries, or passenger carts. Occasionally there was the rumble of a car. As the water trickled gently over me, Dudley, Bill's Siamese cat, padded past, and looked at me disapprovingly.

When I came in from exploring the garden Khalil, the butler who had opened the door when we first arrived, appeared again with a big glass jug of pomegranate juice; it was a purply scarlet colour, like a dark ruby. The juice had been squeezed from the big glowing fruit I had noticed on a tree in the garden. I gulped it down; it was deliciously refreshing and became, especially when mixed with orange juice, one of the Damascus tastes I craved. I had yet to try what became my favourite juice in late summer, the intensely flavoured so called 'black mulberry juice' from the many mulberry trees in and around Damascus, which the cook also pressed from the fruits of the large mulberry tree beside the fountain outside my room.

Khalil was tall and thin with rippled black hair, shiny with hair oil, which contrasted with his light complexion; his neatly clipped moustache looked as if it might have been stuck on. He had worked for the British for many years, coming to work each day from the old Christian quarter of the city. He smiled at the way I drank the juice so eagerly, then took my hand and led me into the kitchen, where a wonderful and unfamiliar smell filled the room. The cook, Joseph, greeted me effusively; he was Armenian, quite podgy and pale, with a round friendly face and a rather incongruous bony nose. Enthusiastically, he showed me some lamb he was cooking for the evening meal.

On the other side of the room a far larger, darker man was chopping fresh mint and grinding some spices with a rolling pin on a stone; the crushed mint and spices combined with the roasting lamb created a mouth-watering fusion of aromas. Khalil, who spoke good English and some French, told me that the huge man was the *marmiton*, which meant 'cook's boy'. I was astonished. I had never seen anyone less like a boy; his belly was enormous under a stained cook's apron, he had bags under his eyes and a thick black moustache. His name was Mohammed, and he was twenty-four. Noticing my confused look, Mohammed laughed in a good-natured way and gave me a light, crispy little pastry, sticky with honey and tasting like perfume, and then popped two of them in his own mouth. This aromatic kitchen and the affectionate presence of Khalil, Joseph and Mohammed became an important part of my days in Damascus; many years later the memory of dishes produced in that kitchen proved to be my inspiration when I created my first recipes.

The next morning Shafiq dropped my mother and me near the main entrance to the al-Hamadiye souk in the centre of the old city. Holding hands, we walked into the dim light of what seemed like a vast arched corridor without end, full of mysterious sound and bustle. At the start of the 1950s the souk of Damascus must have looked very like it had done a hundred years before. Only the corrugated iron roof, punctured by bullet holes and held down by stones, dated from a more recent era when the French bombed Damascus in 1945, and the souk was machine-gunned from the air. The holes created thin shafts of sunlight, intensely bright in the darkness, which seemed to shoot down like a laser beam and pierce the ground as if they would burn a hole. The intensified light crisply illuminated parts of the shops on either side. The rich gold brocades, printed cottons and delicate vegetable dyed silks had not yet been replaced by man made fabrics in garish colours; there were no plastic objects, and almost no Western products. Dazzled by the jewellery shops I asked my mother if I was old enough to wear gold bangles on my wrist but she would only buy me a little dagger in a sheath made of silver filigree.

Most people in the souk still wore traditional clothes, and many of the men were in the long striped silk robes typical of Damascus. We saw groups of Bedouin tribesmen with their desert headgear: a large block-printed piece of cotton held by gold or silver rope and floating white robes. My mother said they came from the desert to buy bridles, harnesses, camel gear, traditional tools and things for their goat hair tents. In spite of the summer heat they seemed to be stocking up for winter, buying sheepskin coats, thick woollen jackets and strong leather boots. Their boots came from the shoe souk, off the main corridor on one side, even darker and more crowded; I held my mother's hand tighter. I had never seen so many shoes, slippers and sandals, some simple and some embossed with gold, even studded with bits of sparkling glass. Nor had I smelt leather quite like this, and was told that it was camel leather. In the close atmosphere the smell was quite overpowering; I was relieved when we reached the sweetmeat shops with their pointed mountains of succulent crystallised fruit.

Perhaps the most exciting moment was when we entered the part of the souk devoted to spices. I could not believe that these vast bowls of many coloured powders, seeds and pieces of bark, nor the incredible scent which came from them, could have anything to do with food, but I was intrigued by them, and thanks to Joseph's skill in our kitchen I was soon converted to the kind of dishes that few little English children would have accepted. That introduction to the magical world of spices in the Damascus souk was the start of a lifetime of visits to spice markets wherever I go, and led me to use spices with confidence as soon as I started cooking myself, by trial and error; in the very first dish I ever attempted, a shepherd's pie in the tiny kitchen of my shared student flat in south London, I could not resist adding a little ground coriander and a few cumin seeds.

Soon I met several families from the small British community at the first of many picnics in the Ghouta, the oasis that encircled Damascus. In fact the city was still so small that at night we could hear wolves howling in the desert beyond the oasis and you could walk from the centre to the edge of the Ghouta in ten minutes. Irrigated by streams that filtered out from the Barada, the oasis was a gentle haven between the busy city and the harsh desert on the other side. Little paths connected the orchards where there were almonds, olives, walnuts, pomegranates, vines climbing through the trees, and all kinds of fruit trees. Above all there were apricots, to this day the most delicious apricots I have ever eaten. A local saying was '*Bukra til Mish-Mish*', which means roughly, 'See you tomorrow under the apricots'. In a turbulent land the Ghouta was truly an idyll of peace.

Bill heard that a large stone house in the cooler mountains, about fifty kilometres above Damascus, just outside the village of Bloudan, still belonged to the British. In the early 19th century a British consul, Richard Wood, had acquired it to use as summer quarters for British consuls and their families. But since the most famous British consul, the legendary Richard Burton and his wife Isabel, made it their summer quarters in the early1870s it had not been inhabited. Bill persuaded the Foreign Office to let us use it when his older children from his first marriage came out for their school holidays. It was very shabby and sparsely furnished but new mattresses were found for the rickety bedsteads, walls were whitewashed and my mother bought cotton in the souk with a design of tiny Damas roses, which was made into simple curtains.

It was not luxurious but we spent most of the time outside. We ate well, as Joseph came up with us to cook. Although the rooms were Spartan the house had a large garden with a stream running through it, and spectacular views over six mountain ranges. There were several walnut trees and even an old croquet lawn, a game that Bill loved, specially cheating at. The air was far cooler than in Damascus and incredibly clear; the sky a deep flawless blue by day, seemingly impenetrable, like a dome which at night became an intense blue black, densely sparkling with sharply defined stars.

But it was not silent in the mountains; during the day there was a constant hee-hawing of donkeys and as soon as it was dark a loud chorus of frogs would start up in the stream at the bottom of the garden. This reminded Bill how delicious frogs' legs were. He made a hole in the mud wall on the far side of the stream, chased frogs into it, then put his hand in and pulled the struggling creatures out, flinging them into a sack. Poor Joseph had the job of cutting the little things in half. At one meal seven of us consumed more than fifty pairs of frogs' legs.

My stepsister and I were lent two donkeys which we used to ride, accompanied by someone we called 'the donkey boy', on a track up the mountain behind to the 'swimming pool' of Dr Kahil, a local doctor. In reality the pool was a fairly small but deep stone reservoir full of dark, cold water. It was shaded by a large fig tree laden with light green figs that were like soft little bags of pink honey filled with crunchy seeds; one of the branches of the tree hung so far over the water that we used to pick the figs while we swam and eat them in the water. I remember it as a blissful experience.

Once, on our return to the house, the donkey boy suddenly fell to the ground, jerking alarmingly and frothing at the mouth. Joseph rushed out of the house with a large kitchen knife. He took the boy's head in his hands and thrust the knife into the ground just above it. At this point my governess appeared and tore the knife from the ground, shouting angrily at Joseph. The poor boy, whom we later learnt was an epileptic, came round to the sound of Joseph shouting back at Mrs Rydon; the knife had been put in to ward off the evil spirits who were attacking the boy, he told her, and pulling it out was sacrilegious and would bring terrible bad luck. Mrs Rydon looked mortified and retired to her room for the rest of the day.

Six months after our arrival in Damascus my half-brother Matthew was born in the Victoria Hospital, an old missionary hospital not far from our house. The Edinburgh Medical Missionary Society opened the Victoria Hospital in Damascus in 1897, the Diamond Jubilee year of Queen Victoria's reign. Dr Emrys Cadwaladr Thomas, who became Superintendent of the hospital in 1933, was an exceptional man and a clever doctor who spoke with a strong Welsh accent and had a great sense of humour. When the Vichy French took over the city in 1940 he had to flee from Damascus dressed as an Arab. Loyal Syrian friends took all the movable equipment from the hospital, hid it in villages in the area and themselves guarded the hospital building.

By 1945 Dr Thomas was back at the hospital when Damascus was bombed yet again by the French; he and his team took in four hundred casualties within a few hours. The bombing and machine-gunning continued for three days and nights without cease before the British intervened and evacuated the French forces. Throughout the following turbulent years of continuous political changes and dangers Dr Thomas and his wife remained at the hospital. By the start of the 1950s the building was in a sadly dilapidated state and Dr Thomas admitted that it had not been possible to keep up with progress; the Victoria was put to shame by modern hospitals, such as the University Hospital nearby. But what never changed was the efficient and affectionate care of the nursing staff. Dr Thomas's wife Peggy was praised particularly for her skilled nursing of mothers and babies, and when my mother was pregnant again, two years after the happy experience of Matthew's birth, she planned to go there again. However, about a month before my mother was due to have her baby, in the middle of a formal dinner party, she haemorrhaged; blood soon covered the seat of her chair and trickled down onto the marble floor as the guests looked on in horror. She was rushed to the Victoria Hospital but was very weak from loss of blood by the time she got there. Dr Thomas told Bill that the only way they could hope to save either her life or the baby's would be to perform a Caesarean Section. What Bill did not know was that this operation had never been done at the hospital before and that the only anaesthetic was a cloth soaked in chloroform that my mother had to inhale. However, the operation was rapid, my mother was alive and a girl was born, who cried strongly. Despite the lack of an incubator everyone was hopeful. But the next morning Bill found my mother, exhausted and distressed, holding the tiny infant in her arms and trying, again and again, to feed her with drops of milk from a fountain pen, though the baby seemed too weak to swallow. Towards evening the baby died in my mother's arms. That was the moment, she told me in her old age, which she could never forget, when she felt the warmth leave the little body so quickly.

The death of Barbara's baby touched everyone in the closely-knit ex-pat community of Damascus. Bill was seen carrying a small white coffin out of the Victoria Hospital and putting it onto the back seat of the embassy car. Shafiq drove to the old Protestant Cemetery just outside the city walls. Harold Adkins, the Anglican chaplain, wearing his gown and surplice, was waiting among the dusty tombstones, many of them the sad little graves of babies and young children from missionary families. He conducted a short service and the baby was buried near to the impressive tomb of the famous adventuress Lady Jane Digby, who had married a Bedouin sheikh. My mother was still in hospital, too weak to be there.

My mother never got over the death of her baby; during the last two mentally confused years of her life she used to talk often of 'the baby' and ask me to fetch it from the next room. After she died I thought about my infant sister still buried in Damascus, unvisited and forgotten. I thought about the happy years there before the tragedy had clouded my mother's life, and I wanted to return, to try and find the house we had all loved; even the Foreign Office did not know if it still existed. Above all, for my mother, I felt I must visit the baby's grave.

In October 1998 I flew to Damascus and arrived late at night. The hotel I had booked was the faded Art Deco Omar Khayyam on Merji, or Martyrs Square, which I knew was in the Halbouny district where we had lived. In 1950 there were still weekly public hangings of thieves, murderers and sometimes Israelis in this square. Crowds would watch the hangings at dawn, and the bodies, with placards round their necks stating their crimes, were left hanging until they were cut down at noon. I remembered the astonishment on my mother's face when our chauffeur Shafiq asked her if he could take me to see the hangings, and his look of puzzled surprise when she firmly replied that it was out of the question.

When I walked out of the hotel next morning I could see how shabby this once fashionable area had become; all the expensive houses, flats and diplomatic residences have been in the constantly expanding modern part of the city for decades. But as soon as I started walking down University Street it felt familiar, and I knew I was close. Then on my left, behind a wall, I saw something that made my heart miss a beat. It was a ruin, yet quite unmistakably it was 'our' old house. I was told that sixteen years before someone had bought it and started to demolish it for development, but because of a squabble over the ownership of the land the work had stopped. So there the half-ruined house still stood, with the familiar wide staircase now leading to a non-existent upper floor, in a large area of parched wasteland, the devastated remains of our lovely garden.

The strangest thing about returning to the ruin of our house, which could have been such an upsetting reminder of a lost and enchanted time, was that I didn't feel sad. Instead I felt comfortingly at home. Even in its dying state I found the house welcoming. The street and surroundings, although so changed, gave me a feeling of security. A small part of me imagined that I had experienced no other life, never grown up, and that if, standing here on the street on that sunny morning, I shut my eyes and opened them again the house would be just as it used to be; the ruin would have been a dream.

The old Protestant cemetery in Damascus is now unromantically sandwiched between two main roads leading to and from the airport. It was easy to find the prominent tomb of Lady Jane Digby, who died in 1881. And a few feet away, placed flat on the ground, was the simple marble cross that my mother and Bill had chosen for their lost child. Above my head branches of a pink peppercorn tree, with its feathery leaves, gave the graves a delicate lacy shade in this bleak and sun-scorched corner of Damascus. Nearby I noticed a little boy of about ten years old, holding a hosepipe. I asked him if he could wash the thick dust and dirt from the marble cross so that the words could be read once more. He sprayed water on the marble and then rubbed it with an old cloth. Gradually the words, tarnished brass set in the marble, appeared:

> In loving memory
> of the infant daughter of
> William and Barbara Montagu-Pollock
> Died March 16th 1953
> Aged two days

I felt that at least I had done something for the tiny baby who had lain alone in this distant place for so long, for the sister I had never known, and for our mother.

II: The Syrian Desert

A PORTUGUESE, AN ITALIAN, a Frenchman, an Englishman and a German, their lives spanning as many centuries, wrote superbly of their journeys through the Syrian desert. An entire anthology could be devoted to this area alone. Although the writers selected have been drawn from different nationalities, and from over different periods, there is consistency in what they observe. They are linked, at least until the early part of the twentieth century, when the introduction of the motorcar dissolved distance, by *what does not change*. This said, stylistically they are sufficiently diverse to warrant inclusion. The Syrian desert, which ranges from the semi- to the non-arable, was where the early Christian mystics became 'fools for Christ's sake' and it was there, too, the later Muslim poets went in order to purify their language. The Bedouins were always said to be in possession of the finest Arabic. The desert was for over three thousand years part of the Great Trade Route, with the two main centres in Syria being Aleppo and Damascus with connections between them and Baghdad and Basra. The Syrian desert was dangerous to go through, with armed bandits everywhere, either that or local chiefs exacted heavy tolls for passage.

The earliest detailed account of a desert journey is by the Portuguese Jew, Pedro Teixeira, about whom we know little other than that he seems to have converted, perhaps out of convenience, to Christianity during the course of his travels that took him as far as the Philippines. Once settled in the then Spanish city of Antwerp, where he wrote up his *Travels*, he reverted to his old faith. Probably he was a physician, or at any rate '*un hombre inteligente de medicinas*', and may have dealt in gems on the side. Christina Phelps Grant, author of *The Syrian Desert: Caravans, Travel and Exploration* (A & C Black, 1937), says of him: 'He was an observant, well-informed traveller, and one who took the trouble to be as accurate as possible in every way. He found no feature of his trip uninteresting or unworthy of comment; and he allowed neither fear nor discomfort to interfere with the conscientious, daily recording of all that he observed.' Teixiera began his travels in 1586 when he sailed to India. In the winter of 1604 and 1605 he travelled from Basra to Aleppo. Accompanying him was a troublesome Portuguese, Diego de Melo, of whom Teixeira writes, 'he would not consider and distinguish times and places; which, if a man cannot do, he had better stay at home.' One must choose one's company carefully in the desert. We begin with Teixeira's efforts to get out of Ana, which stands on the Iraqi side of the Euphrates, and which in Arabic means 'groaning' but which he translates, perhaps understandably, as 'pain' or 'vexation'. This Portuguese traveller, Pedro Teixeira, is *not* to be confused with the Portuguese traveller, Pedro Teixeira, who a few years later explored the Amazon.

One of the strangest *kafilas* (caravans) to have ever crossed the Syrian desert was the one led by the Italian, Pietro della Valle (1586-1652), who after a romantic disappointment quit Rome (and two illegitimate children, by someone other than his paramour), and in 1614 set off for Jerusalem where he prayed for a favourable turn in his romantic fortunes. As George Bull writes in the introduction to his translation of a selection from the *Travels*, 'Young, rich and eager to learn, Della Valle, with his patrician style of travel, anticipated many elements of the Grand Tour, as well as expressing the old medieval motives of piety and pilgrimage.' After travelling from Jerusalem, first to Damascus and then to Aleppo, he finally found the answer to his prayers in Baghdad where he met and married an eighteen-year-old Nestorian Christian by the name of Maani Joerida. Della Valle provides a physical description of his 'Babylonian love', remarking on her finely proportioned body, her long eyebrows 'which are quite gracefully arched, and eyelids, made up with kohl', and, as the translation of her Arabic name suggests, her fine intelligence. Maani accompanied him on his further travels into Persia. There she lost a child through miscarriage and then, after eating 'a fine bass which, fresh from the sea, and cooked very well with a lemon dressing to excite her appetite', she fell seriously ill. Della Valle describes movingly her somewhat operatic death, which in the 1664 Dutch edition of the *Travels* is illustrated with a wood engraving. It was then that Della Valle made a most extraordinary decision. Not wishing to have her buried in non-Christian ground, but rather in Rome, he had her remains embalmed and covered with camphor and travelled with them for the next five years, going first through India and then, on the return journey, from Basra to Aleppo, where, in the Syrian desert, in July 1625, he and his strange cargo met with the experiences recounted here. Della Valle did finally get Maani to Rome where, prior to burying her in the church of Ara Coeli, he opened the coffin and wrote a graphic description of her decomposed body. Some years later, Della Valle married his adopted daughter by whom he had fourteen sons. His only other published work is an essay in praise of modern music.

The French *savant* Constantin François de Chasseboeuf Volney (1757-1820) spent four years in the Near East and published his *Voyage en Egypte et en Syrie* in 1787. An English translation was published the following year. Volney states clearly his reasons for travelling there: 'Those are the countries in which the greater part of the opinions that govern us at this day have their origin. In them, those religious ideas took their rise, which have operated so powerfully on our private and public manners, on our laws, and our social state. It will be interesting, therefore, to be acquainted with the countries where they originated, the customs and manners which gave them birth, and the spirit and character of the nations from whom they have been received as sacred.' Volney wrote his impressions of the Bedouin and in his determination 'to see them such as they really are', displayed the attitudes we associate with the Enlightenment. We shall meet him again in Palmyra, wearing philosopher's robes.

There is no shortage of nineteenth-century accounts, but rather than dwell upon the most famous names it may be instructive to reproduce a chapter from a writer about whom we know very little. The anonymous author of *Rambles in the Deserts of Syria and among the Turkomans and Bedaweens* (John Murray, 1864) may have been James Henry Skene, who was British consul at Aleppo at the time, and was the man who taught the Blunts all he knew about Arab horses. The journeys he made between 1858 and 1862 recount tribal skirmishes in which he occasionally took part, the Damascus revolt of 1860 and the massacre of Christians there, and his subsequent failed attempts to rescue some Christian women who had been sold to the Amarat Aneza tribe. The book is presented as a series of letters, these being addressed to the author's father. The opening chapter is reproduced here. There are few accounts that better conjure the spirit of the tenth-century poet al-Mutanabbi's most famous line: 'I am known to night and horses and the desert, to sword and lance, to parchment and pen.'

Arguably the most vivid twentieth-century record of life among the Bedouin is Carl R Raswan's *The Black Tents of Arabia* (1935), in which the author describes his experiences with the Ruala tribe who divided their time between the Syrian and North Arabian deserts. Born Carl Reinhard Schmidt, in 1893, at the Castle of Reichstedt, near Dresden, he changed his name after his favourite horse 'Raswan' was accidentally killed. 'Raswan shall not die,' he said, 'I shall write under his name.' He fought at Gallipoli on the Turkish side, was imprisoned in 1937 by the Nazis, and served with British Intelligence during the Second World War. An expert on the Arabian horse, his monographs on the subject are still considered the best. Raswan spent twenty-two years off and on among the Bedouin, actually living as one, 'migrating, hunting, raiding, starving and feasting with them.' A 'blood-brother' by chance, he was dubbed 'Aziz' by his companions. He died in 1966, from silicosis, which he contracted years earlier after being caught in desert sandstorms.

The two chapters selected from *The Black Tents of Arabia* recount Raswan's experiences in 1926 when the Ruala tribe, suffering from famine, made their way towards the pastures of Abu Rijmeyn, just north of Palmyra. Although deep in enemy territory, this sparsely fertile area offered their only hope of survival. Raswan visited Mijhem ibn Meheyd, chief of the hostile Fid'an tribe, and extracted from him a promise of peace, but one of the shakyhs of the Ibn Meheyd alliance, Rakan of the Saba tribe, withdrew from the meeting, which Raswan rightly interpreted as an ominous sign. After leaving the camp, or, more precisely, after the camp left them, Raswan and his travelling companion, Faris ibn Naif es-Sa'bi, a young Shammar Bedouin, 'the truest friend I have ever known', headed back to join the Ruala tribe when the events described here befell them. Their party also included Abd el-Karim, a Wuld'Ali chieftain from Syria, his slave, Sleyman, and two other people. Tuëma, the young woman with whom Faris had earlier fallen in love, was of the Ruala tribe. A passage earlier in the book describes her on a sacred camel 'enthroned on high like a desert queen above her people ... Tuëma had risen and stood erect in the lofty frame. Her face became transfigured in an ecstasy of joy. Suddenly she put both her hands to her throat and tore open her dress and broke into jubilant song. With bared breast she rose, straining her supple body until she was poised high above the ark, holding aloft a bunch of ostrich plumes. She looked like a goddess – the bravest and most beautiful maiden of her great tribe. She cried to the youth words of passionate eloquence. She inflamed them with war-like ardour.' As well as being a stirring first-hand account of desert rivalries, Raswan depicts the Bedouin at a historical juncture, between the demise of the camel and the ascendancy of the automobile. The desert would never again be the same. It may be claimed, too, that Raswan's book, with its many *thee's* and *thou's*, was perhaps the last to be written in a somewhat heightened, antique style.

This section concludes with two paragraphs, the first from William Beawes, a delicious morsel of prose, dating from 1745, describing the discomforts of travelling in a *mohaffa*, the heavily curtained wooden box whose declared purpose was to make a wealthy traveller comfortable. A pair of these would be slung from a pole placed over the pivot of a camel's back, with care taken to see that each was of equal weight, otherwise their inhabitants might find going by foot a better alternative. And final word goes to the camel, the poet George Sandys's description of him, in *A Relation of a Journey Begun An. Dom. 1610* (1615), which is couched in lovely Jacobean prose.

Pedro Teixeira
From *The Travels of Pedro Teixeira (1605)*

How we started from Ana, and took our way through the desert to Sukana.

On Thursday January 13th, 1605, at nine in the morning, already weary of new debates and squabbles, we turned our backs upon the river, and ascended the mountains, here more rugged than lofty. After about a league of toilsome travel, we gained more level ground, if not more fertile, and halted, until the cafila should pull itself together. The Arabs call that spot Tel Alyud, or 'the Jews' Hill,' because these have their houses below it in the city, near the river, and give name to that quarter. In this same place, the night before, robbers had fallen on some Turkyman shepherds, who fed great flocks there. These, seeing us halt and pitch tents, thinking to be safer, drew around us with their stock, whence we feared some violence. For these shepherds are also, upon occasion, stout and stubborn thieves. The first watch of that night was mine; as throughout that journey, by land and sea, in town or field, I took my watch every night, save only in the great cities. I kept it with trouble enough from a great fever that I felt come on me; and on relief I took shelter, and threw myself, dressed and booted, on my bed. This was but a cloak thrown over a chest, and all rough with its knotted lashings. I had scarce lain down, and was beginning to feel still more fever and headache, when my comrade, who had relieved me, called me up in haste. I rose, and took my arms, seeing him in the tent-door with his gun levelled. Thieves had attacked the flocks by stealth, and at the bleating of the sheep, the shepherds and others had made hue-and-cry, and driven them off with the loss of one sheep only.

On Saturday the 15th, we remained here in trouble enough. For the others who had agreed to follow us failed therein, hindered by the Anales. These, after our departure, dissuaded the other merchants' camel-men from crossing the river, with their stories of a second siege of Aleppo, and of the roads being closed by El Dendal and Fyad, the Amir's nephews.

In this affliction, whereof was left us no cure but what we hoped for of God and our own patience, there came that morning a *cafila* from Damascus, which passed our camp on its way to the city, and assured us that Aleppo was open and in good order, and our route safe. This was so true that eight or ten unarmed men brought hither, over its whole length, a hundred loaded camels without mishap. With this news we were in a little better heart, and hoped to get away the sooner. On Monday the 17th, came eighty camels more from Iuba and Haddyt, with the Amir's dates, to go in our company; and that same morning the Kurds and some of the Mosulis came out of Ana, and the departure of the *cafila* began to be warmly pressed forward.

On Friday January 21st, 1605, at eight in the morning, the *cafila* began to move. We led off, and some followed us, to the number of one hundred and twenty camels in all. We marched westwards about four leagues, over barren and rugged hills, and presently came out on level ground with abundant pasture, where many flocks of sheep were grazing. In the midst of this plain were two high round mountains standing apart, from which all that district is called by the Arabs Rumam-hen, meaning 'the Two Pomegranates': a name most fitly derived from their form.

These we passed, and after three leagues' further march we halted at four in the evening, in a pleasant field full of green grass, but waterless. The rest of the *cafila* had failed to follow us, hindered by the customs officers, for the dues that some had not paid. They had waited for that day, because these payments are used to be managed with least confusion in the open country, when the *cafila* is ready to march; and as all dues are upon the load or bale, they are then most easily settled. Herein we find, amongst the Moors, a milder and easier method than that in use amongst Christians in Europe.

On Saturday the 22nd, we marched westwards, in terrible cold and tempest; now over very level and good land, and again amongst broken glens and hills. After about five leagues we came to a *manzel*, where caravans used to halt. We passed it, because there was no water, and that next day's march might be less, up to the river, short of which we should find none. This *manzel* is called Iubab, that is, 'the Wells of rain-water.' At five pm, after a march of eight leagues, we halted in a plain without water, which the Arabs call Mekaçar Iubab*· All along our route were many flocks of sheep at pasture.

On Sunday the 23rd, after sunrise, we left this place; marching north-westwards over varying country, until we descended into the channel of a great dry watercourse. All its bottom, as far as we could see, was of living rock, white and hard as marble, and smooth as if paved by hand. Herein were many pot-holes, made, as the Arabs say, by the rains, and full of rain-water. We drank of it, men and beasts, and filled our water-skins with what remained over, for hereabouts is no other. Scarce was this done when there came two mounted Turkymanis with bows and quivers, stout and well equipped, who came in search of water for their flocks. Small joy had we at the sight of them, for on those ways the best security lies in meeting with no man.

We wanted to go on that day to the river; but one of the Kurds objected, who expected the caravan to overtake us. So we got out of the watercourse, and went a little further on, to halt at the foot of one of two hills, standing, like the

---

* Our traveller does not translate Mekaçar. Probably it stands for maksur, and the name means 'the rain-water pools amid the pasture,' and, in fact, is hardly a name at all. It reminds one of the marches of our own armies in Asia and Africa, fittingly described by an Irish private as 'marches from nowhere to nowhere else, for nothing at all.'

last, in the midst of great plains, to which they give their name, in Arabic Aden then, or 'the Two Ears': and well it fits them. They are of the same form and equal height. I climbed one, whence I could see far all around, for the land was level. We halted here at one o'clock in the afternoon, having marched five leagues. That night it was so cold that next morning we found all the water frozen in the skins.

On Monday the 24th, we marched at dawn westwards, over country like the last, until we came to the river, whose current is here very gentle. Here is a *manzel* of caravans, called in Arabic Kahem, after a turret or tomb of that name, standing on the river bank. Probably it was built by, or for, someone of that name. Kakem, in Arabic, is the same as our Cayn [Cain]. Here, the Arabs say, according to their tradition, was of old an important city, astride of the river, which they magnify with many words. But now no trace of it is to be seen.

We had come about six leagues to this place, and two hours before, the Amir's date-laden camels, which were most of our company, had parted from us, taking another road; their owners were householders of Sucana, and went thither to await the main caravan, and rest themselves until it came up. Only we and the Mosulis, with under forty camels, came on to this place (Kahem). We thought it an unsafe place for so few folk, being much infested with thieves; and resolved to go in search of the other party for their company's sake. The Mosulis wanted to wait here for the caravan, fearing to cross the desert, that begins here, with so few folk, and not without reason. As each side persisted in maintaining their own opinion, they came to ill words and well nigh to blows. But my comrade Diego Fernandes, who was chief of the merchants and strangers in that company, made up his mind, and, in spite of the Mosulis, caused us to set out in search of the other party. At nightfall, after two leagues' journey, we found them at a place called Tel ul Manahyat, that is, 'the Well Mounds,' because of one there which we found full of rain water, foul and disgusting; but our need made it seem pure and sweet. The Mosulis, who wanted to make us stay by the river, when they saw that we had really marched were frightened, and followed us, sore against their will. They came into camp when the night was well spent.

On Tuesday the 25th, at sunrise, we marched north-westward, over land of varying surface and quality, until five in the evening, when we entered upon great plains. Amidst these we found about forty tents of Turkymanis who used those pastures, with their families and cattle, sheep, camels and mules. The tents are all round, their tops like half an orange cut across. Their inner frame is of rods or canes, and the outer covering of pieces of felt. They are all portable and divisible, so that they can be taken to pieces, and carried in balanced camel-loads. Some were very clean and handsome, well hung and carpeted* within, especially that of the Sheikh, which was spacious and very well ordered.

These Turkymanis are true Turks, of such as came first from Turkestam. And being content with life on the plains they remained on these, which had been possessed, before their coming, by the Arabs with their herds and households. They are divided into what they call *tayffas*, the Arabs *cabiley*, and we *cabilda*, and the Tartars *orda*, all meaning 'a tribe.' They are stout fellows, afoot and mounted, strong-limbed, patient of toil, and resolute in action. They live by their herds, but lose no chance of plunder.

While the sheep are at pasture they keep the lambs shut up under shelter, but let them out when the flocks return in the evening. Then every lamb finds out his own mother, as if she were alone. This done, they hobble the ewes, that they may not stray, and the lambs suck at their ease. When we came there, I saw more than six hundred lambs come out of one pen, and their meeting with the ewes was a sight to see. When these are full they are penned up again, and the sheep return to pasture: which method of stock-raising seems good to me, both for profit and security.

These people live on dairy produce, and though they have so great stock, yet never would they sell us a sheep, but hung carcases of those dead of disease, or by accident. We did not want these, and the camel-men bought them.

Here we were in fear of some mischief from the ill-disposition of that folk. Wherefore Mostafá, who came with Diego de Melo, set himself up for a *chaús* or special messenger of the Amir, and him who was in charge of the dates for the Amir's servant. And they put me also into their tale, saying that I was a physician sent with them to Aleppo by the Amir, to look to some things he would have them buy there. Partly on this account they used us with some civility and respect, and gave us some of their sheep's milk, which was no small treat to us.

Their women do not hide themselves, but, being robust, are foremost in the management of their stock. These dress somewhat after the Galician fashion. They have all cow-hide boots, short skirts, and tight bodices, and on their heads great rolled hats, like a sort of pyramid. The Arabs call this place Meçenáh, and there is no water there.

We left this place on Wednesday the 26th, and after about three leagues' march northwards we came into a very wide plain, almost surrounded by a

---

*This description of the felt tent of Central Asia, distinguishing it from the southern tents of rough blankets or cotton canvas, is interesting. All have been often described, and a chief's white felt tent was on show at South Kensington some years ago. I have translated one word, *entapitadas*, as 'hung and carpeted.' The same materials are still often used in Asia for both purposes, in both houses and tents; and the French *tapis* and *tapisserie* indicate similar usage in mediæval Europe, though now applied to two different things.

ridge of earth, like a great rampart. Right across the middle of it there ran the bed of a watercourse, equally level and of very uniform width, fifty or sixty paces. Dry as it was, one could conceive how fine it would look when full.

In this plain was another clan of Turkymanis, with great flocks of sheep, many camels, and other beasts. They were clean and well dressed, but not so manageable and easy-going as the last. They begged for dates, and were answered that these could not be given, being the Amir's goods, but that they had it in their power to take them. They made no reply; but it was well seen that for a little they would take the dates and everything else, and ill-pleased were we to see their greed.

There were here near the watercourse three wells, where they watered their cattle. Our camel-men filled the water-skins and other vessels, and then we moved off. The Arabs call this place Muy al Meçenah, or Methenàh, that is, 'the water of Mesnáh.' We marched over varying country, mostly very fertile and level, until sunset; meeting some more herdsmen with cattle and camels, and starting many hares. After about ten leagues' march, we halted in a very level plain, without water, called by the Arabs Tabakt Seguer. Here we suffered fearfully from thirst, for all the water we had brought on was so foul and stinking that none would drink it.

On Thursday the 27th, we marched at sunrise, heading north-westwards, over very good and level land. After about three leagues, we crossed the ravine and channel of a wondrous great watercourse, then dry, which the Arabs call Sehel, a common *manzel* of caravans. Here were some wells of good water, from which we partly quenched our thirst, and continued our march, until five o'clock in the evening, when we encamped in a very level plain of hard sand. Here were some wells of good water, and the Arabs call the place Iubeba. This day's march was seven leagues.

On Friday the 28th, we started at dawn, and marched northwards, over level, clear, and fertile land, albeit stony in some places. We met with a great herd of the Turkymanis' camels at pasture; and after rather more than seven leagues' march, just before sunset we halted in a place without water, called by the Arabs Ragem al Kayma. This means 'the Tent Cairn,' and there is one there, of stones heaped up in the shape of a tent, as a landmark.

In all this march we saw no hill, mound, nor high land, except, when we halted, a very distant range which the Arabs call Gibel el Bexar, or 'the Mount of Bexar:' the name of a clan that inhabits it. Perhaps it was in memory of this that the Arabs gave the name to Bexar in Spain whence the Duke takes his title. We saw many hares, and coursed some with a dog that my comrade had with him, called Marzoko, which means in Arabic 'Good Luck;' but had never enough of it to catch one. It is true that, of all hares ever I saw in the world, none seemed to me as swift as these.

On Sunday we started half-an-hour after sunrise, and marched north-westwards, over very flat and good land, leaving the Bexar range on our right. At sunset, having made about seven leagues, we halted amongst ten or twelve tents of Turkymanis, who were pasturing their cattle and camels there.

Here, when the camels were unloaded, arose a bloody and dangerous strife between our camel-men and those of the Mosulis. They came from words to blows and broken heads, and we had enough ado to quiet them; wherein we spared no pains, more for our own sakes than for theirs. The quarrel was over our going to Sucana, a village where the Amir's camel-men, who had his dates, had their homes; and meant, as I have said above, to await therein the arrival of the main caravan at Tayba, another village on our direct route. As it did not suit us to part company with them in those deserts, we had to follow them where they chose, against the will of the Mosulis and our own. For they had promised to come with us to Tayba. The Mosulis urged that we should march to Tayba without the others [the Sucana men]. Ours objected to the danger of parting company, and they came to such strife that some had faces all bloody at their parting. In the end our men prevailed, and we settled to accompany the date-carriers. This place is called Ketef el Hel, and has no water, so we had provided some beforehand. Here, and on the previous march, we saw many hares and great herds of wild asses.

On Sunday the 30th, we started before sunrise, and marched north-westwards over good plain country. Since the middle of the previous march, we had high mountain ranges in sight ahead. In the plains we saw many and great herds of the Turkymanis' cattle, and many of their tents, but each alone and far apart. These were of the *tayfa*, or clan, calling themselves Beghdely, which alone of the Turkymanis using these pastures owns not the Amir's authority. For it has as many as eight thousand mounted archers, and some firearms, wherefore they are exempt from vassalage. We saw many hares and wild asses.

One hour and a half before sunset, we began to descend through ravines and uneven ground, but fertile; and one hour after it we came to some wells of bad water, where Turkymanis were watering their cattle and camels. That day we may have made nine leagues up to this place, which the Arabs call Naquib, meaning the deputy of any master. Here we spent the night in little safety and great fear. A little above us, on our left, was a watercourse, famous in those parts, called Gadyr a Ther, at that time dry.

On Monday January 31st, we started two hours before dawn, though the night was very thick and dark. We marched north-westwards through a very wide and level valley, between mountains and lower hills, at our best pace, for fear of robbers. At nine o'clock of the morning, under rain enough, we came to a village called Sucana, set in the gorge of two ranges, and took shelter in a *khan*, ancient indeed, but great and strong. It is one hundred paces without the place. This may contain one hundred and fifty houses, all little and poor, of unbaked bricks, mud, and small stones, the abodes of Arabs and Turkymanis.

The origin of this place was a fort, yet standing amidst it, though in bad condition. It was set here in aid of the caravans, or *cafilas*, passing between Damascus and Tripoli on one side, and Bagdad and Baçora on the other; as Tayba serves those of Aleppo. A sufficient escort brought them hither, turned them over to the garrison, and went home again. This arrangement has ceased altogether since the Turkish conquest of these regions. I remember that there was on the fort's platform an iron falconet, as a scarecrow, I suppose, to plundering raiders.

About two hundred paces to the south is a spring of sulphurous water, hot and stinking, rising in and filling a natural round basin. Thence it flows southwards, and waters some gardens and fields thereabout. This water gives its name to the place; for in Arabic *sukan* means 'hot.' All the people drink mostly of this, and bathe in it, men and women alike, with little modesty, and go out of it into a mosque thereby. Of what is left after watering the land, and of another water, not so bad, which joins this from afar in a distant salt valley, they make their salt.

To conclude: the place is a very poor open hamlet. Everything is scarce and dear, especially wood, for want whereof they burn dry dung of camels and other beasts. The climate is unhealthy, provisions scanty and bad; and, for all that, I saw in this town some women as beautiful as angels.

We stayed here five days, not without trouble from the importunity of the inhabitants. For there is no village but hath its *alcalde*, and no *alcalde* but would be greater than the king*; and in this and the like matters it is in Syria as in Spain. So we kept good watches, fearing townsfolk and plain-dwellers alike. But Diego de Melo, forgetting that he was not in India, where passion is wont to heed reason but little, lost his temper with a camel-man, and threatened him with a sword. This had been a sore game for Diego, but for our earnest entreaties and excuses. And other unpleasant things befell him during this journey, for that he would not consider and distinguish times and places; which if a man cannot do, he had better stay at home.

Here we awaited news of our caravan's arrival at Tayba, where we kept one to bring us word. This came on the morning of February 5th, and we loaded up and marched forthwith.

---

* Referring apparently to a Spanish proverb. Pinelo, in his Spanish-English Dictionary, quotes the following: '*Alcálde de Aldéa, el que lo quiérre, esse lo sea*: let him that desires to be Alcalde of a Village; that is, let them that are fond of foolish Honours, which bring Trouble and no Advantage, enjoy them.'

Pietro della Valle
From *The Travels of Pietro Della Valle (1625)*

July 7th, We travell'd from day-break till noon, passing over clayie and slippery ground, where the Camels went with much difficulty. We rested at a place full of prickly shrubs, the leavs whereof are less than a Man's naile, and of the shape of a heart; the fruit was round and red, like small coral-beads, of taste sweet, mixt with a little sharpness, having little stones in them; it was very pleasant to the taste, and afforded no small refreshment to us in these Desarts. The Mahometans celebrated their Bairam, the Fast of Ramadhan being now ended.

July 8th, We came to several places of stagnant waters, and baited at one, two or three hours before noon; but the water was sulpherous and ill-tasted, as most of the rest were also, in regard of the many Minerals where-with the Earth of the Desert abounds. We departed not from this place at night, because we were to pay a Gabel to Emir Mudleg Aburise whose Territory here-abouts begins. Emir Aburise is the greatest Prince of the Arabians in *Arabia Deserta*; and this Prince (whose proper name is Mudleg) succeeded his deceased Uncle Feiad, who was living and reign'd when I went from Aleppo to Baghdad nine years before, having upsurp'd the Government from Mudleg, who was very young at the time of his Father's decease. At night we were visited by some pilfring Arabians, who finding us prepar'd with our Arms, betook themselves to their heels, and escap'd unhurt from us, though we persu'd them a while.

July 9th, The Morning was spent in paying Gabels: I pay'd for my part for a load and half of portage, as they reckon'd it, fifteen Piasres, and two more towards the abovemention'd Gabel of the Camels to Emir Nasir's Brother, besides other fees. They open'd my Trunks, and took away two Velvet Caps, much good Paper, and several other things; and had it not been more for the Capigi Ibrahim entreaties than authority, they would also have broken open the Chest, wherein I carri'd the Body of Sitti Maani my wife. Three hours before night, we put our selves upon the way, and travell'd till about an hour before night, when we came to a place of water.

July 10th, We travell'd till Noon, and rested in a great Plain surrounded with certain Hills, in the midst whereof stands erected a Stone, fashion'd at the Top like the bowl of a Fountain. After which, we proceeded till an hour after sunset, and came to a place where we found good water between two little Hills. Here we staid to refresh our selves and our Camels till three hours before night; the *Capigi's*, who were to go by the way of Anna, to find the *Serdar* at Mardin, or elsewhere, departing before us: but we, who intended to go to Aleppo without touching at Anna, for compendiousness of the way, and for avoiding payment of some kind of Gabel there, left the way to Anna on the right hand, and took that within the Desert more Southward. We travell'd all the remainder of this day, and all the night, with part also of the next day, without staying; to end we might the sooner arrive at water, of which we had no less desire then need.

July 12th, About three hours after Sunrise we baited, being weary, at the foot of certain little Hills, without finding water; so that we were fain to drink that little which remain'd in the Goat-skin borachoes which we carri'd with us. About three hours before Sunset, we proceeded again till almost Noon the next day, when we arriv'd at water, to wit, the famous River Euphates, lighting upon a place of the ordinary way to Aleppo, where I had formerly pass'd when I went from thence to Baghdad, and where the road between the River and certain little Hills full of that Talk or shining Mineral is very narrow. Our further stirring at night was prevented by the supervening of some Soldiers, sent by the officers of Anna, (whom the *Capigi's* had informed of our passage) to demand those Tolls or Gabels which we had fought to avoid, although we pass'd not through that City.

July 14th, Most part of this day was spent in paying the said Gabel. I paid for my part six Piasters, and gave two more as a gratuity to the soldiers; besides which, I was oblig'd to pay twenty to the chief Camelier, whose money was all gone; and in this manner I was constrain'd both to profit and pleasure him who never did me other than disprofit and displeasure. But for all this, they afterwards open'd the two greatest Trunks I had, and tumbled all my Goods about, treating me with all rigor and discourtesie. Only I took it well (and upon that account willingly pardon'd them all the rest) that seeing the Chest wherein the body of Sitti Maani was, and understanding what it was (for I was glad to tell them, lest they should have broken it open) they not only gave me no trouble about it, as I thought they would, (being a thing contrary to custom and their Laws) but rather accounted it a piece of piety that I carri'd her with me to bury her in my own Country, both pitying and commending me for it: which hapning beyond all expectation I attributed to God's particular favour, and to her own effectual prayers, which undoubtedly helpt me therein.

This being over, about three hours before night, We set forth and travell'd till night. Some of the above-mention'd Soldiers return'd to Anna, but others, who were carrying I know not what moneys to their Emir Mudleg; accompani'd with us. In the Evening the Leader or Chieftain of these Soldiers made me open my Trunks once again, (namely the two little ones which they had omitted in the day) and putting all my Goods in disorder, took away many things, as a Mantle of Sitti Maani of deep azure silk, according to the mode of Assyria, a Ball of Amber, an Alabaster Vessel curiously wrought, and consign'd to me in India by Sig Antonio Baracho, to present in his name to Sig Francesco del Drago at Rome; many exquisite Porcellane Dishes miniated with Gold; an Arabick Book, though of little importance; a great watchet Cloke or Mantle to keep off rain after the Persian mode; much paper besides and other such things. At night we staid to rest, but the Soldiers went onwards; before their going, I redeem'd from them the Mantle of Sitti Maani, and Sig Francesco del Drago's Alabaster Vessel, giving them in exchange two Abe's, or Arabian Surcoats which I bought of one of our company for seven Piastres; the Amber and the other things I could not recover, but they carri'd them away; for they would neither restore them freely, nor take money for them, and our *Cafila* was so small that I could find nothing to give them instead thereof which pleas'd them. It was no small good luck that I sav'd the Sword and Ponyard of Sitti Maani, with many of her jewels, bracelets, and other ornaments of Gold from their rapacious hands; hiding them under a trunk: for, if they had seen them, 'tis ten to one but they would have taken them from me. I relate these things that it may be known what Tyranny these Barbarians exercise in their own Counties towards us, who in ours very often, with ill-employ'd courtesie, are wont to be undeservedly caress'd and honour'd when they come thither.

July 15th, We travell'd from Day-break till Noon, and three hours after till night, when we took up our Station not far from the River, amongst many shrubs which to me seem'd to be Juniper, or else that plant which in Persia they call *Ghiez*. The next two days we travell'd and rested at our usual hours, and on the latter, we rested near a Pit or Well of bitter and stinking water in a mineral Soil, all full of Talk, of which I brought away a parcel with me. In like manner we proceeded the two next days; and on the twenty first, we pass'd by a ruinous Castle call'd Hheir, which I had seen only by night when I went from Aleppo to Baghdad. I took a better view of it now, and found it to be a great Building, all of good and large white Marble Stones; the form of it is a long Square, with walls round about, here and there distinguish'd with small round Turrets; within are many contrivances of Rooms, all likewise of white stone, but so ruinous that it cannot be known what they were. From hence we travell'd about three hours further, and at night arriv'd at Taiba, a Town which I had formerly seen, and lodg'd in a by-place amongst the walls of the Houses near the Gate.

July 22nd, this day was spent in paying the usual Gabels, which every day are enhaunc'd in these Countries, and are now become insupportable. Though I had nothing of Merchandise, but only goods for my own use; yet I could not come off under twenty Piastres between Gabels and Donatives to the Officers, which they demanded as equally due. Here I found an Arabian nam'd Berekiet, who spoke a little Italian, and pass'd for Factor or Procurator of the Franks, saying, he had authority so to be from the Consuls of Aleppo. He presently offer'd himself to speak to the Officers in our behalf, gave us an Entertainment, and invited us to lodg in his House, and, if we had been so minded, would have conducted us thither; but his services tended only to get some money of us, and by his speaking with the Officers to make us pay more than perhaps we should otherwise have done.

July 23rd, Two hours after Sunrise, we departed from Taiba, whence the said Officer sent an Arabian with us, to conduct us first to Emir Mudleg (who they said was at Hhamah, between Aleppo and Damascus) and afterwards to Aleppo; they having done the same to the great *Cafila* of Bassora which had pass'd by Taiba a little before us. This going to the Emir, was a troublesome thing, both in regard to the diversion out of the way, and the inconveniences we imagin'd the Emir himself would put us to, after all the Tyrannies we had hitherto met with in the Desert. We travell'd till past Noon, and after a short rest till sunset, having a continu'd ridge of little Hills always on the left hand.

July 24th, We travell'd again from daylight till past Noon, and two hours more in the Evening, taking up our Quarters an hour before Sunset.

July 25th, we set forth an hour before Sunrise, travelling till Noon, when the Arabian assign'd to us by the Officers of Taiba to conduct us to the Emir, being so perswaded, as I believe, by the Cameliers, who alledg'd that the Camels were very weary (as indeed they were, and over-laden, in regard that many of them dy'd by the way, so that they could travel but gently) resolv'd to go alone before us by a neerer way over the mountains, and leave us to follow him leisurely, as the Cameliers said they would. I was glad of this going, and intended to take a different course from what the Cameliers imagin'd; but because it was not yet seasonable, I held my peace. After two hours rest, we travell'd till an hour before night, when we took up our station neer certain Pits, a little distant from the reliques of certain ancient Fabricks call'd Siria by me formerly seen and describ'd in my journey to Baghdad.

July 26th, Setting forth by daylight, we came to rest after Noon near a water which springs up in a place full of small Canes, whence we remov'd not this night, partly, that our tir'd and over-laden Camels might recover themselves a little, and partly, because the Cameliers were minded to eat a Camel there conveniently, which falling lame of one leg they knockt on the head in the morning; and indeed they had eaten all the others which fail'd by the way, either through Disease or otherwise. Of this, which was not infirm, I was willing to take a trial, and lik'd the roasted flesh well enough, only it was something hard.

July 27th, Setting forth early, we wav'd the directest way to Aleppo, (which was by the town of Achila) and took another more Southwards, and to the left hand, which led to the place where the Emir resided; intending to leave the Camelier at a certain Town upon the way, from whence he was to go alone to the Emir, to carry him a present, and excuse our going to him by alledging the death and weariness of our Camels. Hereby we endeavour'd to avoid (if possible) the troubles and disgusts which we were likely to meet with from the Emir and his Arabians, in case we should have gone to him ourselves. At Noon, we came to the design'd Village, call'd Haila; they account it a *Mezar*, that is, a place to be visited, and of devotion, in regard of some persons buried there whom the Mahometans hold for Saints: yet it consisted only of four poor Cottages, and those uninhabited and abandoned, as is credible, by reason of the Tyrannies which the Arabians of the Desert, especially the Soldiers, exercis'd in these troublesome times upon the poor Peasants. The Camelier, because he could not leave us here, by reason the Village was without people, purposed to carry us to the Emir; doubting, lest if he did otherwise, it might turn to his prejudice. Whereupon, considering what disgusts and perhaps dangers too I might meet with there, both by reason of the women whom I carri'd with me, and of whom the Mahometans use to be very greedy; and also by reason of the body of Sitti Maani, and upon other accounts; I set my foot against the wall, and resolutely told the Camelier, that I would by no means go to Emir Mudleg, with whom I had nothing to do, now I had pay'd all his Gabels; I would go directly to Aleppo; whither if he would not carry me with his Camels, I would go on foot with my people, leaving all my Goods there on the ground to his care; of which, if any were lost, he should be responsible to me for the same at Aleppo: And indeed, had the Camelier been obstinate, I was resolv'd to do as I said, having little heart to trust to the mischievousness of the Emir, (which was very infamous); or to expose to so great danger, not onely the few good I had, but also the body of Sitti Maani, our lives, and the women's both Liberty and Souls (which was a great consideration); and little caring to present to the Emir the letter which I had for him from the Basha of Bassora in my recommendation, because I had found by experience what little good the two former did me, which I had presented to Sceich Abdullah at Cuvebeda, and to Sceich Abitaleb the Son of Nasir in the Desert. The chief Camelier try'd a good while to prevail with me to go with him to the Emir; but at length seeing me obstinate, and some other Cameliers of his companions of the same mind, he resolv'd at last to leave the Camels with me to carry my Goods directly to Aleppo, together with some few other companions of the journey, and to go himself alone with all his loads to the Emir, purposing also to tell him, that we by force, and against his will, had freed our selves from going to him; with which I was very well contented.

After he was gone his own way, we took ours directly to Aleppo, and after two hours travel, took up our station in a bare champian place, where night had over-taken us.

July 28th, From Sunrise we travell'd almost till noon, but the Camels being few, weary, over-laden, made no great progress. After three hours baiting, we journey'd again till almost night, and lodg'd by a water near the Tents of some Arabian Beguin shepherds who were there.

July 29th, Setting forth early, we saw some number of Horse cross the way before us at a good distance, and finding the place a plain inclos'd with Hills, and consequently, fit for Ambuscades and Treacheries, we suspected that they were Thieves, and that they went to wait at some pass to assault us. Wherefore we put ourselves in order, and march'd a good while on foot with our Arms ready to defend ourselves by fight: But at length these suspicions vanish'd, and we met no body; and, peradventure, they were people that were afraid of us, and fled. Such encounters we frequently had in the Desart, and many times betook our selves to our Arms; some times too in the night we were visited by Pilferers, who attempted to steal something clandestinely; but, God be thanked, no mischief ever befell us, and the Thieves finding us upon our guard, went away always frustrated; and sometimes too, either hurt or terrify'd by our Arms. On this occasion I will not omit, (now we are near the end of this journey), that the Desart between Bassora and Aleppo, is a great Plain with very few inequalities; and some of the soil is dry, some saltish and full of other Minerals, little stony, and less moorish with Reeds; but the greatest part was green with grass at the time of my passing through it, yet with grass most commonly thorny, and good onely for Camels to eat. The heat, even in these Summer-months, was always supportable, and, provided a Man were shelter'd from the Sun, the wind was continually so great and constant that it caus'd coolness, though sometimes it molested us with the dust. The nights were always sufficiently cool, and, to avoid catching cold, it was requisite to be very well cover'd. But to return to my purpose, on the day above-said, a good while before noon we stay'd to rest in a little Village of Arabians, (not subject to the Emir, but Vassals of Aleppo) call'd Ludehi, lying in a fertile Valley irrigated with a running water. From hence I dispatch'd my Servant Giovanni Rubehh with a Camelier to Aleppo, which was about a league off; and I writ Letters by him to the most Illustrious Sig Aluyse de Ca, the Venetian Consul in that City; and also to Doctor Luigi Ramiro his Physisian, a Roman both by Birth and Education, (upon which account I hop'd, that though I was unknown by sight, he would nevertheless be favourable to me) giving them account of my coming, and desiring the Doctor to provide me a convenient residence for my self and the Women with me. The Consul sent some of his servants to introduce us into the City, without disturbance from the Turks or Custom-Officers; which to me, in regard of the Coffin wherein I carry'd the Body of Sitti Maani, was a great happiness; for if it had been seen, I might have found much trouble from the Turks; as also by reason of the Books which I had in their Language, some about matters of Religion, which, (as it had hapned to some others at Aleppo) 'tis likely would have been taken from me. After my Servant was gone, we follow'd him till within a mile of Aleppo, where we stay'd his return in a Meschita or Sepulchre, upon the way, of one Sceich Saadi, venerated for a saint; and because either the Consul's Servants miss'd of me and took another way, or else my Servant arriv'd there late; therefore hearing of no Answer, we remain'd in this place all night.

Constantin François de Chasseboeuf Volney
From *Travels through Syria and Egypt (c. 1784)*

The [Bedouin] Arabs have often been reproached with this spirit of rapine; but, without wishing to defend it, we may observe, that one circumstance has not been sufficiently attended to, which is, that it only takes place towards reputed enemies, and is consequently founded on the acknowledged laws of almost all nations. Among themselves they are remarkable for a good faith, a disinterestedness, a generosity which would do honour to the most civilized people. What is there more noble than that right of asylum so respected among all the tribes? A stranger, nay, even an enemy, touches the tent of the Bedouin, and, from that instant, his person becomes inviolable. It would be reckoned a disgraceful meanness, an indelible shame, to satisfy even a just vengeance at the expence of hospitality. Has the Bedouin consented to eat bread and salt with his guest, nothing can induce him to betray him. The power of the Sultan himself would not be able to force a refugee* from the protection of a tribe, but by its total extermination. The Bedouin, so rapacious without his camp, has no sooner set his foot within it, than he becomes liberal and generous. What little he possesses he is ever ready to divide. He has even the delicacy not to wait till it is asked: when he takes his repast, he affects to seat himself at the door of his tent, in order to invite the passengers; his generosity is so sincere, that he does not look upon it as a merit, but merely as a duty: and he, therefore, readily, takes the same liberty with others. To observe the manner in which the Arabs conduct themselves towards each other, one would imagine that they possessed all their goods in common. Nevertheless, they are no strangers to property; but it has none of that

* The Arabs discriminate their guests, into guest *mostadjir*, or *imploring protection*; and guest *matnoub, who sets up his tent in a line with theirs*; that is, who becomes naturalized.

selfishness which the increase of the imaginary wants of luxury has given it among polished nations. It may be alleged, that they owe this moderation to the impossibility of greatly multiplying their enjoyments; but, if it be acknowledged, that the virtues of the bulk of mankind are only to be ascribed to the necessity of circumstances, the Arabs, perhaps, are not for this less worthy our esteem. They are fortunate, at least, that this necessity should have established among them a state of things, which has appeared to the wisest legislators as the perfection of human policy: I mean, a kind of equality in the partition of property, and the variety of conditions. Deprived of a multitude of enjoyments, which nature has lavished upon other countries, they are less exposed to temptations which might corrupt and debase them. It is more difficult for their Shaiks to form a faction to enslave and impoverish the body of the nation. Each individual, capable of supplying all his wants, is better able to preserve his character, and independence; and private poverty becomes at once the foundation and bulwark of public liberty.

This liberty extends even to matters of religion. We observe a remarkable difference between the Arabs of the towns and those of the desert; since, while the former crouch under the double yoke of political and religious despotism, the latter live in a state of perfect freedom from both: it is true that on the frontiers of the Turks, the Bedouins, from policy, preserve the appearance of Mahometanism but so relaxed is their observance of its ceremonies, and so little fervor has their devotion, that they are generally considered as infidels, who have neither law nor prophets. They even make no difficulty in saying that the religion of Mahomet was not made for them; 'for,' add they, 'how shall we make ablutions who have no water? How can we bestow alms, who are not rich? Why should we fast in the Ramadan, since the whole year with us is one continual fast? And what necessity is there for us to make the pilgrimage to Mecca, if God be present every where?' In short, every man acts and thinks as he pleases, and the most perfect toleration is established among them. Nothing can better describe, or be a more satisfactory proof of this than a dialogue which one day passed between myself and one of their Shaiks, named Ahmed, son of Bahir, chief of the tribe of Wahidia. 'Why,' said this Shaik to me, 'do you wish to return among the Franks? Since you have no aversion to our manners; since you know how to use the lance, and manage a horse like a Bedouin, stay among us. We will give you pelisses, a tent, a virtuous and young Bedouin girl, and a good blood mare. You shall live in our house.' 'But do you not know,' replied I, 'that, born among the Franks, I have been educated in their religion? In what light will the Arabs view an infidel, or what will they think of an apostate?' 'And do not you yourself perceive,' said he, 'that the Arabs live without troubling themselves either about the Prophet, or the *Book* (the Koran)? Every man with us follows the direction of his conscience. Men have a right to judge of actions, but religion must be left to God alone.' Another Shaik, conversing with me, one day, addressed me, by mistake, in the customary formulary, 'Listen, and pray for the Prophet.' Instead of the usual answer, *I have prayed*, I replied, with a smile, *I listen*. He recollected his error, and smiled in his turn. A Turk of Jerusalem, who was present, took the matter up more seriously: 'O Shaik', said he, 'how canst thou address the words of the true believers to an infidel ?' 'The tongue is *light*,' replied the Shaik, 'let but the heart be *white* (pure); but you who know the customs of the Arabs, how can you offend a stranger with whom we have eaten bread and salt?' Then, turning to me, 'All those tribes of Frankestan, of whom you told me that they follow not the law of the Prophet, are they more numerous than the mussulmen?' 'It is thought,' answered I, 'that they are five or six times more numerous, even including the Arabs.' 'God is just,' returned he, 'he will weigh them in his balance*.'

It must be owned, that there are few polished nations whose morality is, in general, so much to be esteemed as that of the Bedouin Arabs; and it is worthy of remark that the same virtues are equally to be found in the Turkman hordes, and the Curds, It is singular, also, that it should be among these that religion is the freest from exterior forms, insomuch that no man has ever seen, among the Bedouins, the Turkmans, or Curds, either priests, temples, or regular worship. But it is time to continue the description of the other tribes of the inhabitants of Syria, and to direct our attention to a social state, very different from that we are now quitting, to the state of a cultivating and sedentary people.

---

* M Niebuhr relates in his *Description de l'Arabie*, that, within the last thirty years, a new religion has sprung up in the Najd, the principles of which are analogous to the disposition of mind I have been describing. 'These principles,' says that traveller, 'are that God alone should be invoked and adored, as the author of all things; that we should make no mention of any prophet in praying, because that too nearly resembles idolatry: that Moses, Jesus Christ, Mahomet, &c. were in truth great men, whose actions are edifying; but that no book was ever inspired by the angel Gabriel, or any other celestial spirit. In short, that vows made in the time of imminent danger are neither meritorious nor obligatory. I do not know,' adds M Niebuhr, 'how far we may trust the veracity of the Bedouin who told me this. Perhaps it was his peculiar way of thinking; for the Bedouins, though they call themselves Mahometans, in general, care very little about either Mahomet or the Koran.'

The authors of this new sect were two Arabs, who, having travelled, in consequence of some commercial affairs, into Perlia and Malabar, reasoned on the diversity of religions they had seen, and thence deduced this general toleration. One of them, named Abdel-el-Waheb, in 1760, erected an independent state in the Najd, the other, called Mekrami, Shaik of Nadjeran, had adopted the same opinions; and, by his valour, raised himself to considerable power in those countries. These two examples render still more probable a conjecture I have already mentioned, that nothing is more easy than to affect a grand political and religious revolution in Asia.

Anonymous
From *Rambles in the Deserts of Syria (1858)*

Letter One

Beles: October 6th, 1858

I write from a camp of the Bedaween, on the right bank of the Euphrates. I shaped my course in a south-easterly direction from Aleppo – not following any road or pathway, for there is none such in the desert. Leaving on my right the Salt Lake of Jibool, supposed to be the Valley of Salt of the second Book of Samuel, in which Hadadezer was routed by King David with a loss of eighteen thousand men, I reached in the evening an Arab camp of the Hanadi tribe, whose chief, Haji Batran, I wished to take with me. He was absent, however; and, after partaking of the hospitality offered by his four wives, I proceeded next morning towards the east, accompanied by a few servants and Arab followers of my own.

The country is woodless, houseless, uncultivated, and inhabited only by the wildest of the Bedaween tribes. Like most denizens of unbounded plains, these are fanatical votaries of freedom. They are also essentially indolent. Poor and lazy, but brave, they find a ready scope for their warlike impulses, and a timely resource for their subsistence, in the levying of black mail from passing caravans. To check their predatory propensities, Ibrahim Pasha of Egypt, when ruling also over Syria some twenty years ago, brought a tribe of African Bedaween, of tried fidelity and good conduct. Some of these he had stationed between Aleppo and the Salt Lake, to guard the villages from the inroads of more unruly Arabs; and this measure answered well until the Hanadi, or Hindawi (for so the Africans were called, from a supposed Indian origin) became connected by intermarriage with the native Bedaween, and their services in opposition to the latter had assumed a merely nominal existence. Still they were recognised as the representatives of the government in the desert, and our progress without Haji Batran was of doubtful issue. The Hanadi have seventeen hundred fighting men.

We had ridden on for a couple of hours in the fine autumn morning without encounter. Suddenly shouts from the rear announced an attack. Our party quickly closed up. There they were, to be sure, at least fifty or sixty horsemen galloping after us abreast, and in open order, to give room for the play of the long lances, which they brandished furiously as they advanced. On they came, making the hard burnt-up earth sound again with the rapid fall of many hoofs, and mingling its rolling growl with the long monotonous notes of the Arab song of onslaught. In front, on a powerful bay mare, thundered along a burly figure of sixteen stone at least, and, as he neared us, I was not sorry to make out the bronzed features and loud laugh of Haji Batran, who was bringing us an escort of Hanadi. This semblance of hostile intentions is a compliment of the Bedaween to their friends, but it renders friendly meetings in the desert doubtful affairs before recognition. I once knew a distinguished foreigner trust to his being well mounted, and turn tail before those who came to do him honour in this fashion: a very pretty chase was performed ere his equanimity was restored. Haji Batran collected his party close behind a mound we had reached; and, after exchanging cordial greetings, we dismounted, and crept cautiously to its summit, to survey together the eastern horizon. No Arabs were to be seen. Batran then had our tents pitched, saying that we must wait there till nightfall, as the two great tribes, Anezi and Shammar, had been fighting for several days not far from us, and we might come in for a share in their warfare if we should not pass unobserved. It was a long halt, but there was no gainsaying the arrangement. To while away the weary hours, stories were told, songs sung, pipes smoked, and various feats of legerdemain displayed. Amongst others of the latter diversions, a snowy-bearded patriarch placed his spear-point on his breast, and pretended to pierce himself by falling against it, while the butt was stuck fast in the bank of the mound. There was a trick in it of course: perhaps a strong leather belt protected him; but, however that might be, it passed for a miracle, and the charmed life received all due honour accordingly.

When the sun had set, and the short twilight faded away, we mounted again, and followed in single file and in profound silence the stalwart form of Haji Batran on his tall mare, who led the way. Eight hours in the saddle brought us, just before dawn, to another tumulus, which we were told was on the bank of the great river. We halted behind it, and two horsemen were sent round to see if no one else was doing the same on the other side. All being clear, we lay down on the short grass, while a messenger went on to the Anezi camp, for it is never safe to approach one unannounced. Mistakes may occur, or are afterwards alleged as an excuse for plunder. Our scout returned with Sheikh Jedaan himself, the renowned chief of the Fedan Anezi, to welcome our arrival; and with the rising sun we proceeded along the broad and shingly bed of the Euphrates.

A strange scene awaited us on the plain of Beles, where the ancient Syrian kings had parks and forests, as recorded by Xenophon, and which is still known as a favourite haunt of wild boars, wolves, and jackals, though now only clothed with clumps of tamarisks. An open space was crowded with black goat-hair tents in such surprising numbers that they formed not only a camp, but a mighty city of camps, while upwards of three thousand Bedaween were careering over the plain on their fleet mares as far as the eye could reach;

rushing at each other lance in rest, wheeling right and left, charging in a mass, their scanty garments and long hair streaming behind them, singing, screaming, dealing around hard knocks with the butt end of their spears, and laughing loud when blood was drawn by a stray touch with the point. Some were mere children, slenderly clad, and riding wildly, without saddles or bridles, their docile fillies yielding at their best pace to the mere tightening of a rope-halter. Such horsemanship is seen nowhere else. The din was deafening, the confusion bewildering. When we reached the tent of the sheikh, who had galloped on to receive us, we were led to the seat of honour, a camel's packsaddle in the centre of a long narrow carpet. No sooner installed, than we were surrounded by two or three hundred Bedaween, squatting on the ground in several ranks, from each of whom we received a formal welcome.

Jedaan is a young man, under thirty years of age, short in stature, light and wiry, with a handsome countenance and deep expressive black eyes. Elected sheikh for his bravery in battle and wisdom in council, he had all the air and bearing of a desert prince amongst his vassals. Before the tent, which contained five large compartments, stood picketed his milk-white mare, a noble animal, the gift of his enemy, Abd-ul-Kerim, Sheikh of the Shammar. Jedaan's father had taken refuge from a feud in his tribe with the father of that great chief. The boys became sworn brothers; and now that each is sheikh of his respective tribe, they always avoid meeting in the many fights between the Anezi and the Shammar. Last year the latter were defeated on one occasion, and Abd-ul-Kerim was with difficulty saved by the speed and lasting quality of this mare. On the following day, he sent to tell Jedaan that he would soon have his revenge when reinforcements should come, and that, as he feared for the life of his boyhood's friend, he sent him his mare, which could distance every other in the Shammar tribe. Jedaan rode her in the next engagement he had with Abd-ul-Kerim, the Anezi were beaten, and she brought him home unhurt after a long pursuit. There is little bloodshed in this desert warfare, considering the frequency of battles and the numbers engaged, for the conquered generally surrenders and is well treated, while deaths are always avenged sooner or later.

Acts of high-minded generosity are greatly appreciated by the Bedaween, who delight in narrating them. One of their favourite anecdotes is that of the owner of a swift mare which a neighbouring sheikh greatly coveted. A reward was in vain offered to any one of his tribe who could take her for him. She was too fleet to be obtained in the usual way. A proposal of a hundred camels in exchange for her was made and refused. A stratagem was resorted to. The sheikh lay groaning on the lonely plain when the man passed on his mare. Dismounting, the latter raised him gently, and placed him on her to lead him home, supposing him to be wounded or sick. The deceiver galloped off, and the dupe called after him to take the mare as a gift on the sole condition of never telling the tale, which might deter others from being compassionate.

The Arab tents are made of long belts of coarse cloth, stitched together, and supported by poles of different lengths, with screens of reeds woven with red and blue worsted in rude patterns. All these materials are home-made. The reeds and poles are found on the banks of the Euphrates, which are covered with jungle in many places. Some of the tents are not less than eighty feet long, in squares partitioned by suspending carpets from the roof. The women and children occupy one end, the men the other, and stores are piled in the centre rooms. During winter the best mares and foals are in very bad weather admitted into the tent, and they go freely about every part of it.

The Bedaween never taste animal food, except when a sheep is slaughtered for a guest. The feast is shared on such occasions by as many as can find a morsel to seize. Their ordinary food is bread dipped in melted butter, but they are often reduced to camel's milk, either alone or with a few dates. I once stayed a week with a tribe which had had nothing but camel's milk for three months; they did not appear unusually emaciated, and I did not myself suffer in the least from hunger. It is no fable of the Arabs to attribute to that kind of milk somewhat of the sustaining quality evinced by the wonderful enduring power of the animal which produces it. They wean their foals when only one month old, in order to rear them on camel's rather than on their mothers' milk, with the view of rendering them capable of long-continued exertion, and they firmly believe in this effect on the constitution.

This singular people seems to be the only one on the face of the globe which has remained in precisely the same state for the last four thousand years. Often conquerors, never subjugated, they have retained the features of the times when the first great empires of the world were founded. They gave sovereigns to Babylonia and Egypt nineteen centuries before Christ. They combated successfully the arms of the Pharaohs and the Assyrian kings; eluded the grasp of Cyrus and Alexander the Great; defied the Roman power; and, when Mahomet united them in a common cause, they carried their Oriental civilisation to the shores of the Bosphorus and the banks of the Tagus, where both the Eastern and the Western Empires had lost the enlightenment of Greece and Rome. The khaliphs of Bagdad, of Cairo, of Cordova, spread the thirst of knowledge around them. Even the Mongolian hordes, which attacked their eastern frontier, derived from them their religion and their intellectual developement. Europe sent her chivalry to assail them, and received back its scattered remnants, bearing only scars and rags from the holy war. Still Arabia, Syria, Egypt, Tunis, Algiers, Morocco, offer the same spectacle of a freedom-loving race, wandering at will over their scorched plains; still the Syrian desert, whose roving tribes have exercised so widely extended an influence on other countries, serves only to furnish a bare subsistence to a people possessing the same habits and ruled by the same principles in their social and political condition as their fathers Ishmael and Esau.

It is a mistake to suppose that their state is in any way analogous to that of the North American Indians or New Zealanders. These Bedaween Arabs are not savages. They have an organisation. It is the highest possible developement of the pastoral life. They are subject to the influence of public opinion. The lawlessness of the people, and the simple despotism of their chiefs, are, therefore, not altogether untempered. A man, who has disgraced himself by a breach of their species of morality, is shunned by his whole tribe, and is finally forced to leave it as an outcast. A chief, who has drawn the bond of allegiance too tight, is deposed or abandoned, and becomes a mere member of a tribe, or remains without one. Their laws are certainly somewhat peculiar, but they are laws, and, as such, they preclude anarchy. Robbery from a hostile tribe, from a village, caravan, or traveller, is honourable according to the Bedaween code; from an Arab of the same tribe, it involves only restitution. Grave offences of some kinds are punished with death. The execution is effected simply by laying the criminal on the ground and cutting his throat, the executioner being the sheikh himself. Murder is subject to retaliation by the relatives of the victim, if not redeemed by the payment of blood-money. Strange to say, no distinction is drawn between assassination, killing in battle, and accidental homicide.

There exists amongst the Bedaween a most salutary institution, which keeps them from waging wars of extermination. This is the ransom of blood. It falls on all kindred within five degrees. Death may thus be avenged on a large number of relatives. If the price of blood is paid in preference to suffering retaliation, the amount is divided amongst many contributors, whose lives are possibly saved thereby. It is generally the value of fifty camels, falling perhaps on fifty persons, which is not a heavy premium of insurance. This system tends greatly to preserve life, and to restrain those fierce passions which roving habits excite.

Another curious feature of Bedaween government is that by which the supreme authority changes hands provisionally when a sheikh is too old to lead the tribe in war, or another is considered a more fit and successful leader, to be restored to him at the conclusion of peace. I know an instance in which an elder brother is the sheikh in favour of his prudence, and a younger brother is the military chief by right of greater valour. The Arab tribes consider this practice to be a guarantee for the liberty of the subject, inasmuch as power is not concentrated, and jealousy prevents a coalition against popular freedom. Jedaan is the military leader of his tribe, and his uncle Deham the sheikh; but in this case the judgment and discretion of the former give him power even when not engaged in war. They are not on good terms, and when Jedaan sees his influence over the tribe diminished by intrigues on the part of Deham, who is a cunning old man, he always looks for another tribe to quarrel with, and by declaring war consolidates his authority.

A further check to the assumption of absolute power is found in the judicial functions of a member of each tribe, distinguished for sagacity, whose award is without appeal, even when it condemns the sheikh, or *aghid*, as the military chief is called. This magistrate enjoys the title of *cadi*, and is generally no mean lawyer. In the Fedan tribe there is really an upright judge, an old man, by name Jemaijem, whom I have heard decide cases with the greatest acumen and impartiality. He can neither read nor write, but he is gifted with a prodigious memory, and quotes a host of precedents in the point of law at issue, preparing his audience for his verdict before pronouncing it.

The Anezi tribe is subdivided into many sections, with distinctive appellations, such as Fedan, Sebaa, Erfuddi, Ibn Haddal, Amarat, Weled Ali, and Beni Sachar. Other tribes, the Aghedat, Sochni, and Aghel, live under their protection; the two former occupying the country between Palmyra and the Euphrates, where they burn herbs producing soda for sale in the towns, and the latter moving from camp to camp to act as brokers for the merchants of Aleppo and Bagdad, while they also form large caravans of camels for the transport of goods between those two marts. The Anezi are in the habit of tracing every year a great migratory orbit, which takes them to Aleppo in summer, towards Urfa, Diarbakir, Moossul and Bagdad in winter, and leads them round by the southern regions of the desert, passing near Damascus, Homs, and Hama, back to Aleppo. They provide themselves with grain and manufactured goods at the last-named city, and with dates at Bagdad, selling their wool, butter, lambs, young camels and horses to raise money for these purchases. All their other wants are supplied by the flocks and herds which they rear, and which oblige them to wander for ever in that vast circle to avoid the barren centre of the desert, and to find fresh pasture-grounds on its skirts in succession when they are exhausted.

As regards their honesty, I can say that I have been a good deal amongst them, and I feel more disposed to join those who have extolled their few virtues than the exponents of their many vices. One cannot with any degree of fairness throw all the responsibility of Bedaween misdeeds on their perpetrators. Treated as they have been, it is only surprising that they should have retained any virtues at all, and should not have pushed their vices much farther.

Carl R Raswan
From *The Black Tents of Arabia (1926)*

The Ambush

On our homeward drive to the Ruala camp, only an hour or so after we had parted from Ibn Meheyd, we were attacked by Bedouins from ambush in a wadi. The ensuing action was brief, but it cost the life of Abd el-Karim, who was particularly dear to Faris, while our assailants left three dead behind. They proved to be Saba of the House of Rakan.

Abd el-Karim's end was most harrowing. Sitting directly behind me in our open car, he was fatally wounded by a bullet which tore his abdomen to pieces. Realizing the inevitableness of the end, he calmly ordered his slave to shoot him through the head, before our very eyes. We scraped a shallow grave for him in the sand, and we were still occupied with the other dead when Sleyman, who had been posted on guard, reported that he had sighted three motor-cars through his binoculars. They were trying to cross the *wadi*, a considerable distance off, and come up on our side.

We pushed our car to a covered position in the *wadi* and made ready for action. The Saba were coming towards us cautiously. The visibility was bad in the dazzling glare, but at last we scored some hits, and the enemy fell back beyond reach of our long-range rifles.

While Faris and Sleyman kept watch on our opponents' movements, we others set to work to change the tyres riddled in the earlier fight and to solder the damaged radiator. This of course we could only very patchily; but luckily we managed to drive the heavy car out of the river-bed and make for the enemy.

The Saba divided on our approach, obviously for the purpose of attacking us on two sides. Mijhem steered for the car on our right, which had wheeled suddenly and stopped broadside on. Its occupants raked us with a hail of bullets, but although a number of these hit our car, we managed to dash in closer. Our carbines answered shot for shot. Steel rang on iron, the wind blew out our cloaks, bullets whistled past, sand and pebbles spattered my face, and wild shouts came from my companions; but I thought there must be some wounded, for our fire lessened. (Faris, Mnahi, and Sleyman had in fact been wounded more or less seriously, but carried on as well as they could.)

With a fresh volley of steel-cased bullets we finally put this car-load of our opponents out of action. If they were not all dead, we could feel sure that none were left fit to fight. Indeed we drove up to within a hundred yards without drawing a shot. But now it was high time for us to turn against the other two cars which appeared on our left, already dangerously near.

We headed for them, but we had gone little more than a mile when our damaged engine stopped abruptly.

There was no time, of course, to attempt repairs. We could no longer manœuvre the car, let alone take to flight. 'Get out,' said Mijhem. There was nothing for it but to stand our ground, with the car for cover. It was then I found out how badly Faris and Mnahi were injured. Faris could not move his right leg, and I had to half lift him out of the car. It was a mercy that the two enemy cars did not attack at that critical moment. They must have suffered losses in the first attack more serious than ours, for they had retreated beyond our range, and were marking time merely watching us.

I took advantage of this respite to get out my surgical kit and dress the wounded. My dear friend Faris was not so badly wounded as I had at first thought. The deep groove made by a bullet in the upper part of his right thigh bled profusely, but it was only a flesh wound. I cleaned it and closed it with half a dozen clamps. The bullet that had wounded Mnahi had gone clean through his shoulder and lodged in the muscles of his neck, and I easily succeeded in extracting it. Sleyman showed nothing worse than some harmless grazes on the wrist. I was bandaging these when Mijhem shouted to me to hurry. A fresh attack was coming.

I picked up my rifle and cartridge-belt and cowered down under the rear end of the car. I felt sick to the point of vomiting, and very weak; I could scarcely raise enough energy to throw open the chamber of my carbine and slide in a fresh cartridge-clip. My nausea was perhaps due to the ether I had involuntarily inhaled when attending to our wounded. I felt better, however, after I had been lying for a while under the car with my carbine under my arm.

Meanwhile the two hostile cars were drawing nearer. They drove one behind the other, so that only the leading car offered a good target. We pumped lead into its iron body, but unfortunately not with steel bullets; for Mijhem had brought along only a few clips of this ammunition and wanted to save it for the decisive moment – an ill-advised economy that was to cost us dear.

Presently the foremost car skidded, then reduced speed, and finally stopped six or seven hundred yards away. The car behind it, however, rushed on us at terrific speed, swerved sharply only about ten car-lengths from us, and was gone as quickly as it had come. The whole thing could have taken no more than thirty seconds.

In these few moments a terrible tragedy befell us, the details of which I fear I am quite unable to give with any degree of accuracy. I recall that at the critical moment I was chiefly conscious of the fact that only two or three shots were fired on our side. We had made the mistake of emptying our carbines almost simultaneously on the leading car. We all had to reload, and that allowed the other car those fatal few seconds in which to make its rush unchecked.

When the first car stopped (really put out of action by our fire) I had not a cartridge left in my magazine.

As I started to load a fresh clip, I heard a dull thud behind me, and a heavy body tumbled over me. I jerked my shoulder to let it slide off, and it collapsed limply on the ground. It was Sleyman. His wide-open eyes stared into emptiness. A bullet had pierced his right temple and come out under his left jaw. At the same moment I became conscious again of the oncoming car not one hundred yards off, and heard a voice cry half in terror, half in warning: 'Merciful One! O God of Grace!'

It was Faris who had cried out. Only then did I notice that he was no longer beside me. He had crept out from cover, to get a clearer sight, and was lying wholly exposed on the sand.

As the death-car thundered past, bullets clashed into the chassis of our vehicle, but in spite of the feverish excitement and the clanging and clatter about me, my ears picked out repeatedly in the fury of noise those dull, hollow thuds known only to those who have taken part in pitched battles – the sound of bullets striking into living flesh. Then I also heard moaning and groans. I straightened up a little to take a hasty look – and my blood ran cold. Faris lay writhing on the ground ahead of me.

My last shots spat venomously after the swiftly retreating car. Then I raised myself and, leaning on my carbine, staggered like a drunken man to my friend's side. He now lay quite still with his face in the sand. I turned him round. His eyes were glassy, but he was still alive. Blood trickled from the corners of his mouth, staining his handsome face and his dress. Near him lay the slave of Abd el-Karim riddled with bullets, a ghastly sight.

I fetched one of our water-bags in which we kept sulphur-charged water from Tudmur and with it washed Faris's face. He was quite unconscious; this made it easier for me to examine his injuries. Apart from the relatively unimportant thigh wound which he had received in the first attack, he had two terrible wounds in the right breast. To me it seemed a miracle that he was still alive. Both bullets had lodged deep down; to extract them with the means at hand was out of the question. I could do nothing but bandage the wounds with Mijhem's assistance.

Mnahi had broken down from sheer weakness and was huddled on the foot-board.

Everything seemed unreal.

Together with Mijhem I started to collect the scattered rifles. We ejected the spent cartridges and reloaded and stacked the arms beside Mnahi.

As we carried our two dead to the car Mijhem was also overcome by faintness. He dropped suddenly as if he had had a stroke, and remained full length on the ground. With my last remaining strength I got Sleyman's body into the back seat. Then I sat down on the running-board beside Mnahi.

I covered Faris with my cloak, for it was getting cool. I now felt thirsty and took the leather bag with the sulphur-water with which I had washed the faces of Faris and the dead men, and drank eagerly. That revived me. I picked up my Zeiss, for it seemed to me as if there was something stirring in the apparently disabled car of the enemy. I had not been deceived. The crew were obviously engaged in repairing their engine; I could clearly see three figures moving about. I handed the glass to Mnahi, asking him to keep watch on the enemy while I tried to restore Mijhem. He soon got up and tried to shake off his faintness. He drank some water and so did Mnahi.

There were two carbines for each of us. Four of these six we had loaded with steel-jacketed ammunition, and these we meant to use first. Mijhem had now recovered enough to stand by me. For Mnahi we made a seat so that, leaning against the car, he could take part in our defence.

The sun was nearing the horizon when the enemy car at last got under way. At first they moved away from us, but that was only to find smoother ground for their charge. We had agreed that Mijhem should open fire alone; Mnahi and I would hold our ammunition for the close fighting.

Mijhem shot deliberately, but quite fast enough. I had handed him another carbine with steel bullets when, after this eighth shot, the advancing car struck side-on, two hundred yards or so away. It must have run wild for the last thirty yards. In its front seat we saw distinctly the huddled figure of the negro. Of the rest of the crew there was no sign. All life seemed to have been extinguished.

Without a word, Mijhem, with rifle at the ready, started for the car at a run. I called to him to come back, but in vain; so I jumped up and ran to overtake him. After I had repeatedly shouted to him, he stopped at last to let me come up; and we advanced side by side, ready to fire at the slightest sign of life. The last fifty yards seemed to me endless, as step by step, every nerve taut, we approached the enemy car.

Nothing stirred.

The car was a ghastly sight. The three negroes huddled in it were terribly wounded and on the point of death; only the one at the wheel was still conscious. Mijhem drew his Mauser pistol, and, reaching behind the man, put a bullet through his brain. He then as quickly put the other two out of their misery, while I gathered up the men's rifles, revolvers, and ammunition. They all had been slaves of Rakan.

Meanwhile it had become nearly dark. My eyes strayed to the tragic vehicle loaded with our dead and with Faris, as I thought, lying beside it, perhaps dying. Still and ghostlike it loomed in the gloaming. But, was I dreaming? Faris, whom we had left lying on the ground unconscious, was sitting in the front of our car!

He raised his hand and waved it at us! It was no hallucination! I left Mijhem standing there and ran to Faris.

When I sat down beside him, he slowly extended his right arm and laid it over my shoulder. So he leaned on me; and we rested awhile side by side. I had switched on the lights on our instrument-board, and a faint glow fell on his pallid face. A sickly, sweet odour came from his blood-soaked garments. He tried to speak, but he was in much pain and could barely draw his bloodless lips away from his teeth.

When Mijhem had come back, we made ready to get under way. With some trouble we got our engine going. One of our head-lamps still worked and could be lighted; the other one had been shot to pieces.

I wanted to drive Faris straight to Damascus, where there were a number of French surgeons, one of whom I knew. But he only shook his head and begged us to carry him to his family and Tuëma. He was convinced he had only a short time to live and that no physician could help him.

I, too, had little hope of his recovery and ceased to persuade, feeling loath to assume the responsibility for his dying far from his kin and without having seen his beloved one again.

'If we go now,' said Faris, with pleading voice, 'God will extend my time so that I may see Tuëma, and take her as my wife. And so I shall raise a 'name' to honour my father's house, even if it please God to take me away.'

Faris – the true Ishmaelite!

Bedouins (and for that matter the Wahhabees also) do not honour the tombs of their dead, but they revere the wombs of the living as blessed.

So we resolved to do the will of Faris. But, before setting our faces homeward, we drove to the Saba car and its three dead. We removed a good tyre and some parts, which Mijhem thriftily thought could be put to use, and also poured most of its petrol into our tank. What remained Mijhem splashed over the car and then set fire to it. As we drove away into the night, this funeral pyre lit up the dark desert and its unseen horrors.

We drove slowly and carefully, and it was morning when we came in sight of the Ruala camp.

'The Cloud in my Eyes'

The sun had just risen when, from a ridge, we saw the black tents in the valleys between gently undulating hills. Some camel herds were already stringing out to pasture. I stopped the car and we looked at the peaceful scene spread out before us. The world could not be more beautiful than it was that morning.

On Faris's face lay the same still light that glorified the land. His eyes shone as with the gleam of a new light; and I was happy to bring him home.

Today he looked on everything with the eyes of one about to say farewell. What at other times he hardly noticed, today he regarded with wonder, as if he saw it for the first time.

He asked me if I thought that the 'other' life would be like this earthly one.

'Surely!' I replied.

He looked at his bloodless hands: 'Once upon a time they were strong,' he said, 'but now no strength is left in them. They are yellow like ripe seed. They will be laid in the earth.' He looked into my face and said earnestly in a low voice: 'Let us go to Tuëma.'

As we made our way through the camp of the tribal division to which Faris belonged, a grave-faced throng pressed round our car and in silence accompanied it to his father's dwelling. Supported only by me and holding his head high Faris dragged himself from the car to the tent. He would show no weakness. But the deathly pallor of his face betrayed his sad condition. There were also Mnahi's wound-dressings and the shot-riddled car to tell their tale. But though hundreds crowded close, grown-ups and children, and looked at us with anxious and inquiring eyes, not a mouth was opened to put a question. The very dogs, usually so joyful and vociferous on the return of a party, were silent; they only snuffed the blood-stained car, laid back their ears, and slunk off as if they had received a beating.

Faris's father, informed of the disaster by the word that had flown from tent-row to tent-row, came in gravely and sat down beside his stricken son. It cost him a terrible effort to preserve the appearance of composure prescribed by the Bedouin code. He made no inquiry as to his son's condition until after coffee had been handed round, and even then he could only ask, according to established usage: 'God willing, Faris, mayst thou stay with us?'

'I am alive, father, God be praised! And there is peace.'

'Peace?' asked Naif and some others in obvious surprise.

'Ibn Meheyd proclaimed peace in the council of Shiyukhs. Yesterday he had already removed his herds to the northern grazing-grounds.'

'Peace – peace,' the cry of 'Peace' ran through the tent and swelled outside into a chorus – 'There is peace – we may move on!'

Behind Faris knelt his little sister and the small sons of Tra'd ibn Sattam. Tears ran down the children's faces, but they bit their lips. Now our adventures were related, to the accompaniment of the free comments of the company. With incredible self-mastery, Faris, marked by Death, sought to hide his sufferings and take part in the general conversation, which ran on and on. Every little detail of the fighting was threshed out in cold blood, and Faris's inevitable fate was discussed with (to anyone of the Western world) cruel disregard of his feelings.

This discussion lasted two hours. When the company finally rose, Faris also tried to get up; but a severe hæmorrhage threw him back on his couch, and he fainted. His mother was sent for. When he came to, she was kneeling at his side, with his hands in hers; and one could see she was hungering for a look from him. 'My son!' she whispered, and kissed him, her face streaming with tears.

When Faris's still-wandering eyes saw her so convulsed with grief, his face quivered. 'Who is this woman?' he said, propping himself on his elbow. 'Take her away! I don't know her.'

The slaves looked at one another uncertainly.

'Take her outside!' Faris called to them again. Then I took the poor woman by the arm and, with some words of consolation, led her from the tent. But at the entrance of the tent she wrenched herself from me, ran back and threw herself at Faris's feet. With both hands she gathered dust from the ground and poured it on her head and cried to God to preserve her son.

Faris touched her bent head and said:

'Go, mother! God will give thee strength. I would have only happy faces about me. Nay, have I lived in order to be afraid of death?'

He motioned to me to lead his mother away.

When I came out of the woman's tent, a rider on a sorrel horse came galloping from another camp at the lower end of the valley and I waited. It was Tuëma, as I had thought.

Her whole body trembled and her voice was choked with tears. I tried to calm her and told her of what passed between Faris and his mother. At this she pulled herself together and kissed my hands and pressed them to her wet eyes.

'What shall I do, Aziz?' she asked.

'Make his last hours cheerful, Tuëma. Show him that you are happy. That is all.'

'Go thou before me,' she begged, and tried to smile; but the tears rolled down her cheeks.

'Go before me,' she repeated. 'I want first to dispel the cloud from my eyes.'

It had been decided that the marriage of Faris and Tuëma should take place that very evening. He had been inquiring after her with growing impatience. When I told him the glad news that Tuëma had come and would be with him at any moment, he begged first to see his mother again.

I went myself to the woman's quarters to bring her. Her grief had made her a frail wraith-like creature: she walked with uncertain steps, but was more composed. She knelt down by Faris's couch. He put his arms round his beloved mother, and hugged her to his breast. Tears came into his eyes and they seemed to soothe the mother's pain. She sat bolt upright by her son's side, arranged his clothes and cushions and replaited his long, thick tresses, with some words of jest about him and his beloved Tuëma. When she had finished she left again, leaning on my arm, and from the threshold called out to her son that she would now send in Tuëma.

We had arranged a broad comfortable couch for Faris and partitioned it off with curtains; but one of them, according to the direction of the wind, was always drawn back, so that Faris, resting with the upper part of his body propped up, could look out.

A smile of happiness mingled with surprise suddenly lit up his face. Tuëma had come in. She had paused at the threshold with a smothered cry and a look of horror in her face at her lover's helpless plight. But so quickly had she mastered herself that I hardly noticed her emotion, and Faris saw only a smiling face as she moved to his bedside. Her silver bangles tinkled faintly. 'Faris! Faris! my Life!' she exclaimed, dropping on her knees; and, twining her arms about his neck, she stroked and caressed his face and body.

When she kissed him I noticed that her mouth was stained with his blood; but she kept her lips firmly pressed to his, so that he should not see that blood was trickling from his mouth on to her neck.

Shortly before sundown the tent began to fill with relatives and friends, who had been invited as witnesses to the wedding.

Tuëma had meanwhile returned to her own dwelling at the lower end of the valley. Her girl friends had been busy selecting the handsomest camel-litter and decorating it for the occasion. With its ornate marriage-canopy it was mounted on a fine, gorgeously-caparisoned camel, which slaves then led to Tuëma's tent. There the bride mounted to her lofty seat between the slender horns of the camel-litter and, with songs and shouts and waving of scarves, her girl friends escorted her to the tent of the bridegroom.

Before the women's quarters, but so arranged that Faris on his couch could see everything, Tuëma made her camel kneel down. Faris's mother and sisters, attended by numerous men and women slaves, greeted and received the bride ceremoniously.

Close by, Mnahi held an old white battle-mare by the halter. Auda, 'The Helper,' she was called, and also the 'Virginal Kuhaylat-Ajuz,' for she had never been mated. The Ruala all but worshipped her as sacred. As a three-year-old she had been presented to Misha'il as a gift on the birth of her son, Amir Fuaz. The mare was thus twenty-seven years old and her body bore the scars of many a raid. Over her back was spread a white lamb's-skin rug, the 'Virgin-Fleece' which, according to immemorial custom, the Bedouin bride brings to the bridegroom as a wedding gift.

Tuëma had disappeared into the harem to be attired in her wedding-dress by Faris's mother and sisters. When she came out again she was resplendent in a rich cashmere gown woven in red and green (it had been worn by Faris's mother at her own bridal ceremony) and a gold-laced shepherd's cloak floating from her shoulders. She took her position beside the white mare; and an aged Bedouin, with a little lamb, only a week old, in his arms, stepped before her, laid the lamb at her feet and slit its throat as a sacrificial offering. Auda snorted and backed away from the blood, but the old man grabbed the halter and, dipping his fingers in the lamb's blood, painted the Wasm (tribal mark) of the Ruala on the mare's neck. Then he calmly passed his gory fingers through his white beard. The slaughtered lamb was given, in accordance with the custom of the Bedouins, to an orphan – a little girl selected by a Sheykh.

Without accepting a helping hand from Mnahi, which he offered because of her trailing garments, Tuëma lightly swung herself on to the back of the white mare and at walking-pace rode through the camp. The huge negro strode beside her, holding over her head the great sword of Janda and Jidua and exclaiming, herald-fashion:

> 'See ye the bride of Faris! See ye the virgin!
> O for Tuëma's eyes and Alya's grazing herds!
> O for the dark hero and his bride!'

Thus the procession made the round of the camp, all the inhabitants of which were lined up in front of their black tents and, as the bride rode past on her white mare, it was with a joyful 'Zarraghrit' they greeted her, even though their hearts were heavy within them.

Returning to Faris's tent, Tuëma dismounted, took the white lamb's-skin rug from the mare's back and spread it on the nuptial couch. Then she disappeared into the harem, to wait there until her bridegroom should call her.

Therewith the simple wedding ceremony was ended. We, who had been with Faris to witness the arrival of the bride, now rose to go.

The first stars were glittering over the hills when I stepped outside. The black tents in the valley melted into the deepening darkness of the evening.

The herds were wending their way homeward, their silhouettes now showing as they crossed high ground, now sinking out of sight in the hollows...

As my friends departed from the tent, each called out to Faris, according to Bedouin custom: 'Vigour! And God be with thee!'

Behind the partition that closed off the women's apartment Tuëma was waiting for our going. When the last farewell was uttered, she pulled the middle tent-pole from its position and laid it on the ground. The roof bulged and drooped low in the middle, almost touching Faris's couch, but the lateral supports and the taut stays kept the rest of the tent fixed at about a man's height. It was the sign to any passer-by that a bride was with her bridegroom.

That night Faris died. When we came to his tent next morning, Tuëma was lying unconscious beside her dead lover.

A stone's-throw from the tent a few slaves were busy digging his grave.

As we committed our dear brother, lying on the white fleece, into the keeping of the desert, the women looked on from a distance and bewailed the dead. Their hair was dishevelled and with smoke-black from their hearths they had painted signs of mourning on their faces.

Tuëma stood silent among them. The red cloak of camelhair flowed from her shoulders. Her head was held high, but in her eyes were tears and a look of ineffable pain.

Once more the sun rose and beamed over the land.

The tent poles dropped and the Ruala marched on...

The living strode over the dead, marching on into the young morning to new pastures and to new life...

Once more I rode on Sadha to the mound where we had buried Faris. It had already become a solitary thing – insignificant in the vast wilderness. A dog which lay on the grave slunk away at my approach. A bunch of white ostrich feathers was stuck between three fire-blackened stones which, the evening before, had formed Tuëma's hearth. This was her farewell to her lover. A gust of wind broke off one 'flower' from this unfading wreath and blew it over the ground. I got off my mare to pick up this broken white feather and to keep it in memory of my dear friend.

I remounted and rode on, but presently pulled rein again and looked back. The lonely dog had returned to the grave: he turned round and round and finally lay down, curled up as if in sleep. He was mourning his dead master. Nobody minded him, nobody looked for him; but where should he be but here, with his dead friend?

I was on the point of guiding Sadha away when I noticed a rider coming in my direction – a Bedouin on a white-stockinged sorrel mare, who had just detached himself from a moving group of Kethebs (riding-litters) and pack camels and was coming along at a tearing gallop.

It was Tuëma.

A short distance from where I was waiting for her she pulled up. Her horse snorted impatiently.

'Peace!' she called to me, lifting her hand.

'Peace! Tuëma,' I called back. The tears came in my eyes.

'Shushan!' she called. The dog on the grave got up and walked slowly and reluctantly toward her, then stopped and turned his head.

'Shushan,' she called again, and as she rode away the dog followed her.

The Ruala were on the march and the land was covered with their camels.

Within a few days Tudmur was engulfed in the maëlstrom. Day after day, with never a pause, fresh swarms of camels came out of the arid waste to stop at the foot of the hills and drink their fill. The sulphurous but wholesome water here issues from the hills in a clear stream, which branches out into a hundred rivulets in the plain and the small gardens surrounding the ancient city.

In the midst of the marching Ruala I rode again with Amir Fuaz beside the Abu Duhur, the hallowed tribal emblem. But it all seemed so different now – no martial body-guard; only the litters containing some chieftain's wives and children. Now there was no Faris among the young men, galloping with them on their mares, with the baying greyhounds about him. In vain also did I look for the young war-goddess.

The melodies of ancient herding-songs came floating back to us as we penetrated deeper into the beautiful pastures, which, with every step we took, became more luxuriant.

Never shall I forget that happy picture of the joyful people and its contented herds browsing, as they wandered onward, the juicy herbage and luxuriant plants.

Nor shall I easily forget the stragglers that vainly strove to reach Ishmaël's promised Canaan. There were thousands of camels dragging themselves along with the futile exertion of the last remnants of their strength. They were still perishing by the wayside, while the more fortunate ones were already walking in the rich meadows that had saved them from death.

Nearly two years passed, and the hardships of that spring were forgotten. Twice since then had I been with the Ruala, but only on my third visit did I fall in with the camp of the Shammar family of Faris ibn-Naif; for in the rainy season the sub-tribes divide and wander sometimes hundreds of miles apart, and it is not so simple a matter to find someone you are looking for. On my arrival I was greeted by the sons of Tra'd ibn-Sattam, whose tents adjoined the Shammar household, and after a while Faris's father came home, and we celebrated our reunion.

In the corner of the women's section of the tent there presently appeared a small, chubby Bedouin boy, who gazed at us new-comers with inquisitive and bashful eyes. He was still a toddler, and had to hold on to the end of the frayed tent-curtain.

'Menwer!' a woman's voice called from within.

The voice was Tuëma's; and this was Faris's son!

She came out and laughingly took the boy by the hand to lead him back, when I called out her name. She turned round in amazement and raised her hand to me in the salutation of peace. Then she bent down and whispered into her child's ear. The little fellow pointed to me and looked into his mother's face. She nodded encouragingly, and he wobbled toward me with outstretched arms. As I picked him up and hugged him to me, I laughed, but there were tears in my eyes.

Tuëma, who was speechless with amazement at seeing me again, at last joyfully exclaimed: 'Aziz!'

At a gesture from her father-in-law she sat down on a camel-saddle beside us. She touched me with shy fingertips in greeting and in her dark eyes was the sadness of memory. Since Faris's death she belonged altogether to Ibn Naif's family. She had been taken into it as a daughter and sister.

She drew the boy to her breast, and the two fondled each other, a picture of maternal happiness.

'In the evening the Beloved one went from me,' said Tuëma. 'In the morning he came back to me.'

'Sabah – the morning,' I whispered to myself. 'Sabah' was the word Faris had said to her in farewell – 'Sabah – thou untouched morning, thou virgin bride.'

Early the following day I rode with Abu-Faris (the 'Father of Faris') to some rising ground. My eyes travelled over the Hamad where the Ruala with their tents and camels were migrating southward. I felt as if invisible hands were carrying off my friends into the wilderness...

'Is not the life of man like a tent and its dwellers?' said the old Shammar Chief. 'The day comes when they go, and the site is forsaken. As Imrul-Kais says: "Pause, wanderer. Let us weep for the beloved one in his resting-place in the shifting sand between ed-Dujayl and el-Hamal. He was like the evening star set in the midst of the firmament!"'

This spring had brought back poignantly to my memory that other spring when Faris and Tuëma had been together. It seemed to me now like a dream.

There arose in me (as it had in another great friend of the Bedouins) the burning hope that always would there be room enough on the earth for my Bedouins.

And as my eyes took in the earth and the sky, the gentle hills and the far, far distances, the boundless expanse of the wilderness became peopled with recollections which, in spite of all that was sad, I count among the most beautiful in my life.

William Beawes
From *The Diary of William Beawes (1745)*

Our mahoffi terribly fatigues us, and was certainly only intended for such who have only no legs or can bestow them independent of their bodies. It is impossible to maintain a tolerable easy posture for two minutes together, and the motions moreover are so diabolical that I have frequently in a day worse qualms than a breeding woman and am sorer bruised by night than Sancho in his government. However, it keeps the immediate heat of the sun from us, which we should probably find at this season [ie August] insupportable; tho' here also the benefit is not much greater than being baked instead of roasted, and therefore the mahoffi is but a trumpery machine, and a wheelbarrow in comparison to a princely carriage.

George Sandys
From *A Relation of a Journey Began An. Dom. 1610*

These are the Ships of Arabia; their Seas are the desarts. A creature created for burthen. Six hundred weight is his ordinary load; yet will he carry a thousand ... Four days together he will travel without water; for a necessity fourteen; in his often belching thrusting up a Bladder, wherewith he moisteneth his mouth and throat ... Their pace is slow, and intolerable hard, being withal unsure of foot, were it never so little slippery or uneven. They are not made to amend their paces when weary. A Beast gentle and tractable, but in the time of his Venery: then, as if remembering his former hard usage, he will bite his Keeper, throw him down, and kick him: forty days continuing in that fury, and then returning to his former meekness.

III: Palmyra

P ALMYRA OR TADMOR, which is its ancient Semitic name, is listed in the
Holy Bible as one of King Solomon's cities: 'And he built Tadmor in the
wilderness ...' (*II Chronicles 8:4*). Often referred to as 'the Queen of the
Desert', Palmyra does indeed exude a powerful feminine presence. The most
legendary of its inhabitants was Queen Zenobia. We have even a physical
description of her, which is useful to recall when visiting, in the ruins of the
city, the marble depression that is said to have been her bath. (At certain hours,
when the sun decides, Palmyrene marble acquires a fleshly hue.) Trebellius
Pollio describes her thus:

> She went in state to the assemblies of the people, in a helmet, with a
> purple band fringed with jewels. Her robe was clasped with a diamond
> buckle, and she often wore her arm bare. Her complexion was dark
> brown, her eyes black and sparkling and of uncommon fire. Her
> countenance was divinely expressive, her person graceful in form and
> motion beyond imagination, her teeth were white as pearls, and her
> voice clear and strong.

She became the tragic heroine of literature, two early examples being Chaucer's
representation of her in *The Monk's Tale* and Christine de Pizan's in *Le Livre de
la cité des dames* (*The Book of the City of Ladies*), both of which draw upon
Boccaccio's *De Claris mulieribus* (*Concerning Famous Women*).

Edward Gibbon's account of Zenobia's rise and fall, although probably
inaccurate in places, pulls together the many strands from earlier classical
accounts, and, in the sheer muscularity of the prose, makes for the most
pleasurable introduction to her life. The description he gives of Zenobia being
led captive into Rome is the most operatic of the several versions we have of
her fate. What is worth adding to Gibbon's history, if only because it serves to
remind us of the horrors so easily forgotten when we take in the beauty of
Palmyra's ruins, is the letter the conquering emperor Aurelian wrote to
Ceionius Bassus:

You must now sheathe the sword. The Palmyrans have been sufficiently slaughtered and cut to pieces. We have not spared women; we have slain children. We have strangled old men; we have destroyed the husbandmen. To whom, then, shall we leave the land? To whom shall we leave the city? We must spare those that remain, for we think that the few who are now existing will take warning from the punishment of the many who have been destroyed.

Aurelian, as Gibbons reveals, was defensive on the issue of his having a woman for a deadly foe. Trebellius Polio in his History cites a letter Aurelian wrote to the senate:

I hear, O conscript fathers, that it has been urged against me that I have not accomplished a manly task, in triumphing over Zenobia. My accusers would not know how to praise me enough, if they knew that woman – if they knew her prudence in council, her firmness in purpose, the dignity she preserves towards her army, her munificence when necessity requires it, her severity when to be severe is just.

The actual site of Palmyra was virtually unknown to Europeans until 1678 when a couple of English merchants travelled there from Aleppo, but the first detailed account was that made by the archaeologist and classical scholar, Robert Wood, in 1752. The book, which he published the following year, *The Ruins of Palmyra, otherwise Tedmor in the Desart*, is one of the great publications of the period, not least because of its magnificent illustrations. A scholar and meticulous draughtsman, he not only introduced the Roman and Palmyrene architecture of Syria to a Western audience, but he also influenced the architectural taste of the period. Horace Walpole wrote: 'The modest descriptions and prefixes are standards of writing: The exact measure of what should and should not be said, and of what was necessary to be known was never comprehended in more clear diction or more clear style.' The passage quoted here comes from his otherwise scholarly introduction.

The work for which Constantin François de Chasseboeuf Volney is best remembered, if at all, is the philosophical meditation, *Les Ruines: ou, méditations sur les révolutions des empires* (1791), which was inspired by a dream he had in the ruins of Palmyra. It is Shelley's Ozymandias speaking prose. President Jefferson co-translated one the early English-language versions and President Lincoln read it.

The French poet, Jacques Réda, born 1929, was awarded the French Academy's Grand Prix in 1993 for a lifetime's work, and, more recently, the Bourse Goncourt de la Poésie. *Treading Lightly: Selected Poems 1961-1975* was recently published, in Jennie Feldman's fine translations, by Anvil Press. The two poems published in this and in the Saint Simeon sections were especially translated for this book. In speaking of the poems which comprise Réda's Syrian sonnet-sequence, Jennie Feldman writes: 'They remind me of the postage-stamp paintings that Réda puts alongside the real stamps on his envelopes – delectably and skilfully crafted. And they somehow recall the seventeenth-century French poets he so prizes (shades of Racine in that depiction of Zenobia).'

The first time I visited Palmyra, in 1985, I spoke to an elderly man who kept trying to explain to me, in fragmentary English, how one of his ancestors had entertained somebody called 'Yadi Astor Sanop'. It was only later, on a bus going back to Damascus, that I realised what I should have been quick enough to figure out at the time, that he was speaking of that other Queen of the Desert, Lady Hester Stanhope. When I returned a year later, I looked for my informant but without success. One of her biographers, Joan Haslip, writes of Lady Hester Stanhope: 'Even in the wilds of the desert, Hester Stanhope worshipped before the altar of her colossal egotism. She saw herself reflected in Zenobia's fame ... But where were the legions for her to command? Where were Longinus and the laden elephants bearing her the spoils of Egypt and Palestine?' She will continue to be promoted and demoted in the eyes of her admirers and detractors, but certainly there can be no arguing with the image. It is one to which others of her acquaintance were happy to add their own voices.

> If Lady Hester succeeds in this undertaking she will at least have the merit of being the first European female who ever visited this once celebrated city. Who knows but she many prove another Zenobia and be destined to restore it to its ancient splendour? Perhaps she may form a matrimonial alliance with Ibn Saud, the great chief of the Wahabees. He is not represented as a very lovable object; but, making love subservient to ambition, they may unite their arms together, bring about a great revolution both in religion and politics, and shake the throne of the Sultan to its very centre.

The author of this letter was Lady Hester's exasperated younger lover, Michael Bruce, and ought perhaps to be considered more for what is contained between its lines, the acidic juices of a man scorned. There are biographies aplenty on this extraordinary and surely impossible woman, but nothing speaks more clearly of her idea of self than the two letters reproduced here.

The section concludes with a letter from another remarkable woman, a queen among travellers, Gertrude Bell, from the recently published *The Arabian Diaries 1912-1914*. It is addressed to Charles Hotham Montague

Doughty-Wylie, a married British army officer with whom she was in love, and provides a vivid account of a journey she made from Aleppo to Baghdad and back again. The approach to Palmyra is not from the west, as is the experience of most travellers, but from the east when she approached it from Baghdad. She had earlier written to Doughty-Wylie, on January 13th, 1915, 'Do you know what it is going to be, this war?' She was still writing to him when, on April 26th, 1915, he died at Gallipoli. Their love was never physically consummated. She had written to him, saying that soon it would be.

Edward Gibbon
From *The Decline and Fall of the Roman Empire (c. 1780)*

Aurelian had no sooner secured the person and provinces of Tetricus, than he turned his arms against Zenobia, the celebrated queen of Palmyra and the East. Modern Europe has produced several illustrious women who have sustained with glory the weight of empire; nor is our own age destitute of such distinguished characters. But if we except the doubtful achievements of Semiramis, Zenobia is perhaps the only female whose superior genius broke through the servile indolence imposed on her sex by the climate and manners of Asia. She claimed her descent from the Macedonian kings of Egypt, equalled in beauty her ancestor Cleopatra, and far surpassed that princess in chastity and valour. Zenobia was esteemed the most lovely as well as the most heroic of her sex. She was of dark complexion (for in speaking of a lady these trifles become important). Her teeth were of a pearly whiteness, and her large black eyes sparkled with uncommon fire, tempered by the most attractive sweetness. Her voice was strong and harmonious. Her manly understanding was strengthened and adorned by study. She was not ignorant of the Latin tongue, but possessed in equal perfection the Greek, the Syriac, and the Egyptian languages. She had drawn up for her own use an epitome of oriental history, and familiarly compared the beauties of Homer and Plato under the tuition of the sublime Longinus.

This accomplished woman gave her hand to Odenathus, who from a private station raised himself to the dominion of the East. She soon became the friend and companion of a hero. In the intervals of war, Odenathus passionately delighted in the exercise of hunting; he pursued with ardour the wild beasts of the desert, lions, panthers, and bears; and the ardour of Zenobia in that dangerous amusement was not inferior to his own. She had inured her constitution to fatigue, disdained the use of a covered carriage, generally appeared on horseback in a military habit, and sometimes marched several miles on foot at the head of the troops. The success of Odenathus was in a great measure ascribed to her incomparable prudence and fortitude. Their splendid victories over the Great King, whom they twice pursued as far as the gates of Ctesiphon, laid the foundations of their united fame and power. The armies which they commanded, and the provinces which they had saved, acknowledged not any other sovereigns than their invincible chiefs. The senate and people of Rome revered a stranger who had avenged their captive emperor, and even the insensible son of Valerian accepted Odenathus for his legitimate colleague.

After a successful expedition against the Gothic plunderers of Asia, the Palmyrenian prince returned to the city of Emesa in Syria. Invincible in war, he was there cut off by domestic treason, and his favourite amusement of hunting was the cause, or at least the occasion, of his death. His nephew, Mæonius, presumed to dart his javelin before that of his uncle; and, though admonished of his error, repeated the same insolence. As a monarch and as a sportsman, Odenathus was provoked: took away his horse, a mark of ignominy among the barbarians, and chastised the rash youth by a short confinement. The offence was soon forgot, but the punishment was remembered; and Mæonius, with a few daring associates, assassinated his uncle in the midst of a great entertainment. Herod, the son of Odenathus, though not of Zenobia, a young man of a soft and effeminate temper, was killed with his father. But Mæonius obtained only the pleasure of revenge by this bloody deed. He had scarcely time to assume the title of Augustus, before he was sacrificed by Zenobia to the memory of her husband.

With the assistance of his most faithful friends, she immediately filled the vacant throne, and governed with manly counsels Palmyra, Syria, and the East, above five years. By the death of Odenathus, that authority was at an end which the senate had granted him only as a personal distinction; but his martial widow, disdaining both the senate and Gallienus, obliged one of the Roman generals, who was sent against her, to retreat into Europe, with the loss of his army and his reputation. Instead of the little passions which so frequently perplex a female reign, the steady administration of Zenobia was guided by the most judicious maxims of policy. If it was expedient to pardon, she could calm her resentment; if it was necessary to punish, she could impose silence on the voice of pity. Her strict economy was accused of avarice; yet on every proper occasion she appeared magnificent and liberal. The neighbouring states of Arabia, Armenia, and Persia, dreaded her enmity, and solicited her alliance. To the dominions of Odenathus, which extended from the Euphrates to the frontiers of Bithynia, his widow added the inheritance of her ancestors, the populous and fertile kingdom of Egypt. The emperor Claudius acknowledged her merit, and was content that, while *he* pursued the Gothic war, *she* should assert the dignity of the empire in the East. The conduct, however, of Zenobia was attended with some ambiguity; nor is it unlikely that she had conceived the design of erecting an independent and hostile monarchy. She blended with the popular manners of Roman princes the stately pomp of the courts of Asia, and exacted from her subjects the same adoration that was paid to the successors of Cyrus. She bestowed on her three sons a Latin education, and often showed them to the troops adorned with the Imperial purple. For herself she reserved the diadem, with the splendid but doubtful title of Queen of the East.

When Aurelian passed over into Asia, against an adversary whose sex alone could render her an object of contempt, his presence restored obedience to the province of Bithynia, already shaken by the arms and intrigues of Zenobia. Advancing at the head of his legions, he accepted the submission of Ancyra, and was admitted into Tyana, after an obstinate siege, by the help of a perfidious citizen. The generous though fierce temper of Aurelian abandoned the traitor to the rage of the soldiers: a superstitious reverence induced him to treat with lenity the countrymen of Apollonius the philosopher. Antioch was deserted on his approach, till the emperor, by his salutary edicts, recalled the fugitives, and granted a general pardon to all who, from necessity rather than choice, had been engaged in the service of the Palmyrenian queen. The unexpected mildness of such a conduct reconciled the minds of the Syrians, and, as far as the gates of Emesa, the wishes of the people seconded the terror of his arms.

Zenobia would have ill deserved her reputation, had she indolently permitted the emperor of the West to approach within a hundred miles of her capital. The fate of the East was decided in two great battles; so similar in almost every circumstance that we can scarcely distinguish them from each other, except by observing that the first was fought near Antioch, and the second near Emesa. In both, the queen of Palmyra animated the armies by her presence, and devolved the execution of her orders on Zabdas, who had already signalized his military talents by the conquest of Egypt. The numerous forces of Zenobia consisted for the most part of light archers, and of heavy cavalry clothed in complete steel. The Moorish and Illyrian horse of Aurelian were unable to sustain the ponderous charge of their antagonists. They fled in real or affected disorder, engaged the Palmyrenians in a laborious pursuit, harassed them by a desultory combat, and at length discomfited this impenetrable but unwieldy body of cavalry. The light infantry, in the meantime, when they had exhausted their quivers, remaining without protection against a closer onset, exposed their naked sides to the swords of the legions. Aurelian had chosen these veteran troops, who were usually stationed on the Upper Danube, and whose valour had been severely tried in the Alemannic war. After the defeat of Emesa, Zenobia found it impossible to collect a third army. As far as the frontier of

Egypt, the nations subject to her empire had joined the standard of the conqueror, who detached Probus, the bravest of his generals, to possess himself of the Egyptian provinces. Palmyra was the last resource of the widow of Odenathus. She retired within the walls of her capital, made every preparation for a vigorous resistance, and declared, with the intrepidity of a heroine, that the last moment of her reign and of her life should be the same.

Amid the barren deserts of Arabia, a few cultivated spots rise like islands out of the sandy ocean. Even the name of Tadmor, or Palmyra, by its signification in the Syriac as well as in the Latin language, denoted the multitude of palm trees which afforded shade and verdure to that temperate region. The air was pure, and the soil, watered by some invaluable springs, was capable of producing fruits as well as corn. A place possessed of such singular advantages, and situated at a convenient distance, between the Gulf of Persia and the Mediterranean, was soon frequented by the caravans which conveyed to the nations of Europe a considerable part of the rich commodities of India. Palmyra insensibly increased into an opulent and independent city, and, connecting the Roman and the Parthian monarchies by the mutual benefits of commerce, was suffered to observe an humble neutrality, till at length, after the victories of Trajan, the little republic sunk into the bosom of Rome, and flourished more than one hundred and fifty years in the subordinate though honourable rank of a colony. It was during that peaceful period, if we may judge from a few remaining inscriptions, that the wealthy Palmyrenians constructed those temples, palaces, and porticos of Grecian architecture, whose ruins, scattered over an extent of several miles, have deserved the curiosity of our travellers. The elevation of Odenathus and Zenobia appeared to reflect new splendour on their country, and Palmyra for a while stood forth the rival of Rome: but the competition was fatal, and ages of prosperity were sacrificed to a moment of glory.

In his march over the sandy desert, between Emesa and Palmyra, the Emperor Aurelian was perpetually harassed by the Arabs; nor could he always defend his army, and especially his baggage, from these flying troops of active and daring robbers, who watched for the moment of surprise, and eluded the slow pursuit of the legions. The siege of Palmyra was an object far more difficult and important, and the emperor, who with incessant vigour pressed the attacks in person, was himself wounded with a dart. 'The Roman people,' says Aurelian, in an original letter, 'speak with contempt of the war which I am waging against a woman. They are ignorant both of the character and of the power of Zenobia. It is impossible to enumerate her warlike preparations, of stones, of arrows, and of every species of missile weapons. Every part of the walls is provided with two or three *balistæ*, and artificial fires are thrown from her military engines. The fear of punishment has armed her with a desperate courage. Yet still I trust in the protecting deities of Rome, who have hitherto been favourable to all my undertakings.' Doubtful, however, of the protection of the gods, and of the event of the siege, Aurelian judged it more prudent to offer terms of an advantageous capitulation: to the queen, a splendid retreat; to the citizens, their ancient privileges. His proposals were obstinately rejected, and the refusal was accompanied with insult.

The firmness of Zenobia was supported by the hope that in a very short time famine would compel the Roman army to repass the desert; and by the reasonable expectation that the kings of the East, and particularly the Persian monarch, would arm in the defence of their most natural ally. But fortune and the perseverance of Aurelian overcame every obstacle. The death of Sapor, which happened about this time, distracted the councils of Persia, and the inconsiderable succours that attempted to relieve Palmyra, were easily intercepted either by the arms or the liberality of the emperor. From every part of Syria, a regular succession of convoys safely arrived in the camp, which was increased by the return of Probus with his victorious troops from the conquest of Egypt. It was then that Zenobia resolved to fly. She mounted the fleetest of her dromedaries, and had already reached the banks of the Euphrates, about sixty miles from Palmyra, when she was overtaken by the pursuit of Aurelian's light horse, seized, and brought back a captive to the feet of the emperor. Her capital soon afterwards surrendered, and was treated with unexpected lenity. The arms, horses, and camels, with an immense treasure of gold, silver, silk, and precious stones, were all delivered to the conqueror, who, leaving only a garrison of six hundred archers, returned to Emesa, and employed some time in the distribution of rewards and punishments at the end of so memorable a war, which restored to the obedience of Rome those provinces that had renounced their allegiance since the captivity of Valerian.

When the Syrian queen was brought into the presence of Aurelian, he sternly asked her, How she had presumed to rise in arms against the emperors of Rome? The answer of Zenobia was a prudent mixture of respect and firmness. 'Because I disdained to consider as Roman emperors an Aureolus or a Gallienus. You alone I acknowledge as my conqueror and my sovereign.' But, as female fortitude is commonly artificial, so it is seldom steady or consistent. The courage of Zenobia deserted her in the hour of trial; she trembled at the angry clamours of the soldiers, who called aloud for her immediate execution, forgot the generous despair of Cleopatra, which she had proposed as her model, and ignominiously purchased life by the sacrifice of her fame and her friends. It was to their counsels, which governed the weakness of her sex, that she imputed the guilt of her obstinate resistance; it was on their heads that she directed the vengeance of the cruel Aurelian. The fame of Longinus, who was included among the numerous and perhaps innocent victims of her fear, will survive that of the queen who betrayed, or the tyrant who condemned, him. Genius and learning were incapable of moving a fierce unlettered soldier, but they had served to elevate and harmonize the soul of Longinus. Without uttering a complaint, he calmly followed the executioner, pitying his unhappy mistress, and bestowing comfort on his afflicted friends.

Returning from the conquest of the East, Aurelian had already crossed the Straits which divide Europe from Asia, when he was provoked by the intelligence that the Palmyrenians had massacred the governor and garrison which he had left among them, and again erected the standard of revolt. Without a moment's deliberation, he once more turned his face towards Syria. Antioch was alarmed by his rapid approach, and the helpless city of Palmyra felt the irresistible weight of his resentment. We have a letter of Aurelian himself, in which he acknowledges that old men, women, children, and peasants had been involved in that dreadful execution, which should have been confined to armed rebellion; and, although his principal concern seems directed to the re-establishment of a temple of the Sun, he discovers some pity for the remnant of the Palmyrenians, to whom he grants the permission of rebuilding and inhabiting their city. But it is easier to destroy than to restore. The seat of commerce, of arts, and of Zenobia, gradually sunk into an obscure town, a trifling fortress, and at length a miserable village. The present citizens of Palmyra, consisting of thirty or forty families, have erected their mud cottages within the spacious court of a magnificent temple.

Another and a last labour still awaited the indefatigable Aurelian; to suppress a dangerous though obscure rebel, who during the revolt of Palmyra, had arisen on the banks of the Nile. Firmus, the friend and ally, as he proudly styled himself, of Odenathus and Zenobia, was no more than a wealthy merchant of Egypt. In the course of his trade to India, he had formed very intimate connexions with the Saracens and the Blemmyes, whose situation on either coast of the Red Sea gave them an easy introduction into the Upper Egypt. The Egyptians he inflamed with the hope of freedom, and, at the head of their furious multitude, broke into the city of Alexandria, where he assumed the Imperial purple, coined money, published edicts, and raised an army, which, as he vainly boasted, he was capable of maintaining from the sole profits of his paper trade. Such troops were a feeble defence against the approach of Aurelian; and it seems almost unnecessary to relate that Firmus was routed, taken, tortured, and put to death. Aurelian might now congratulate the senate, the people, and himself, that in little more than three years he had restored universal peace and order to the Roman world.

Since the foundation of Rome, no general had more nobly deserved a triumph than Aurelian; nor was a triumph ever celebrated with superior pride and magnificence. The pomp was opened by twenty elephants, four royal tigers, and above two hundred of the most curious animals from every climate of the North, the East, and the South. They were followed by sixteen hundred gladiators, devoted to the cruel amusement of the amphitheatre. The wealth of Asia, the arms and ensigns of so many conquered nations, and the magnificent plate and wardrobe of the Syrian queen, were disposed in exact symmetry or artful disorder. The ambassadors of the most remote parts of the earth, of Æthiopia, Arabia, Persia, Bactriana, India, and China, all remarkable by their rich or singular dresses, displayed the fame and power of the Roman emperor, who exposed likewise to the public view the presents that he had received, and particularly a great number of crowns of gold, the offerings of grateful cities. The victories of Aurelian were attested by the long train of captives who reluctantly attended his triumph, Goths, Vandals, Sarmatians, Alemanni, Franks, Gauls, Syrians and Egyptians. Each people was distinguished by its peculiar inscription, and the title of Amazons was bestowed on ten martial heroines of the Gothic nation who had been taken in arms. But every eye, disregarding the crowd of captives, was fixed on the emperor Tetricus and the queen of the East. The former, as well as his son, whom he had created Augustus, was dressed in Gallic trowsers, a saffron tunic, and a robe of purple. The beauteous figure of Zenobia was confined by fetters of gold; a slave supported the gold chain which encircled her neck, and she almost fainted under the intolerable weight of jewels. She preceded on foot the magnificent chariot in which she once hoped to enter the gates of Rome. It was followed by two other chariots, still more sumptuous, of Odenathus and of the Persian monarch. The triumphal car of Aurelian (it had formerly been used by a Gothic king) was drawn, on this memorable occasion, either by four stags or by four elephants. The most illustrious of the senate, the people, and the army, closed the solemn procession. Unfeigned joy, wonder and gratitude swelled the acclamations of the multitude; but the satisfaction of the senate was clouded by the appearance of Tetricus; nor could they suppress a rising murmur that the haughty emperor should thus expose to public ignominy the person of a Roman and a magistrate.

But however, in the treatment of his unfortunate rivals, Aurelian might indulge his pride, he behaved towards them with a generous clemency which was seldom exercised by the ancient conquerors. Princes who, without success, had defended their throne or freedom were frequently strangled in prison, as soon as the triumphal pomp ascended the capitol. These usurpers, whom their defeat had convicted of the crime of treason, were permitted to spend their lives in affluence and honourable repose. The emperor presented Zenobia with an elegant villa at Tibur, or Tivoli, about twenty miles from the capital; the Syrian queen insensibly sank into a Roman matron, her daughters married into noble families, and her race was not yet extinct in the fifth century.

Robert Wood
From *The Ruins of Palmyra (1751)*

Our account of Palmyra is confined merely to that state of decay in which we found those ruins in the year 1751. It is not probable that the reader's curiosity should stop here: The present remains of that city are certainly too interesting to admit of our indifference about what it has been; when and by whom it was built; the singularity of its situation (separated from the rest of mankind by an uninhabitable desart,) and the source of riches necessary to support of such magnificence, are subjects which very naturally engage our attention. The following Enquiry is an attempt, in some measure, to satisfy that curiosity.

It seems very remarkable, that Balbeck and Palmyra, perhaps the two most surprising remains of antient magnificence which are now left, should be so much neglected in history, that, except what we can learn from the inscriptions, all our information about them, would scarce amount to more than probably conjecture.

Does not even this silence of history carry with it instruction, and teach us how much we are in the dark with regard to some periods of antiquity?

It is the natural and common fate of cities to have their memory longer preserved than their ruins. Troy, Babylon and Memphis are now known only from books, while there is not a stone left to mark there situation. But here we have two instances of considerable towns out-living any account of them. Our curiosity about these places is rather raised by what we see than what we read, and Balbeck and Palmyra are in a great measure left to tell their own story.

Shall we attribute this to the loss of books, or conclude that the Antients did not think those buildings so much worth notice as we do? If we can suppose the latter, it seems to justify our admiration of their works. There silence about Balbeck, gives authority to what they say of Babylon, and the works of Palmyra scarce mentioned, become vouchers for those so much celebrated of Greece and Egypt.

Any authority I can collect from the Antients, immediately relating to Palmyra, might be thrown into a very small compass; but as persons of more leisure may, if they think it worth while, enlarge and correct these hints, I shall not only produce such materials as I have met with, but also give the historical order in which I searched for them, by taking short view of the most remarkable revolutions of Syria, from the earliest account of this place, which may at least be of some use towards a more diligent and accurate enquiry.

A Journey through the Desart

Our journey to Palmyra was that part of our tour through the East, in which we expected to meet with the greatest difficulties, as it was much out of the common road, and where the protection of the Grand Signior could do us no service.

Aleppo and Damascus seemed to be the places where we might most effectually consult our ease and safety in this undertaking. Having unsuccessfully attempted to make the first of those cities our road, we left our ship at Byroot on the coast of Syria, and crossed Mount-Libanus to Damascus.

The Bashaw of this city told us, he could not promise that his name, or power, would be any security for us in the place to which we were going. From what he said and from all the information that we could get, we found it necessary to go to Hassia, a village four days journey north from Damascus, and the residence of an Aga, whose jurisdiction extends as far as Palmyra.

Since we propose this work merely as an account of the ruins of Palmyra, and not of our travels, we shall here only premise such a short sketch of our passage through the Desart, as may give a general idea of our manner of travelling in a country, which no body has described.

Hassia is a small village upon the great caravan-road, from Damascus to Aleppo, situated near Antilibanus, and at a few hours distance from the Orontes. The Aga received us with that hospitality, which is so common among all the ranks of people in those countries; and though extremely surprized at our curiosity, he gave us instructions how to satisfy it in the best manner.

We set out from Hassia on March 11th, 1751, with an escort of the Aga's best Arab horsemen, armed with guns and long pikes, and travelled in four hours to Sudud, through a barren plain, scarce affording a little browsing to antilopes of which we saw a great number. Our course was a point to the south of the east.

Sudud is a poor small village, inhabited by Maronite christians; its houses are built of no better materials than mud dried in the sun. They cultivate as much ground about the village as is necessary for their bare subsistance, and make a good red wine. We bought a few manuscripts of their priest, and proceeded after dinner through the same sort of country, in a direction half a point more to the south, to a Turkish village called Howareen (where we lay) three hours from Sudud.

Howareen has the same appearance of poverty as Sudud, But we found a few ruins there, which shew it to have been formerly a more considerable place. A square tower, with projecting battlements for defence, looks like a work of three or four hundred years, and two ruined churches may be of the same age, though part of the materials, awkwardly employed in those buildings, are much older. In their walls are some corinthian capitals, and several large attick bases of white marble. Those and some other scattered fragments of antiquity, which we saw here, have belonged to works of more expense than taste. We remarked a village near this entirely abandoned by its inhabitants, which happens often in those countries, where the lands have no acquired value from cultivation, and are often deserted, to avoid oppression.

We set out from Howareen on the 12th, and in three hours arrived at Carietein, keeping the same direction. This village differs from the former, only by being a little larger. It has also some broken pieces of marble, which belonged to antient buildings, as some shafts of columns, a few corinthian capitals, a dorick base, and two imperfect Greek inscriptions. It was thought proper we should stay here this day, as well to collect the rest of our escort, which the Aga had ordered to attend us, as to prepare our people and cattle for the fatigue of the remaining part of the journey, which, though we could not perform it in less time than twenty four hours, could not be divided into stages, as there is no water in that part of the desart.

We left Carietein on the 13th, about ten o'clock, which was much too late: but as our body became more numerous, it was less governable. This bad management exposed us to the heat of two days, before our cattle could get either water or rest; and though so early in the season, yet the reflection of the sun from the sand was very powerful, and we had not the relief of either breeze or shade during the whole journey.

Our caravan was now increased to about two hundred persons, and about the same number of beasts for carriage, consisting of an odd mixture of horses, camels, mules and asses. Our guide told us, this part of the journey was most dangerous and desired we might submit our selves entirely to his direction, which was, that the servants should keep with the baggage immediately behind our Arab guard; from which one, two, or more of their body were frequently dispatched, for discovery, to whatever eminences they could see, where they remained until we came up. Those horsemen always rode off from the caravan at full speed, in the Tartar and the Hussar manner. We doubted whether all this precaution was owing to their being really apprehensive of danger, or whether they only affected to make us think highly of their use and vigilance. Our course from Carietein to Palmyra, was a little to the east of the north, through a flat sandy plain (without either tree or water the whole way) about ten miles broad, and bounded to our right and left by a ridge of barren hills, which seemed to join about two miles before we arrived at Palmyra.

The tiresome sameness, both of our road and manner of travelling, was now and then a little relieved by our Arab horsemen, who engaged in mock fights with each other for our entertainment, and shewed a surprising firmness of seat, and dexterity in the management of their horses. When the business of the day was over, coffee and a pipe of tobacco made their highest luxury, and while they indulged in this, sitting in a circle, one of the company entertained the rest with a song or story, the subject love, or war, and the composition sometimes extempory.

In nine hours from Carietein we came to a ruined tower, on which we observed, in two or three places, the Maltese cross. Near it are the ruins of a very rich building as appeared by a white marble door-case, which is the only part standing and not covered with sand ... At midnight we stopt two hours for refreshment, and the fourteenth about noon we arrived at the end of the plain, where the hills to our right and left seemed to meet. We found between those hills a vale through which an aqueduct (now ruined) formerly conveyed water to Palmyra.

In this vale, to our right and left, were several square towers of considerable height, which upon a nearer approach we found were the sepulchres of the antient Palmyrenes. We had scarce passed these venerable monuments, when the hills opening discovered to us, all at once, the greatest quantity of ruins we had ever seen, all of white marble, and beyond them towards the Euphrates a flat waste, as far as the eye could reach, without any object which shewed either life or motion. It is scarce possible to imagine any thing more striking than this view: So great a number of Corinthian pillars, mixed with so little wall or solid building, afforded a most romantic variety of prospect.

After this general view (by which we found things rather exceed than fall short of our expectations) we were conducted to one of the huts of the Arabs, of which there are about thirty in the court of the great temple. The contrast between the magnificence of that building and the poverty of our lodging, was very striking. The inhabitants, both men and women, were well shaped, and the latter, though very swarthy, had good features. They were veiled, but not so scrupulous of shewing their faces, as the eastern women generally are. They paint the ends of their fingers red, their lips blue, and their eyebrows and eyelashes black, and wore very large gold or brass rings in their ears and noses. They had the appearance of good health, and told us, that distempers of any sort were uncommon among them.

We concluded from this, that the air of Palmyra deserves the character which Longinus gives it, in his epistle to Porphyry. They have seldom rain, except at the equinoxes. Nothing could be more serene than the sky all the time we were there, except one afternoon, that there was a small shower, preceded by a whirlwind, which took up such quantities of sand from the desart, as quite darkened the sky, and gave us an idea of those dreadful hurricanes which are sometimes fatal to whole caravans.

We were tolerably well provided with mutton and goat's flesh, by the Arab inhabitants; which, however, would have become very scarce, had we remained there longer than fifteen days, in which time we satisfied our curiosity.

Constantin François de Chasseboeuf Volney
From *The Ruins: or, A Survey of the Revolutions of Empires (1791)*

The dusk increased, and already I could distinguish nothing more than the pale phantoms of walls and columns. The solitariness of the situation, the serenity of evening, and the grandeur of the scene, impressed my mind with religious thoughtfulness. The view of an illustrious city deserted, the remembrance of past times, their comparison with the present state of things, all combined to raise my heart to a strain of sublime meditations. I sat down on the base of a column; and there, my elbow on my knee, and my head resting on my hand, sometimes turning my eyes towards the desert, and sometimes fixing them on the ruins, I fell into a profound revery.

Meditations

Here said I to myself, an opulent city once flourished; this was the seat of a powerful empire. Yes, these places, now so desert, a living multitude formerly animated, and an active crowd circulated in the streets which at present are so solitary. Within these walls, where a mournful silence reigns, the noise of the arts and the shouts of joy and festivity continually resounded. These heaps of marble formed regular palaces; these prostrate pillars were the majestic ornaments of temples; these ruinous galleries present the outlines of public places. Here a numerous people assembled for the respective duties of its worship, or the anxious cares of its subsistence; their industry, the fruitful inventor of sources of enjoyment, collected together the riches of every climate, and the purple of Tyre was exchanged for the precious thread of Serica; the soft tissues of Cassimere for the sumptuous carpets of Lydia; the amber of the Baltic for the pearls and perfumes of Arabia; the gold of Ophir for the pewter of Thule.

And now a mournful skeleton is all that subsists of this opulent city, and nothing remains of its powerful government but a vain and obscure remembrance! To the tumultuous throng which crowded under these porticos, the solitude of death has succeeded. The silence of the tomb is substituted for the hum of polite places. The opulence of a commercial city is changed into hideous poverty. The palaces of kings are become the receptacle of deer, and unclean reptiles inhabit the sanctuary of the gods. What glory is here eclipsed, and how many labours are annihilated! Thus perish the works of men, and thus do nations and empires vanish away!

The history of past times strongly presented itself to my thoughts. I called to mind those distance ages when twenty celebrated nations inhabited the

129

country around me. I pictured to myself the Assyrian on the banks of the Tigris, the Chaldean on those of the Euphrates, the Persian whose power extended from the Indus to the Mediterranean. I enumerated the kingdoms of Damascus and Idumea; of Jerusalem and Samaria; and the warlike states of the Philistines; and the commercial republics of Phœnicia. This Syria, said I to myself, now almost depopulated, then contained a hundred flourishing cities, and abounded with towns, villages, and hamlets. Every where one might have seen cultivated fields, frequented roads, and crowded habitations. Ah! what are become of those ages of abundance and of life? What are become of so many productions of the hand of man? Where are those ramparts of Nineveh, those walls of Babylon, those palaces of Persepolis, those temples of Balbec and of Jerusalem? Where are those fleets of Tyre, those dock-yards of Arad, those workshops of Sidon, and that multitude of mariners, pilots, merchants, and soldiers? Where those husbandmen, those harvests, that picture of animated nature, of which the earth seemed proud? Alas! I have traversed this desolate country, I have visited the places that were the theatre of so much splendour, and I have beheld nothing but solitude and desertion? I looked for these ancient people and their work, and all I could find was a faint trace, like to what the foot of a passenger leaves on the sand. The temples are thrown down, the palaces demolished, the ports filled up, the towns destroyed, and the earth stripped of inhabitants, seems a dreary burying-place. Great God! from whence proceed such melancholy revolutions? For what cause is the fortune of these countries so strikingly changed? Why are so many cities destroyed? Why is not that ancient population reproduced and perpetuated?

Thus absorbed in contemplation, new ideas continually presented themselves to my thoughts. Every thing, continued I, misleads my judgment, and fills my heart with trouble and uncertainty. When these countries enjoyed what constitutes the glory and felicity of mankind, they were an *unbelieving* people who inhabited them: It was the Phœnician, offering human sacrifices to Moloch, who brought together within his walls the riches of every climate; it was the Chaldean, prostrating himself before a serpent*, who subjugated opulent cities, and laid waste the palaces of kings and the temples of the gods; it was the Persian, the worshipper of fire, who collected the tributes of a hundred nations; they were the inhabitants of this very city, adorers of the sun and stars, who erected so many monuments of affluence and luxury. Numerous flocks, fertile fields, abundant harvests, everything that should have been the reward of *piety*, was in the hands of *idolators*; and now that a *believing* and *holy* people occupy the countries, nothing is to be seen but solitude and sterility. The earth, under these *blessed* hands, produces only briers and wormwood, Man

---

* The Dragon Bel

sows in anguish, and reaps vexation and cares; war, famine, and pestilence, assault him in turn. Yet, are not these the children of the prophets; this Christian, this Mussulman, this Jew, are they not the elect of heaven, loaded with gifts and miracles? Why then is this race, beloved of the Divinity, deprived of the favours which were formerly showered down upon the heathen? Why do these lands, consecrated by the blood of the martyrs, no longer boast their former temperature and fertility? Why have those favours been banished, as it were, and transferred for so many ages to other nations and different climes?

And here, pursuing the course of vicissitudes which have in turn transmitted the sceptre of the world to people so various in manners and religion, from those of ancient Asia down to the more recent ones of Europe, my native country, designated by this name, was awakened in my mind, and turning my eyes towards it, all my thoughts fixed upon the situation in which I had left it*.

I recollected its fields so richly cultivated, its roads so admirably executed, its towns inhabited by an immense multitude, its ships scattered over every ocean, its ports filled with the produce of either India; and comparing the activity of its commerce, the extent of its navigation, the magnificence of its buildings, the arts and industry of its inhabitants, with all that Egypt and Syria could formerly boast of a similar nature, I pleased myself with the idea that I had found in modern Europe the past splendour of Asia; but the charm of my reverie was presently dissolved by the last step in the comparison. Reflecting that if the places before me had once exhibited this animated picture; who, said I to myself, can assure me that their present desolation will not one day be the lot of our own country? Who knows but that hereafter some traveller like myself will sit down upon the banks of the Seine, the Thames, or the Zuyder sea, where now, in the tumult of enjoyment, the heart and the eyes are too slow to take in the multitude of sensations; who knows but he will sit down solitary amid silent ruins, and weep a people inurned, and their greatness changed into an empty name?

The idea brought tears into my eyes; and covering my head with the flap of my garment, I gave myself up to the most gloomy meditations on human affairs. Unhappy man said I in my grief, a blind fatality plays with my destiny! a fatal necessity rules by chances the lot of mortals! But, no: they are the decrees of celestial justice that are accomplishing! A mysterious God exercises his incomprehensible judgments! He has doubtless pronounced a secret malediction against the earth; he has struck with a curse the present race of men, in revenge of past generations. Oh! who shall dare to fathom the depths of the Divinity?

And I remained immoveable, plunged in profound melancholy.

* In the year 1782, at the close of the American war.

The Apparition

In the meantime a noise struck my ear, like to the agitation of a flowing robe, and the slow steps of a foot upon the dry and rustling grass. Alarmed, I drew my mantle from my head, and casting round me a timid glance, suddenly, by the obscure light of the moon, through the pillars and ruins of a temple, I thought I saw at my left a pale apparition, enveloped in an immense drapery, similar to what spectres are painted when issuing out of the tombs. I shuddered; and while in this troubled state, I was hesitating whether to fly, or ascertain the reality of the vision, a hollow voice, in grave and solemn accents, thus addressed me:

How long will man importune the heavens with unjust complaint? How long, with vain clamours, will he accuse Fate as the author of his calamities? Will he then never open his eyes to the light, and his heart to the insinuations of truth and reason? This truth everywhere presents itself in radiant brightness; and he does not see it! The voice of reason strikes his ear; and he does not hear it! Unjust man! if you can for a moment suspend the delusion which fascinates your senses; if your heart be capable of comprehending the language of argumentation, interrogate these ruins! read the lessons which they present to you! and you, sacred temples! venerable tombs! walls, once glorious! the witnesses of twenty different ages, appear in the cause of nature herself! come to the tribunal of sound understanding, to bear testimony against an unjust accusation, to confound the declamations of false wisdom or hypocritical piety, and avenge the heavens and the earth of man who calumniates them!

What is this blind fatality, that, without order or laws, sports with the lot of mortals? What this unjust necessity, which confounds the issue of actions, be they those of prudence or those of folly? In what consists the maledictions of heaven denounced against these countries? Where is the divine curse that perpetuates this scene of desolation? Monuments of past ages! Say, have the heavens changed their laws, and the earth its course? Has the sun extinguished his fires in the region of space? Do the seas no longer send forth clouds? Are the rain and the dews fixed in the air? Do the mountains retain their springs? Are the springs dried up! and do the plants no more bear fruit and seed? Answer, race of falsehood and inquity, has God troubled the primitive and invariable orders which he himself assigned to nature? Has heaven denied to the earth, and the earth to its inhabitants, the blessings that were formerly dispensed? If the creation has remained the same, if its sources and its instruments are exactly what once they were, wherefore should not the present race have everything within their reach that their ancestors enjoyed? Falsely do you accuse Fate and the Divinity? injuriously do you refer to God the cause of your evils. Tell me, perverse and hypocritical race, if these places are desolate, if powerful cities are reduced to solitude, is it he that has occasioned the ruin? Is it his hand that has thrown down these walls, sapped these temples, mutilated these pillars? or is it the hand of man? Is it the arm of God that has introduced the sword into the city and set fire to the country, murdered the people, burned the harvests, rooted up the trees, and ravaged the pastures? or is it the arm of man? And when, after this devastation, famine has started up, is it the vengeance of God that has sent it, or the mad fury of mortals? When, during the famine, the people are fed with unwholesome provisions, and pestilence ensues, is it inflicted by the anger of heaven, or brought about by human imprudence? When war, famine, and pestilence united, have swept away the inhabitants, and the land is become a desert, is it God who has depopulated it? Is it his rapacity that plunders the labourer, ravages the productive fields, and lays waste the country; or the rapacity of those who govern? Is it his pride that creates murderous wars, or the pride of kings and their ministers? Is it the venality of his decisions that overthrows the fortune of families, or the venality of the organs of the laws? Are they his passions that, under a thousand forms, torment individuals and nations; or the passions of human beings? And if, in the anguish of their misfortunes, they perceive not the remedies, is it the ignorance of God that is in fault, or their own ignorance? Cease, then, to accuse the decrees of Fate or the judgment of Heaven! If God is good, will he be the author of your punishment? If he is just, will he be the accomplice of your crimes. No; the caprice of which man complains is not the caprice of destiny; the darkness that misleads his reason is not the darkness of God; the source of his calamities is not in the distant heavens, but near to him upon the earth; it is not concealed in the bosom of the Divinity; it resides in himself, man bears it in his heart.

You murmur and say: Why have an unbelieving people enjoyed the blessings of heaven and of earth? Why is a holy and chosen race less fortunate than impious generations? Deluded man! where is the contradiction at which you take offence? Where the inconsistency in which you suppose the justice of God to be involved? Take the balance of blessings and calamities, of causes and effects, and tell me – when those infidels observed the laws of the earth and the heavens, when they regulated their intelligent labours by the order of the seasons, and the course of the stars, ought God to have troubled the equilibrium of the world to defeat their prudence? When they cultivated with care and toil the face of the country around you, ought he to have turned aside the rain, to have withheld the fertilizing dews, and caused thorns to spring up? When, to render this parched and barren soil productive, their industry constructed aqueducts, dug canals, and brought the distant waters across the desert, ought he to have blighted the harvests which art had created; to have

133

desolated a country that had been peopled in peace; to have demolished the towns which labour had caused to flourish; in fine, to have deranged and confounded the order established by the wisdom of man? And what is this *infidelity* which founded empires by prudence, defended them by courage, and strengthened them by justice; which raised magnificent cities, formed vast ports, drained pestilential marshes, covered the sea with ships, the earth with inhabitants, and like the creative spirit, diffused life and motion through the world? If such is impiety, what is true belief? Does holiness consist in destruction? Is then the God that peoples the air with birds, the earth with animals, and the waters with reptiles; the God that animates universal nature, a God that delights in ruins and sepulchres? Does he ask devastation for homage, and conflagration for sacrifice? Would he have groans for hymns, murderers to worship him, and a desert and ravaged world for his temple? Yet such, *holy and faithful* generation, are your works! These are the fruits of your *piety*! you have massacred the people, reduced cities to ashes, destroyed all traces of cultivation, made the earth a solitude: and you demand the reward of your labours! Miracles are not too much for your advantage! For you the peasant that you have murdered shall be revived; the walls you have thrown down shall rise again; the harvests you have ravaged should flourish; the conduits that you have broken down should be renewed; the laws of heaven and earth, those laws which God had established for the display of his greatness and his magnificence, those laws anterior to all revelations and to all prophets, those laws which passion cannot alter, and ignorance cannot pervert, should be superseded. Passion knows them not; ignorance, which observes no cause and predicts no effect, has said in the foolishness of her heart, 'Everything comes from chance; a blind fatality distributes good and evil upon the earth; success is not to the prudent, nor felicity to the wise.' Or else, assuming the language of hypocrisy, she has said: 'Every thing comes from God; and it is his sovereign pleasure to deceive the sage and to confound the judicious.' And she has contemplated the imaginary scene with complacency. 'Good!' she has exclaimed: 'I then am as well endowed as the science that despises me! The cold prudence which evermore haunts and torments me, I will render useless by a lucky intervention of Providence.' Cupidity has joined the chorus: 'I too will oppress the weak; I will wring from him the fruits of his labour: for such is the decree of heaven; such the omnipotent will of fate.' For myself I swear by all laws human and divine, by the laws of the human heart, that the hypocrite and the deceiver shall be themselves deceived; the unjust man shall perish in his rapacity, and the tyrant in his usurpation; the sun shall change its course, before folly shall prevail over wisdom and science, before stupidity shall surpass prudence in the delicate art of procuring to man his true enjoyments, and of building his happiness upon a solid foundation.

Jaques Réda
Palmyra [Palmyre]

Palms! exclaimed the poet – and that was enough:
The word itself becomes palm and knows how much
A palm weighs in the air, its soaring unchallenged.
Beneath mud walls the pitiless heat subsides

And drowses along canals, or like a sufi
Meditates in the manner of palms. A donkey
Lolls contented by an olive tree ringed with sapphire
On powdery soil. So close to the furnace

Its dead centuries blazing where I've just walked,
I might finally, under these palms, dissolve
In eternity itself, nothing remembered, but

For the crazy notion that inside this maze
Whose walls she illumines, it's me she awaits
Amid palms, Zenobia, proud and doomed.

Translated by Jennie Feldman

Catherine Lucy Cleveland
From *The Life and Letters of Lady Hester Stanhope* (1813)

Having visited the tribes of the Melhem, the Beni Hez, the Beni something else, and the Sebáhs, we arrived on the eighth day at Palmyra. We met two thousand of the Sebáhs upon their march, descending into the plain where we were reposing, from the Beláz, a mountain pass, with all their fine mares, little colts, little camels, little children, and hideous women, with the most extraordinary head-dresses and extraordinary rings at their noses, and preposterously tatooed in flowers and frightful figures.

You must not understand Palmyra to be a desolate place, but one in which there are fifteen hundred inhabitants. The chief and about three hundred people came out about two hours' distance to meet us. He and a few of the grandees were upon Arab mares, and dressed rather more to imitate Turks than Arabs, with silk shawls and large silk turbans. The men, at least many of them, had their whole bodies naked, except a *pestimal*, or petticoat, studded or ornamented with leather, blackamoors' teeth, beads, and strange sorts of things that you see on the stage. They were armed with matchlocks and guns, all surrounding me and firing in my face, with most dreadful shouts and savage music and dancing. They played all sorts of antics till we arrived at the triumphal arch at Palmyra. The inhabitants were arranged in the most picturesque manner on the different columns leading to the Temple of the Sun. The space before the arch was occupied with dancing girls, most fancifully and elegantly dressed, and beautiful children placed upon the projecting parts of the pillars with garlands of flowers. One, suspended over the arch, held a wreath over my head. After having stopped a few minutes, the procession continued. The dancing-girls immediately surrounded me. The lancemen took the lead, followed by the poets from the banks of the Euphrates, singing complimentary odes and playing upon various Arabian instruments. A tribe of hale Palmyrenes brought up the rear, when we took up our habitation in the Temple of the Sun, and remained there a week.

I must tell you that the difficulty of this enterprise was that the King of the Desert was at war with some very powerful Arabs, and it was from them we were in dread of being surprised, particularly as it was known that they had said that they could sell me for twenty-five thousand piastres, or three hundred purses, and which they certainly thought they could get for my ransom at home. This was the most alarming part of the business. Our people, nevertheless, went out robbing every day, and came home with a fine *khanjár*, and some visible spoil. We heard of nothing but the advance of the enemy to the east of Palmyra, and we believed it, as we had taken five of their scouts prisoners, which we thought well secured at Palmyra; but unfortunately one night one got out, and fearing that he would give the intelligence of what day we were to begin our journey back again, we set off before our intended time. We were, nevertheless, pursued by three hundred horses a few hours off, which fell upon the tribe of the Sebáhs, and killed a chief and took some tents; and the Sebáhs, on their side, carried off twenty-two mares. We returned a different way, having made acquaintance with the tribe of the Amoors, the Hadideens, the Wahabees, and another battalion of Sebáhs, including Wahabees, and a party of hunting Arabs that are dressed in the skins of wild beasts. We arrived in safety at the tents of the Grand Emir, Mohanna El-Fadel, who gave us a fine Arab feast and killed a camel, of which we partook. At two hours from Hamar, we were met by a corps of Delebaches, who were sent as a complimentary escort by Moli Ismail, a man of great note in Syria, who conducted us to his house, where dinner was prepared for three hundred people, and corn provided for all the Arab mares. Within a mile of Hamar, full ten thousand people were assembled out of curiosity, half of which were women, and many women of distinction, with Nasif Pacha's children, carried by slaves. *Mashallah* echoed from every mouth. *Selámet, ya meleky; seláme, ya syt* (welcome, Queen; welcome, Madam). *El hamd Sillah* (thank God). *Allah kerym* (the Lord is gracious). And this very interesting scene proved my Ladyship's popularity in Hamar.

Nothing in the world could have been so well managed, which proves me an *élève* of Colonel Gordon's, for I was at once quartermaster, adjutant, and commissary-general. We were as comfortable upon our road as we were at home, and the Duke of Kent could not have given out more minute orders, or have been more particular in their being executed, which, in fact, is the only way of performing a thing of that sort with any degree of comfort.

We were excessively entertained with the different conversations of these people, and the extravagant though elegant compliments they paid me. They have got it into their heads that the only power which can affect them is Russia. They were always thanking God I was not Empress of Russia, otherwise their freedom would be lost. I am now getting translated into Arabic all the real achievements of the Emperor Alexander, on purpose to send to my friends in the Desert. They are the most singular and wonderfully clever people I ever saw, but require a great deal of management, for they are more desperate and more deep than you can possibly have an idea of. It would have very much amused you to see me riding like a Bedouin woman in a bird's nest made of carpeting upon a camel, and upon one of the fleet dromedaries like a Wahabee. I am enrolled as an Anisy Arab in the tribe of the Melhem, and have now the rights of the Desert, particularly that of recommending my friends who may wish to visit them.

After my return to Hamar, the immense number of Arabs that waited on me from all quarters was quite surprising. You think we have wasted our time in Syria, but certainly we have seen in great perfection what nobody else has, not even your friend Shaykh Ibrahim' (Burckhardt), who, going under consular protection, was stripped stark naked in coming from Palmyra, and after having marched some days in this happy state, got a pair of *shalwars* (trousers) at a village, and in this figure entered Damascus ... I only saw one mare, a Wahabee, that I thought perfection. The owner said he would not part with her for less than one hundred purses. The generality of their horses and mares is by no means so beautiful as you would imagine, but beyond anything excellent for swiftness and fatigue. I could write volumes upon different circumstances that took place on this interesting journey, which I certainly recommend to no traveller to undertake without being well aware of the *carte du pays*, and having considerable abilities to plan and great energy to go through with it. When you are once in the scrape nobody can get you out of it, for no Pacha has sufficient authority over them to be the least depended upon. They no sooner heard of our intention of going with the Pacha's people than they said they should cut off all their beards and send them naked about their business. For my part I believe they would have been as good as their word. The idea of telling them cock-and-bull stories, and treating them like fools, is perfectly incorrect; they are much more difficult to manage than any

Europeans I have ever seen ... There was a chief that Lord Petersham would die of envy before, as he was as *éveillé* as a Frenchman, and presented himself with the air of Lord Rivers or the Duke of Grafton. Respecting etiquette and politeness, these people certainly far exceed even the Turks; but for eloquence and beauty of ideas (though one can hardly be a judge of it) they undoubtedly are beyond any other people in the world.

To expect a frigate upon this coast till the plague is quite gone is out of the question, and to pop into a nasty infected ship would be folly.

Latakia, June 30th, 1813

Dear Wynn, – Without joking, I have been crowned Queen of the Desert under the triumphal arch at Palmyra! Nothing ever succeeded better than this journey, dangerous as it was, for upon our return we were pursued by two hundred of the enemy's horse, but escaped from them. They were determined to have the head of the chief who accompanied us, yet sent me an ambassador in secret to say that I need fear nothing, that everything belonging to me should be respected; such were the orders given out to this powerful tribe by five of their chiefs assembled in the neighbourhood of Baghdad. The Slepts (the Arabs who live by hunting and are dressed in the skins of beasts), the bands from the banks of the Euphrates, story-tellers, and Wahabees, all paid me homage. If I please I can now go to Mecca alone; I have nothing to fear. I shall soon have as many names as Apollo. I am the sun, the star, the pearl, the lion, the light from Heaven, and the queen, which all sounds well in its way; for example, 'Salutation from the Warrior Hedgerez, son of Shallun, to our great Mistress, Pearl of Friends and Standard of High Honour.' I have five hundred letters from these people, one more amusing than the other. Old 'G' would be six months squeezing out as many beautiful ideas as they produce in ten minutes, both in conversation and upon paper. I am quite wild about these people; and all Syria is in astonishment at my courage and my success. To have spent a month with some thousand of Bedouin Arabs is no common thing. For three days they plagued me sadly, and all the party but B almost insisted on returning. The servants, frightened out of their senses, always had their eyes fixed upon their arms or upon me. The dragoman could not speak, he had quite lost his head. All the people about me were chosen rascals, and having primed a fellow who was once with the French army in Egypt, I rode dash into the middle of them and made my speech; that is to say, I acted and the men spoke. It so surprised them and charmed them that they all became as humble as possible; and here ended any unpleasant scenes with them. I really believe that some of them now have a sincere affection for me, as their conduct proved on several occasions. One in particular: a chief not resenting, or allowing his people to resent, a blow that had been given him by an Arab of another tribe, an outrage to be punished with death. He said: 'Were we to fight, you might lose your life in the confusion, and inevitably be robbed; therefore we shall put it off and have the man's blood another time.' This was neither cowardice nor indolence, but an act of real friendship, which any one who saw the effect the blow had produced could not have doubted. I had been riding upon a camel like a Bedouin woman for my amusement, and was just going to mount a dromedary to ride like a Wahabee, all those about me ran away in an instant and left me with a troublesome beast who would not keep on his knees long enough for me to get up. Had you witnessed the fury of these people when they saw their chief struck! To me it was quite delightful; they were all ready to die in a moment; yet were quiet, however, as soon as the chief spoke. But revenge was painted in the countenances of all his people. When the world becomes still more corrupt, when people – civilized people – become still more brutal and still more incisive, it is a pleasure to reflect that there is a spot of earth inhabited by what we call barbarians, who have at least some sense of honour and feeling, and where one is sure never to be bored with stupidity or gabble, for they are the most brilliant and eloquent people I ever knew. Nobody must ever give an opinion about the charms of the desert who has not seen above fifteen hundred camels descend the Belap mountains into the enchanting vale of Mangoura, and a tribe of Arabs pitch their tents upon beds of flowers of ten thousand hues, bringing with them hundreds of living creatures only a few days old, children, lambs, kids, young camels, or puppies. But it would be quite in vain for me to attempt to give a G (Grenville) an account of my empire, they who can enjoy nothing but grand walks and trim shrubs; if I could inspire any one of them with a different taste, I should be blamed, and be unhappy when obliged to admire the dulness and grandeur of S (Stowe) and the confined missified beauties of D (Dropmore); as for B (Boconnoc), it was made for its late owner, and for a *great mind* ...

Here I am in the midst of the plague; it is all over Syria, Aleppo only is free from it as yet. This is a great bore, for, though we ride out every day, still it would not be prudent to travel... Above seven thousand people (above half the population of Tripoli) have died of the plague. Here it is only slight, but the French Consul has left the place for a village, and not a Frank hardly will put their head out of window. We are very well off in a house, to make up for what we suffered last winter. You will hardly believe me when I tell you that the cold made me so ill that for more than two months I never walked upstairs, and I mounted my horse to go into the desert in this state. I would go – I would keep my word with the Arabs. I improved daily, and in a fortnight generally travelled from seven, eight, nine or ten hours per day. I came back vastly improved, both in health and spirits; but although I am not myself afraid of the plague, yet I think it right to take proper precautions; and the servants are such bores, frightened out of their senses, fancying if they have got a little dust in their eyes, or have eaten too much, it is the plague, and yet so careless, it is all I can do to prevent them from buying things out of Egyptian shops to get the plague and getting out upon all occasions. You must not consider this scrawl as the picture of my mind, which is tolerably composed in all its troubles, and much more anxious about others than myself, and not a little for absent friends... E (Ebrington?) came into my head every quarter of an hour while passing through some beautiful valleys inhabited by the Kurds, and filled with myrtles fourteen or twenty feet high; the shepherds all play upon reeds, and vastly well too. This place is very beautiful; trees down to the edge of the sea, olives covered with grape vines, fig-trees of an immense size, and every other luxuriant plant which the country abounds with. And *I feel myself* in the dominions of Soliman Pacha, every thing *bows* before me at his command and that of my dear friend the Jew. There is talent! He would turn old G round his finger... The Captain Pacha it is said is coming up this way, but I think he is in all probability only gone to seize the treasure of a Pacha who died lately in Caresmania. I have heard that the plague is at Malta, and am in great tribulation about General Oakes, Colonel Anderson, and poor Williams and her sister. To be isolated in this manner is not pleasant; but, however, I ought to thank God that the plague here is slight. It is said here to have got to Russia, how there I know not, but heaven avert its reaching England, the fleet, and Spain... Too much care cannot be taken at the different ports.

From *The Arabian Diaries 1913-14*

Gertrude Bell to Doughty-Wylie   *April 26th, 1914*

We were off before dawn, a clear still morning. And before we had been on our way two hours a great storm marched across our path ahead of us. We, riding in a world darkened by its august presence, watched and heard. The lightening flickered through the cloud masses, the thunder spoke from them and on the outskirts companies of hail, scourged and bent by a wind we could not feel; hurried over the plain and took possession of the mountains. Do you remember Shelley's song to the Spirit of Delight? –

I love snow and all the forms
of the radiant frost;
I love wind and rain storms, anything almost
That is Nature's and may be
Untouched by man's misery.

And after the pageant and the splendour had all passed, malicious little scuds of rain drove before us and tormented us for several hours. What with the weather and what with his anxiety at observing footprints of a large *ghazzu* – so he held it to be – 'Assaf missed the way and we went a good deal further north than we need have gone. Finally we hove up against tents and camel herds of the Sba ('Anazeh of Fahd Beg's people) and the herdsmen set us right. We were in fact within sight of Palmyra and I can see the bay of desert wherein it lies from my tent. For we have not reached Bukharra – I don't think we should have reached it even if we had gone straight to it. Palmyra from the desert – it must be nearly ten miles from us – is a very different Palmyra from the city you come to along the Roman road from Damascus. It is very different in spirit. One looks here upon the Arab Palmyra, facing the desert, ruler of the desert and dependent upon the desert for its life and force. I am wrong to call it Palmyra; that was its bastard Roman name. Tudmor, Tudmor of the Wilderness. And the Sba know it by no other name. In the middle of the morning we met a man walking solitary in the desert. We rode up and accosted him in Arabic – he made no answer. 'Assaf opined that he must be a Persian dervish. We addressed him in Turkish, Fattuh and I, but he continued to regard us in complete silence. Then we tried what words of Persian we could muster – with the same result. With this we left him, after giving him a handful of bread, his acceptance of which was the only act on his part which might be described as intercourse with us. We rode off into the rain clouds to the west and he continued his lonely way into the rain clouds to the east. And what will become of him I cannot tell. He was heading for the heart of an uninhabited desert. Don't you think that an odd story?

IV: Aleppo

ACCORDING TO LEGEND, the prophet Abraham, on his journey to Canaan, stopped and milked his cows on the mound where the citadel now stands. The Patriarch would distribute milk to the poor who assembled at the bottom of the hill, crying '*Ibrahim haleb*' ('Abraham has milked'). Haleb is the Arabic name for Aleppo. The question of which is the older of the two, Aleppo or Damascus, is best left to the natives of those cities to resolve. It will not be done without some rancour because both lay claim to theirs being the world's oldest continually inhabited city. What is striking is how different they are, not just in terms of architecture but also in the temperament of their natives. While the psychologist can deal with the latter, and it will be to no avail, what is beyond dispute is that Aleppo's souq is not only the greatest in Syria but probably in the whole of the Middle East. Aleppo was one of the greatest centres of commerce, and such was its economic and cultural importance that Shakespeare – or, as the Arabs would have it, that great Muslim writer, Shaykh al-Spear – refers to it twice.

Aleppo was also home, at varying times, to the two greatest poets of their respective ages, al-Mutanabbi and al-Ma'arri. The Persian traveller, Nasir-i-Khursrau (b. 1003/394), visited al-Ma'arri's house, south of Aleppo, in January, 1047. This was roughly two years after Nasir-i-Khursrau who was greatly fond of wine, dreamed of a holy man who rebuked him for his iniquities. Soberly he made his way towards the holy cities and Mecca. There is still some debate as to whether the Nasir-i-Khursrau who forsook wine is the same Nasir-i-Khursrau who later wrote erotic verses.

The English poet, Nigel Wheale, together with his co-translator, Walid Abdul-Hamid, have breathed fresh life into al-Mutanabbi's often difficult to translate verse. Whether he can be properly called a traveller, when for Arabs of his station travel was a fact of existence, Abu 'l-Tayib Ahmad ibn al-Husain al-Mutanabbi (303/915) originally came from al-Kufa in what is now Iraq. Arguably the most famous line in Arabic poetry is his: 'For the

143

horsemen know me, and the night, and the desert, and the sword, and the lance, and the paper and pen.' And, as a modern poetic response – and it is to be wondered why Syria has not appealed to Western poets in the way that, say, Egypt has – we have the once American, latterly Canadian and now British-domiciled poet, essayist and Arabist, Eric Ormsby, author of several volumes of prose and verse, including a remarkable poetic sequence entitled *Araby*. I have suggested elsewhere that his is 'a species of Dixie rococo'. The poems here are based on certain elements in al-Mutanabbi's life.

The most important foreign perspective on Aleppo is Alexander Russell's *The Natural History of Aleppo: containing a description of the city, and the principal natural productions in its neighbourhood; together with an account of the climate, inhabitants, and diseases; particularly of the plague, with methods used by Europeans for their preservation* (1756). A second edition, greatly enlarged by Alexander's half-brother, Patrick, and containing magnificent illustrations, was published in two volumes, in 1794. The Russells were products of the Scottish Enlightenment and in their capacity as physicians to the Levant Company in Aleppo brought to bear their scientific knowledge on all that they wrote. There was no area of Aleppine life that was not of interest to them. The city and its inhabitants are described with much emphasis on manners and customs, religion and culture; the fauna and flora are given equal space. Their book, which only rarely lapses into prejudice, stands as a masterpiece in its own right and served as the model for Edward William Lane's better-known *An Account of the Manners and Customs of the Modern Egyptians* (1836). A selection of passages has been drawn from Russell's great book. Certain scenes, such as the religious practice of *dhikr* (remembrance), can be seen to this day, unchanged, at the Mosque al-'Adiliyya.

In the second edition of Russell's book, there are several passages devoted to Arabic music. It is most fitting, therefore, that there be included here a modern piece by Mark Hudson who is not only hugely knowledgeable on the matter of 'world music', enough to be able to satirise certain of its western aficionados, but is also a travel writer, his book *Our Grandmothers' Drums* (1989), being a study of village women in Gambia.

The career of T E Lawrence covers almost too large a canvas for the purpose of this work, but rather than exclude him altogether I chose these two peeks at Aleppo, the first an extract from a letter he wrote to his brother 'Worm', A W Lawrence, a piece of whimsy, which neglects all mention of the cholera epidemic which was then in force, and the second a couple of paragraphs from the book that most people own but never get around to reading. Maybe it's because they like the title. When in Aleppo, Lawrence stayed at the Baron's Hotel.

A visitor to Aleppo will have to get up at midnight to catch the calligrapher Mohammed Imad Mahhouk on his way to work at the Madrassa as-Sultaniye. There, opposite the great citadel, in a monkish cell, he spends the night in solitude, the breaths he takes caught visibly in the swell of the letters he writes. It is an activity that brings him close to the Divine and which places him firmly in the great tradition of Islamic art.

Nasir-i-Khursrau
From *Diary of a Journey through Syria and Palestine (1047)*

Six leagues further we came to Ma'arrah an Nu'mân, which has a stone wall, and is a populous town. At the city gate I saw a column of stone on which something was inscribed in a writing other than Arabic. One whom I asked concerning it said it was a talisman against scorpions, and thereby no Scorpion could ever come into or abide in the town; and even were one to be brought in, and then set free, it would flee away and not remain in the place. The height of this column, according to my estimation, might be ten cubits. The bazaars of Ma'arrah an Nu'mân I saw full of traffic. The Friday mosque is built on a height, in the midst of the town, so that from whatever side it may be you would enter the Mosque, you go up thereto by thirteen steps. The arable land belonging to the town is all on the hillside, and is of considerable extent. There are here also fig-trees and olives, and pistachios and almonds and grapes in plenty. The water for the city is from the rains, and also from wells.

There was living here (at this date) a certain personage called Abu'l 'Alâ Ma'arrî, who, though sightless, was the chief man of the city. He possessed great wealth, and slaves, and very numerous attendants; for it was as though all the inhabitants of the city were of his people. As for himself, he had adopted the way of the ascetics, being clothed in a rug (*gilîmi*), sitting quiet in his house, and taking for his daily bread half a *Mann* (or about one and a half pound) of barley bread, and beyond this eating nothing more. As I heard, the gate of his house is ever open, and his lieutenants and servants do regulate the affairs of the city, but in all matters take reference to him for orders. He refuses of his goods to no man, and, the while, himself remains fasting by day and constant in prayer by night; for he is occupied in no worldly affairs (of his own). This personage, too, has attained such renown as poet and writer that the learned of Syria, Maghrib and Irâk, all agree that no one of these days is his equal, nor can be. He has written a book under the name of 'Al Fusûl wa-l Ghâyat' (The Divisions and Conclusions), wherein enigmatical words are employed, with such wonderful and eloquent conceits and similitudes that it is only a very

145

small part thereof that one can understand, and that only when one may have perused the work under the author's direction. (So enigmatical and wonderful is this book) that they even calumniate him by averring that he has attempted therein to rival the Kurân itself. There are continually with him some two hundred persons, come from all parts of the world, to attend his lectures on poesy and diction; and I heard that he had himself written over one hundred thousand couplets. A certain one inquired of him why, since God – may He be praised and magnified! – had endowed him with all this wealth and goods, was it that he thus gave all to other men and used none for himself. The answer was, 'No more than what I must eat, can I take.' Now when I passed through Ma'rrah this Abu'l'Alâ was still living.

Al-Mutanabbi
A Poem (963)

Sayf al-Dawla sent his son from Aleppo to Kufa, where Mutanabbi was staying after leaving the court of Kafur, ruler of Egypt. Mutanabbi replied to Sayf in the year 352, saying,

Why do we both have longing O messenger?
    I love, and your heart is as sick with love.
Every time whomever I send to her returns
    He has become envious, and betrays his message.
Her eyes have spoiled my trust in him,
    And the messenger's heart overcomes his mind.
She complains of what I have lamented – pain
    Of longing, but the real longing shows in my poor state.
When love touches the heart of the lover
    The proof of love is what every eye can see.
Provide for us from the beauty of your face
    While it persists, for the beauty of faces wanes,
And court us so that we may court you in this life
    Where residence is brief.
Whoever sees life through life's eyes will find it difficult
    To watch people depart as a caravan departs.
If you see my flesh fade with age
    It is as the litheness of spears after battle.
I was accompanied over the desert by a shining girl, I

Always young, though she changes the colour of others.
You are curtained from her by veils,
    But your lips are kissed red by that sun.
Like the sun you have changed my colour and sickened me,
    But the more beautiful of you both has the greater impact.

Although we know the road, we kept asking in Najd,
    'Is our journey long or prolonged?'
Asking many questions is provoked by desire,
    And not responding to the question is a form of denial.
We did not pause anywhere, however pleasant,
    And those places could not travel with us.
Every time gardens welcomed us we said to them,
    Aleppo is our aim and you are merely the route.
You are the pasture for our camels and horses
    And our canter and gallop are the passage to Aleppo.
Those called emirs are many,
    But in Aleppo's emir all hopes lie.

I deserted him, flying to the furthest east and west,
    Yet his bounty goes before me wherever I turn,
And is with me whatever path I take.
    In every journey I make I have a guarantor.
And if he is criticised for his generosity
    May the critics be sacrificed for him,
And everyone be rewarded from his hand.
    The gifts with which enemies are killed –
Flying horse, long spear,
    Bright shield and the whetted sword –
When they raided an enemy camp at dawn,
    The enemy would say, these rains are our destroying flood.
They surprised them, shattering strong surcoats
    As if they scattered feathers.
His horses hunt their horses like beasts,
    And his cavalry captures the whole army.
When war breaks out, catastrophes
    Appear in his eyes as exaggeration.
When he flourishes the time flourishes,
    And when he is ill time is afflicted.
When his face is no longer present,
    His presence is his beautiful praise.

No one but thou Ali is a hero,

Whose sword is unsheathed for his honour.
How should Iraq and Egypt not feel safe,
    When your horses and squadrons shield them?
If you move a fraction from the path of the enemy
    Their horses will bind the date palm with the date plum,
And those empowered by your defence
    Will know how degraded and submissive they are.
You are continually fighting the Rum,
    When may your warriors return?
Beside the Rum, there are others at your back;
    To which threat will you attend?
Mere men have given up trying to follow you,
    And spears and blades now fulfil your aims.
He who serves death in his company
    Sets himself apart from those who merely serve wine.
Distance has robbed me of the intimacy of your gift giving,
    My pasture is green but my body is wasting.
Even if I died into the life where other gifts are granted,
Your gifts would surely follow me.
If you live, I shall have a thousand Kafurs for my slaves,
    And from your generosity both land and a Nile.
I do not care, so long as the binding ropes of night spare you,
    Whoever else is cut down in their strength and sanity.

Translated by Nigel Wheale & Walid Abdul-Hamid

Notes: *Kafur, a former slave who took over power in Egypt in 355AH, 966CE, after the death of Ibn Tughj. Line 19, 'shining girl', the sun, feminine gender in Arabic. Rum: The Rum: Byzantine forces which were then dominant in the region under the command of Nicephorus Phocas, capturing Aleppo in 351AH, 962CE.*

Alexander & Patrick Russell
From *The Natural History of Aleppo (1794)*

The Bagnio, or Hammam

A custom much more prevalent at Aleppo than that of taking opium, and common to both sexes, is the frequent use of the Bagnio, or Hummam. The Mohammedans are under religious obligation to go oftner to the Bagnio than the other natives; and many persons of rank have private baths, in their own houses: but as these are too small for the reception of a large company, their women, on occasions of ceremonial invitation, are obliged to hire one of the public Bagnios.

A description of the interior of the Hummam was reserved for this place. The first, or outer room, called the *burany* is large, lofty, covered with a dome, and paved with marble. It has windows towards the street, but is lighted chiefly by the lanthern of the dome. A broad stone platform, or *mustaby*, four feet high, is built close to the wall on each side, which, being spread with mats and carpets, forms a *divan*, on which the bathers may undress and repose. A large marble fountain in the middle, serves both as an ornament, and for rinsing the Bagnio linen, which is afterwards, hung to dry on lines extended above. The bathers, as well as the waiters, walk in this outer chamber in *kabkabs*, for the stoves having but small influence there, the pavement, which is always wet, is cold to the naked feet. In the month of February, when the mercury in Farenheit's thermometer stood at fifty-four, in the open air, it rose in the *burany* to sixty-four.

From this chamber a door opens into a narrow passage, leading to the *wustany*, or middle chamber, which has a *mustaby* for the accommodation of such as may choose to fit there, and is furnished with several round or oblong, stone basons, about a foot and a half in diameter, into each of which two pipes open with brass cocks, the one conveying hot, the other cold water. These are called *jurn*, and are fixed to the wall two feet from the pavement. There are also brazen bowls for laving the water duly tempered upon the bathers. The thermometer in the passage rose to seventy-five, and in this chamber to ninety.

From the middle chamber a door opens immediately into the inner chamber, or *juany*, which is much larger than the *wustany*, and considerably hotter, the mercury rising here to one hundred. It has no *mustaby*, so that the bathers sit, or recline on the pavement, which towards the centre is excessively hot. Both the middle and inner rooms are less lofty then the outer one; and are covered with small cupolas, from which they receive a dull light, by means of a few round apertures, glazed with a thick, coloured glass. At each corner of the *juany* is a small open recess, in one of which (in some Bagnios), there is a bason about four feet deep, serving occasionally for a temperate bath. It is called the *murtas*; but as the Turks seldom use immersion, it is found only in some Bagnios.

The Bagnios are heated by stoves underneath. The ordinary heat of the *juany* is about one hundred degrees, but when particularly desired, it is considerably increased. The men remain in the inner room about a quarter of an hour; the women continue much longer. Some Bagnios are for women only, others are appropriated to the men; but in general both sexes are admitted: the men from morning till noon, the women from noon till sunset.

The bather, when undrest, ties a towel round his head, and a wrapper, named a *fouta*, round his middle, reaching like a petticoat to the ankles. Thus attired he passes at once into the *juany*, where he soon begins to perspire profusely, and remains dripping wet, all the time he continues there, partly from sweat, and partly from the moisture of the chamber. The first operation is that of applying the *dowa*, or depilatory, to the pubes and armpits, which, after it has remained about two minutes, or till the hair becomes loose, is carefully washed off: but it is not unusual for accidents to happen from negligence in this point. The depilatory is composed of quick lime, and orpiment, in the proportion of one dram of the latter to an ounce of the former. These are intimately rubbed together in a mortar, to a powder, which is moistened a little with water, at the time of application.

When the *dowa* has been washed off the bather sits down on the pavement, and one of the attendants begins to press and handle the tops of the shoulders, the muscles of the arm, and successively the whole body; first gently, then by degrees increasing the pressure, till he comes to handle pretty roughly, but without giving pain. This is repeated at short intervals till the skin is perfectly softened. The attendant then taking hold of the bather's fingers, with a dexterous jerk makes each joint crack successively; after which, laying him flat on his back, and bringing the arms across the breast, the shoulder joints are made to crack in like manner last of all (and to strangers a part of the process the most alarming) the neck is made to crack, by raising the head and bringing the chin forward on the breast. These operations finished, the attendant, having his hand armed with a coarse camelot bag, begins from the breast, to scrub the body and limbs, pouring warm water from time to time on the parts, and turning the bather in order to reach his back. He then makes a strong soap lather, and with a rubber, made of the fibrous part of the palm leaf, which is brought for this purpose from Bassora and Egypt, lathers the body universally, except those parts concealed by the *fouta*, which the bather washes himself. Nothing now remains but to wash off the soap, which is done by repeated effusions of warm water, the bather removing close to one of the *jurn*. Some instead of soap use the saponaceous earth Byloon. The bather is now reconducted to the middle chamber, and a dry towel and wrapper are presented to him, in which he returns on *kabkabs* to the *divan*, where he left his clothes, and, being covered with fresh towels, or if the season requires it, with a fur, he smokes a pipe, drinks coffee, or eats water melon, before dressing. Persons of condition, particularly women, sometimes send their own Bagnio linen, consisting of towels and a wide gown; as also the *tasa* or cup for laving water, the camelot bag, &c. – but most of the men content themselves with what is furnished by the Bagnio. M Grelot has in most circumstances given an exact account of the practice in the Bagnios at Constantinople.

The process, as now described, takes up a considerable time, although the attendants are very expert; but the Turks seldom go through the whole. In common they go into the inner, or perhaps only the middle chamber, receive a few bowls of water on their body, are lightly rubbed, and retire in a few minutes.

The women remain much longer in the Bagnio than the men. The washing and plaiting the hair is a tedious operation, and they are obliged also to attend the children. They do not however continue all the time in the hot Room, but amuse themselves in the *burany*; for the number of *jurn* not being sufficient to serve so great a crowd at once, they are obliged in succession to take their turn: a circumstance which produces much clamorous altercation.

On ordinary days, women of every rank are admitted promiscuously, till the rooms are quite full. The confusion that reigns in such an assembly, may easily be conceived; the noise is often heard in passing the street, and, when there happens to be a number of young children, the women themselves acknowledge the din to be intolerable. They however are fond to excess of going thither, amid inconveniences of which they perpetually complain. But the Bagnio is almost the only public female assembly; it affords an opportunity of displaying their jewels and fine clothes, of meeting their acquaintance, and of learning domestic history of various kinds; for particular Bagnios being more in vogue than others, the ladies are assembled from remote districts, and if accidentally placed near each other on the same *divan*, it is reckoned sufficient for joining in confidential conversation, though they were not acquainted before.

When ladies of different Harems make a party for the public bath, they take all the females of the respective families along with them, and sometimes carry fruit, sweetmeats and sherbets, with which they regale in the outer room, on their return from the *juani*. Besides these refreshments, the attendants are charged with carpets, small cushions, pipes, copper utensils, soap, byloon, henna, apparel, and the linen appropriated to the Bagnio, consisting of a peculiar habit, with various ornamented wrappers, and towels; whence it will appear, how much female delicacy is respected by national custom; and that the Eastern ladies are not less attentive in the Hummam, than on other occasions, where an opportunity offers of displaying their ornaments.

Each company is also provided with a *keiam*, or woman whose province it is to see that every thing be properly prepared, and to attend the ladies in the hot room. It is requisite for her to be acquainted with the rules of the Bagnio, and well qualified to contest all disputable matters, with fluency of language. The Turks and Jews often retain Bidoween women as *keiams*.

Besides the ordinary times of bathing, the women go to the Bagnio after childbed, after recovery from sickness, before and after the marriage feast, and at a stated period after the death of relations. On these ceremonial occasions it is usual for persons of condition, to hire a Bagnio on purpose, and form select assemblies, where such only are admitted as have been invited. The ladies with their suit, come drest in their richest apparel; the *divan*, and the refreshments have been previously prepared; a band of singing women is retained, and, the company being known to one another, gaiety, decent freedom, and youthful frolic, are less under formal restraint than in the mixed assemblies at the common bath.

As these private assemblies last four or five hours, the women go several times into the inner rooms, but pass a great part of the time in the *burany*, where they either sit in the Bagnio habit, or covered with furs, for they do not dress till determined to enter no more into the hot rooms. The music and refreshments are placed in the outer chamber.

The ladies, as before remarked, are provided with a habit made expressly for the Bagnio; but their slaves and servants are equipped much in the same manner with the men, and the younger girls, especially the slaves, claim a privilege of romping in the Hummam. Dashing water at one another is no uncommon frolic; the *fouta*, or the wrapper, may easily drop by accident, or be drawn away in sport, and should the girl at the time happen to be employed in carrying a cup of coffee, or sherbet, she may possibly advance to deliver it, without stooping to recover the *fouta*. To this, or some such accident, it must be owing, if the women in the Bagnio are ever seen walking about, in a pure state of nature, at least at Aleppo.

The first time a woman goes to the Bagnio after childbed, she is attended by the midwife, who, placing her near one of the *jurn*, anoints her belly and limbs, with a composition named *shidood*, consisting of ginger, pepper, nutmegs, and other hot ingredients, beat up with honey; which, after lying on a certain time, is washed off with warm water: while this operation is performing, the numerous train of women, make the domes of the Hummam reecho with that shrill, warbling shout, which is the female mode of expressing exultation, and which at all festivals, may be heard to a great distance. It is termed *ziraleet*, and, by Shaw, has been confounded with the dismal conclamation of the women at funerals. Belon thought it resembled the last part of the cry of the village women, who sell milk at Paris. But Pietro della Valle describes it more accurately; 'a sharp and loud cry of joy, made in concert, by a quick and somewhat tremulous application of the tongue to the palate, producing the sound heli li li li ii li li li'. The *shidood* is supposed to prevent many disorders consequent to childbed; and is sometimes also applied to convalescents from chronic distempers.

Coffee Houses

The coffee houses are not frequented by persons of the first rank, but by all others indiscriminately. Some of them are large, and handsome rooms, and, for the entertainment of the customers, a band of musick, is retained, a puppet show, and a story-teller. These exhibit at different hours of the day, the audience, by a voluntary contribution, raising a trifle towards defraying the expence.

The Concert, which consists of vocal and instrumental musick, continues more than an hour, without intermission. They make no pause between the airs, but slide from one into another, as if so many movements of the same concert. At inferior coffee houses, not provided with a regular band, the company are occasionally entertained by some volunteer performer, who sings *gratis*.

The puppet show is performed by shadows, in the manner of *Les Ombres Chinoise*, but much inferior in point of execution. The stage is very simple, and constructed in a few minutes. One person with great dexterity conducts the whole, changing his tone of voice, and imitating the provincial dialects, or other peculiarities of the characters introduced in the piece. Some faint attempts towards dramatic fable may be traced in these shows which are moreover diversified and decorated by the march of caravans, bridal processions, and other gaudy pageants. But the whole is too often interrupted by the disgusting indecency of Kara-guze, the punch of their theatre: except where women happen to be present, as at private houses, when the most exceptionable parts of the dialogue are supprest. At the coffee houses, the puppet show, in point of obscenity, is under no restraint, but the magistrate sometimes interposes to protect individuals from being introduced on the stage, and exposed to the derision of the populace. In the beginning of the Russian war in 1768, the Aleppo Janizaries, who had returned from the field rather in disgrace, were introduced on the stage giving a ludicrous account of their achievements; and Kara-guze could not well miss the opportunity of throwing out some severe sarcasms on their prowess. This, though received with great applause, was soon most judiciously put a stop to; for though little was then to be apprehended from the Janizaries in their state of humiliation, it was probable that they might, when in motion the next campaign, have taken ample vengeance. In an affair of bankruptcy which had occasioned much popular clamour, certain persons concerned applied to the Seraglio for protection against the petulance of Kara-guze, who had, on the stage assumed the character of a merchant, and, in allusion to recent transactions, represented a number of fraudulent intrigues, to the great entertainment of the populace.

Satyre must be cautious of descending to too pointed reflection on persons immediately in power; but has full scope to lash in general, the follies of private life, the perversion of public justice, and the corruptions of government. I have known a *bashaw* ridiculed on the stage, after his departure from the city; and a *cady* seldom or never escapes.

The recitation of Eastern fables and tales, partakes somewhat of a dramatic performance. It is not merely simple narrative; the story is animated by the manner, and action of the speaker. A variety of other story books, besides Arabian nights entertainment, (which, under that title, are little known at Aleppo) furnish materials for the story teller, who, by combining the incidents of different tales, and varying the catastrophe of such as he has related before, gives them an air of novelty even to persons who at first imagine they are listening to tales with which they are acquainted. He recites walking to and fro, in the middle of the coffee room, stopping only now and then when the expression requires some emphatical attitude. He is commonly heard with great attention, and, not unfrequently, in the midst of some interesting adventure, when the expectation of his audience is raised to the highest pitch, he breaks off abruptly, and makes his escape from the room, leaving both his heroine and his audience, in the utmost embarrassment. Those who happen to be near the door endeavour to detain him, insisting on the story being finished before he departs, but he always makes his retreat good; and the auditors, suspending their curiosity, are induced to return at the same hour next day, to hear the sequel. He no sooner has made his exit, than the company, in separate parties, fall a disputing about the characters of the drama, or the event of the unfinished adventure. The controversy by degrees becomes serious, and opposite opinions are maintained with no less warmth, than if the fate of the city depended on the decision.

Excepting the public entry of *bashaws*, or of European consuls, and the sports exhibited on certain occasions in the Seraglio courtyard, there are no public spectacles, at which the two sexes assemble promiscuously. Fireworks, at the great feasts, and other times of rejoicing, are exhibited at the Seraglio, but the women, as observed before, do not come abroad at night.

Sufis and Holy Fools

Another kind of holy Sheihs, known to the Franks by the name of Barking Sheihs, are in somewhat better repute among the middle rank of people, and reside constantly at Aleppo. They are often heard in a still evening, from different parts of the town, and may be seen sometimes at the gardens, performing their rites in the open air. They do not perform alone, like the Dervises, but may be joined by any Moslem who has previously prepared himself by ablution. The Sheih, placed in the centre of a circle, consisting perhaps of twenty persons, begins the service by chanting a prayer, while all the rest remain in an attitude of devout attention. He then repeats the words Ullah hu! Ullah hu! accompanying them with a flow of movement of the body backward and forward, the whole circle at the same time following his example. After a short while, moving the body more quickly, they drop the word Ullah! and continue incessantly to repeat the word hu! This ceremony lasts near an hour, the Sheih all the while barking like the others, and from time to time turning slowly, so as to front the circle successively. His countenance appears strangely agitated, and he at length sits down as if quite exhausted by the exercise. It is justly remarked by Chishul 'that as they grow hoarser and weaker, both their sound and action resemble the barking and snarling of dogs.' M du Loir compares the sound they utter, when nearly spent by fatigue, to the howling or bellowing of an expiring beast which has not been knocked down. This order of Sheihs is described under different names by different authors. They are called Santons by Du Loir; but by Porter and others, Kadrie. The dance of the dervises affords a much more amusing spectacle than this strange mixture of fanatacism and indecency; for of those who compose the circle, there are always some who appear, from their demeanour, to have joined merely in sport.

These fanaticks, as well as the itinerant Shiehs, are equally reprobated by most of the sensible Turks, who assert that the Koran does not countenance such extravagancies. But while they give this suffrage in favour of common sense, they exhibit an instance of superstition not less absurd, in the veneration paid to idiots, and harmless madmen.

The power of invisible spirits over the human frame, a notion of such ancient date in the East, is still universally received; and in various diseases, recourse is had to exorcism, as often as to medicine. Insane persons are not however all treated alike. The furious madman is kept in chains, and configured to the care of doctors, or exorcists; mere drivellers are kept within doors, or, become the sport of idle boys in the street; whilst those who are but slightly disordered in mind, and who are guilty of no alarming excesses, are always used with the most compassionate tenderness; and if, happening to take a religious turn, they are capable of prayer, or can occasionally repeat some sentences of the Koran, they are then considered as persons divinely inspired, and sometimes admitted, in tattered garments, with their limbs naked, to sit down familiarly with people of the first rank, and even allowed to kiss their cheek.

The inspired Sheihs are sometimes also consulted as physicians, and return advice truly oracular. It is diverting to observe men, in other respects of strong plain sense, make serious exertions to unravel the incoherent wanderings of a madman.

Of this, the following instance may serve as an example. While I sat one morning with an eminent merchant, who had long suffered with a rheumatic complaint of the shoulder, and had unsuccessfully applied a variety of remedies, he was told by a friend who came to visit him, that meeting in the street with a famous holy madman, he took the opportunity of asking the Sheih's advice in this singular case, which had baffled the doctors; and received the answer that 'the best remedy was oil from the grocers.' The company present immediately approved of applying the oil, but a doubt arising what particular oil was meant, amid the variety to be found at the grocer's shop, a discussion most ridiculously serious ensued, whether the experiment might not safely be made with several sorts. A page, in the mean while, was despatched to obtain a clearer revelation, and soon returned. The Sheih at first seemed to listen to the messenger with much attention, looking him steadfastly in the face, but remained silent, and then, turning away from him, began to mutter to the wall with which he had been conversing when the page came up to him. Upon the messenger pressing for an answer to carry back to his master, the Sheih fell into a violent passion, gave him abusive language, and continued to curse the page as long as he remained in sight. Another servant was then sent to the grocer's shop, to ask simply for oil, in the precise words of the Sheih, and to take the first that should be offered. The oil was immediately applied, but the pain, as usual, becoming worse at night, the failure in the cure was ascribed to not having properly understood the oracle.

Hospitality

Hospitality has always been enumerated among the Eastern virtues. It still subsists in Syria, but prevails most in villages and small towns; among the Bidoween Arabs, and the inhabitants of the Castravan mountains. The hospitable reception that European travellers experience on the road, the officiousness of persons who offer their houses, and services, have been unjustly suspected of always being mercenary. The traveller would oftener find himself at a loss, was his sole dependence for lodging, placed in the covetousness of his host, the value of the present, or *bakhsheesh*, would hardly induce a person at his ease, to derange the economy of his family, and incur an action in itself deemed honorable, and which, if neglected, would subject him to the contempt of his fellow villagers.

Magic, Sorcery and Alchemy

Magic, or sorcery, with various modes of divination, are practiced in private; for these occult sciences are not approved of by the Ullama, and sortilege, which had been so much in use among the Pagan Arabs, was expressly forbidden by the Prophet.

The influence of evil eyes, is of all the species of fascination, that which meets with most general credit. Children and young animals, being supposed peculiarly liable to the malignant influence, are provided with various charms by way of defence, and it is owing to a superstitious apprehension of evil eyes, that the peasants consent with reluctance to let any person enter the rooms where their silk worms are feeding.

Nescio quis teneros oculus mihi fascinat Agnos.

The Greeks and the Romans were not more addicted to this superstition, than the Orientals are at this day. Among a variety of instances universally believed in Syria, I have heard it asserted that there was a *kurdeen*, lately deceased, who had been known to crack a large chrystal vase, by merely looking at it from a distance. It would have been unpolite to have betrayed incredulity on this occasion. 'The being ignorant of the cause takes from the credit of history, but innumerable things have evidently existence, although the causes of them are hidden from us.' Yet it would have puzzled the subtilty of a Greek sophist, to have saved so extraordinary a story from ridicule.

The universal belief in sorcery and occult influence of various kinds, naturally maintains the credit of talismans, and amulets; some of which, being sanctified by religious superstition, are employed in one form or other by the natives of all ranks. The talisman consists of certain caballistical characters engraved on stone, metal, or other substances, or else written on slips of paper. It is not requisite to their effect, that they should be constantly carried about, for they may be deposited with equal success in particular places; and in this respect seem to stand distinguished from the amulets, which are always fixed to some part of the body.

Though the Turks frequently have recourse to charms they are less expensive in their talismans, than some of the more Eastern people, and do not so much give way to that superstition. They have charms against scorpions, serpents, bugs, and other vermin; but one employed to protect the houses from musquetoes deserves particular notice. This charm consists in certain unintelligible characters contained in a little slip of paper, which is pasted upon the lintel of the door, or over the windows. The charm, or rather divine gift, has descended hereditarily in one family, which distributes the papers *gratis*, on a certain day of the year, and some of the gravest effendees are employed in writing them previously to the anniversary. On the appointed day, the people repair to the gate of the house early in the morning, and to each in turn is delivered the papers required, together with a quantity of paste sufficient to fix them up. Certain conditions are indispensably necessary to give efficacy to the charm. The person must be fasting, and must preserve inviolable silence, till after the paper has been fixed in its proper place. It may be easily conceived that a multitude parched with thirst, and crowding close together in a May morning, some pushing forward, others endeavouring to return with the prize, amid a hundred obstacles; the mischievous petulance of such as mingle in the crowd merely to provoke others to a breach of the conditions, and the hard task exacted of the females to remain mute amid numberless temptations to scold; should in the event prove favourable to the musquetoes. The effendees who distribute the papers, go through their part of the farce with admirable solemnity of countenance, and in most of the Turkish houses of lower rank, those and other papers of the like kind may be observed formally pasted up.

The amulet is composed chiefly of certain names of the Deity, verses of the Koran, prayers, or the like, comprehended in small bulk, in a form convenient to be worn. Little slips of paper of this kind rolled up are often concealed in the shash of the turban.

There is commonly at Aleppo, one, or more, of the medical tribe, who have acquired a sufficient smattering in alchymy to beggar themselves by the expense of a laboratory, and the neglect of better business; but the alchymist is in general to be met with among the adepts in astrology, and other occult arts. The possibility of the transmutation of baser metals into gold, is believed in speculation by many of the Ullama; but the fraudulent practices of pretended artists have so often been detected, that people are become more cautious, and instances are now rare of their falling into the snare. Giaber Ebn Heian is one of the most celebrated Arabian alcyhmists. Herbelot says there is a book of his entitled *Kitab Giaber*, and a great number of works on the subject of the philosopher's stone. He lived about the middle of the ninth century, which is two hundred years later than the era assumed by some writers. He is mentioned in the arabic literary history of philosophers, but it does not from thence appear when he lived.

Music

The Aleppeens, in general, have a correct ear, and are fond of music. They have technical names for the notes, as well as for the different measures, but they have no written music. They learn the airs and symphonies by ear, retain them by memory, and communicate them to others in the same manner they themselves were taught. The Arab musical scale, in the subdivision of intervals, differs considerably from that of Europe. They have no music in parts; the performers in a concert, constantly play in unison; but both voices and instruments have sometimes rests of several bars, which they observe with great exactness, being for the most part excellent timeists.

The instrumental music is of two kinds. The one martial and loud, intended for the field; the other less sonorous, adapted to the chamber. The martial band is composed of hautboys, shorter and shriller that the European; trumpets; cymbals; drums of a large size, the head of which is beat with a heavy drumstick, and the bottom, at the same time, struck gently with a very small stick; lastly, drums of a much smaller size which are beat in the manner of a kettle drum. There are nine great drums in the band of a *vizir bashaw*, and eight in that of a *bashaw* of two tails; the number of other instruments is not so strictly limited. A band of music, belonging to the castle, smaller than that of the *bashaw*, performs regularly twice a day from the battlements.

The *bashaw's* band performs also twice a day in the court of the Seraglio. The concert, which lasts above half an hour, is divided into three parts, not distinguished by intervals of pause, but by a close executed by the first hautboy, who in the length of his swell, and his shake, out-trills all patience, as well as melody. The measure of

This plate exhibits a Turkish concert drawn from the life, and the several performers are dressed in the habits perculiar to their rank. The first is a Turk of the lower class, his white shash tied loosely round the *kaook*, which gives the turban a clumsy appearance, compared with those worn by persons of fashion. He beats the *diff*, and sings at the same time. The person next to him is an ordinary Christian, dressed in a slovenly manner, he sings also, and plays the *tanboor*. The middle figure is a dervise in his ordinary *kaook*, without a shash, he is playing the *naie*, or *dervis's* flute. The fourth is a Christian of middle rank. He sits in his *curtak*, and has a *dulaman* which, being tucked under his legs, hides his *kunbaz*, or waistcoat; he has a knife in his girdle, the handle of which appears above the cincture. The shash of the turban is blue and white striped, like that of the other Christian, but a difference may be remarked in the dress; for the first is without a *kurtak*, and has only a long outer garment made fast with a *cincture*, under it a *kunbaz*. He plays the *kamangi*, in the manner it commonly is held resting on its foot. The last man is dressed much in the manner of the Turk, but the head dress is after the fashion of what is sometimes worn by the Janizaries, and very often by the Arabgeers, or Armenian grooms, in the service of the Europeans. He beats the *nakara* with his fingers, in order to soften the sound for the voice, but the drumsticks, appear from under his vest. The slippers of the band, lye at the end of the *mustaby* on which the musicians are placed, they are all of the same form, but the Turkish slippers as mentioned before, are yellow, and the Christian red. The only instrument wanting to complete the band is the dulcimer, or *santeer*.

159

the symphony is commonly slow at first, but by degrees changes into a pretty quick *allegro*, and it is usual, in these movements, to introduce some of the *cantabile* airs which happen to be most in vogue.

The chamber music consists of voices accompanied with a dulcimer, a guitar, the Arab fiddle, two small drums, the dervis' flute, and the *diff*, or *tambour de Basque*. These compose no disagreeable concert, when once the ear has been some what accustomed to the music; the instruments generally are well in tune, and the performers, as remarked before, keep excellent time.

The vocal music, to an European ear, seems at first not less uncouth than the Arabic language, and it seldom happens that time, which by degrees reconciles the language, goes further in music than to render it merely tolerable. There is in particular, one species of song, between an air and a recitative, named *mowal*, held universally in the highest esteem. It is performed by a single voice unaccompanied with instruments, and the singer, placing a hand behind each ear, as if to save the drum of that organ from destruction, exerts his voice to the utmost stretch. The subject of the poetry is generally of the plaintive kind. Some hapless wight laments the absence of his mistress, recals the memory of happier times, and invokes the full moon, or the listning night, to bear witness to his constancy. The performer frequently makes long pauses, not only between the stanzas, which are very short, but in the middle of the line, and, taking that opportunity of recovering breath, he begins anew to warble, swelling his notes till his wind is quite exhausted. Fond as the natives are of this *mowal*, there are few strangers who can hear it with any patience, or without lamenting the perversion of voices, which are often strong, clear and wonderfully melodious.

Although there are a great number of Arabian airs, there is no great variety, a strong similitude being observable in most of them. The verses set to music are commonly amorous, sometimes jovial; and the song is executed by one or more voices, accompanied with several instruments. The dulcimer serves instead of the harpsichord, and the *diff*, or *nakara*, mark the time. Some of these songs are pleasing, but the voices in general are too loud, especially in the choruses: they are perhaps more agreeable to an European ear, when executed by a single voice, accompanied solely by the guitar.

Notwithstanding music is so much esteemed, and a constant attendant at all entertainments, none of the people of condition are themselves performers; nor are the youth of either sex taught it as an accomplishment. Few of the free women bestow pains on their voice; and, though some of the younger ladies may now and then join in the chorus, they do not think it consistent with decorum to lead. Many of the men of inferior rank, sing readily in company, and it often happens, unfortunately for a delicate ear, that there are few who do not think themselves qualified to join occasionally in the chorus.

Besides the musical instruments already mentioned, there are others which are not admitted into the concert. A hautboy much inferior to the zummer, several varieties of rude common flutes, and a bagpipe. The first and latter of these are played by fellows who find employment at weddings, in the villages; and on holidays, they may be heard playing wretchedly, in the skirts of the town.

The syrinx, or Pan's pipe, is still a pastoral instrument in Syria; it is known also in the city, but very few of the performers can sound it tolerably well. The higher notes are clear, and pleasing, but the longer reeds are apt, like the dervis's flute, to make a hissing sound, though blown by a good player. The number of reeds of which the syrinx is composed varies in different instruments, from five to twenty-three.

The natives, rather frugal in the general economy of their family, are on certain occasions, profusely liberal. Their feasts have every appearance of plenty, and hospitality. The master of the house deputes his sons, or one or two of his kinsmen, to assist the servants, in attendance on the guests. A band of music, placed in the court yard, plays almost incessantly; the fountains are well set a spouting; the attendants deck their turbans with flowers; and the company, drest in their best apparel, assume an air of festivity and cheerfulness. This last circumstance however respects more especially the Christians and Jews; for the Turks of condition, in mixed company, very seldom lay aside their usual solemnity.

A set of buffoons commonly attend at all great entertainments. These are composed of some of the musicians, and of others who for hire, assume the character of professed jesters. Some of them are good mimicks, taking off the ridiculous singularities of persons who happen to be well known, and sometimes, in an extempore interlude, make burlesque allusions to persons present in the company: but their wit borders too near on the obscene, and, though the natives appear to be highly entertained, the mummery soon becomes insipid to a stranger.

There is hardly a man of rank who has not a jester among his dependants, with whom he may divert himself at pleasure, and who, being invested with the liberty of saying whatever he chooses, often exercises his privilege with tolerable humour, both on his patron and the company. The *bashaw's* chauses occasionally assume the character of buffoons, and perform interludes for the entertainment of their master.

The women at their festivals are much more noisy than the men; their choruses consist of more voices, and are often interrupted by the *ziraleet*, in which all the young females join cheerfully. They have musicians and buffoons of their own sex, among the latter of which some of the *keiams*, who attend them at the Bagnio, usually distinguish themselves.

Mark Hudson
Aleppo '99

I'm lying on a rooftop in Aleppo, one of the oldest cities in the world. Pigeons gust over the ramparts of the ancient citadel, as the call to prayer goes up from first one mosque, then another – the long wavering notes overlapping, filling the darkening sky with their conference of yearning and wonder.

Situated amid the rocky plateaux of northern Syria, at the hub of ancient trade and pilgrim routes, Aleppo is a place where everything, no matter how old, is built on top of something older: mosques atop Byzantine basilicas, atop Greek and Roman temples, synagogues, Zoroastrian fire temples. Millennia of wars, fires and earthquakes mean that most of what you see is merely medieval. But you're profoundly aware of the layers of ancient culture, not only beneath your feet, but also in the very air of the place. It's as though you're inhaling the dust of monuments along with aromas of cinnamon and cloves, drains and traffic fumes. But lying here, bathing in sounds of otherness in the heart of the oldest quarter of the city, I feel I'm far from getting to grips with the place.

Aleppo doesn't rush to reveal itself. In fact, everything about it is maddeningly enigmatic. In the narrow streets of the old city, the studded doors of the mansions are set deep, the walls high and windowless, while the women come sheathed in black: buttoned-up in coats of strangely Edwardian cut, their faces draped in shawls – with no gaps for lustrous kohl-rimmed pools, just an utter ghost-like blankness. In the immediate vicinity of where I'm staying are the meeting places of no less than twenty Sufi orders – mystical Muslim brotherhoods, for whom music, song and dance are a means towards union with the divine. But how, if you don't speak Arabic, are you supposed to contact them? I feel that around every corner I may step into some mysterious adventure, or that I may be disgorged by the place in a week's time, its essence having eluded me completely.

It was music that brought me here – a recording of Syrian Sufi music heard at a friend's house in London: a rasping, breathy flute, a slow, ominous drumbeat and a low voice, magnificently rounded as though resonating through some dark and cavernous chamber. I had a sense of music that has

162

absorbed something from all the civilizations that have existed in that part of the world; music that, far from being purely Islamic, embodied knowledge too deep and too ancient to be contained by any one tradition. The man behind this recording was a Frenchman named Julien Weiss, a student of Arab music for more than twenty years, who had converted to Islam and now lived in a fourteenth-century palace in Aleppo. He has given himself the name of the medieval Sufi poet Rumi, founder of the whirling dervishes – Jalal Eddine, the 'Splendour of Faith'. I pictured him rattling around in his palace – as orientalist beatnik with a touch of the T E Lawrence. Then one day, discovering we had a friend in common, I phoned him.

When someone tells you that where they live is like Marrakesh without tourists, that they have many rooms and you are welcome to stay, you don't think twice. Syria was effectively closed to westerners for decades. It still sees few tourists. Visas are complicated, flights expensive or tortuously indirect. But six months later I flew into Aleppo at four in the morning, a pick-up driven by Jalal Eddine's servant taking me through the deserted streets, along boulevards lined with burning rubbish, through a narrow gateway into the old city. We carried my luggage along narrow passages into a tree-lined courtyard, where my host appeared on a staircase – tall, silver-haired, in his mid-forties, but with a glow of elfin youthfulness. I was shown to a cell-like chamber off the domed atrium, where I lay as the dawn call to prayer rang our over the city. The house was designed to keep out the heat. The walls of the central living space soar, their elegant arabesques interlocking beneath the light-filled dome. But a certain dimness lingers in the well of the room. The floors and fountain are of polished orange marble. The walls glow with richly coloured kilims, with embroidered hangings, and brass salvers, six feet in diameter and fabulously engraved. A huge beaded chandelier from a Cairo mosque dangles from the dome.

For several hours a day, Jalal Eddine sits on the banquette of Bedouin cushions, intent over his instrument, the *qanun* – the plucked zither that gives that archetypal ring of 'eastern promise' to oriental music. The rippling phrases answer, repeat, overlay each other in dazzlingly complex patterns – all imbued with the same ominously dramatic inflection as the call to prayer, that sense of yearning, of reaching out towards something vast and unknowable. Aleppo is famous for music throughout the Arab world. Many great singers live here, though traditionally they perform not in cafés or at concerts but at soirées in private houses, which in the past would have been carefully sealed (how typical of this place!) so that not one note would be audible to passers-by. Fortunately, Jalal Eddine has just announced that he is holding one in a few days' time.

Aleppo's reticence vanishes the moment you hit the souks: twenty two kilometres of vaulted, dimly lit thoroughfares, one of the largest covered markets in the world. A central corridor runs dead straight through it all – and you're in the way! Shoulders, elbows and hands shove at you from every direction. I see Jalal Eddine's giraffe-like frame plunging off into the throng as barrows ram straight for my shins. Donkeys, thrashed by bareback boys, come bucking out of nowhere, while a spluttering three-wheeler van with a lambada-playing horn, piled high with boys and dirty laundry, lurches backwards out of a side alley. But even more than energy and ceaseless movement, the souk exudes a sense of fatalism and indifference. The traders sprawled behind their glass cases of cumin and cloves, their sacks of hibiscus petals; the men and boys bellowing, tearing open great sacks of trainers, stacking bars of laurel soap in ziggurat formations; all have the air of being locked into another rhythm, another ethos that will keep this place going whatever the competition from the forces of globalisation. And that ethos, according to Jalal Eddine, is Sufism.

Often mistakenly referred to as a sect, Sufism is a broad and diffuse phenomenon, a current of mysticism taking many forms throughout the Islamic world, but often drawing on pre-Islamic belief. Near-eastern Sufism is believed to contain echoes of some of the world's oldest religious ideas – of ancient Persian fire worship, of the dualistic philosophies of the Gnostics, which fed into the medieval Christian heresies, the teachings of the desert hermits and ascetics. From the perspective of the West, it all seems risibly abstruse. Like shamanism and transcendental meditation, Sufism has been absorbed into the pantheon of new-age esoterica; like Zen, it seems less comprehensible the more you learn about it. But here in Syria, it becomes suddenly matter of fact. It's what goes on. The market traders have been closing their stalls on a Friday afternoon, going to the mosque and then on to the *zikr* – the ecstatic ceremonies of the Sufi orders – every week for a thousand years. Nonetheless, finding someone who can not only explain Sufism, but also impart that sense of knowledge linking back into the ancient world, is not going to be easy.

'What you have here is popular Sufism,' says Jalal Eddine. 'For them the *zikr* is a rave. It's gestalt therapy! To find someone with the higher knowledge is nowadays very difficult.'

I must try to meet Sheikh Hilali, the head of the Q'adri brotherhood in Aleppo, possessor of a library of ancient books. It is said that he was once a doctor in Germany, and still has a German wife hidden away in his house. Our taxi pulls out into a Brands Hatch tide of rusting Buicks, horse drawn carts and murderous three-wheeler vans. A lone cyclist comes meandering from the other direction, apparently indifferent to his imminent oblivion. The imposing buildings of the new city are a legacy of the period 1918-45, when Syria was under French mandate and Aleppo was the final terminus of the Orient Express. They look like the blackened hulks of a forgotten civilisation, yet

French is still the language of the cultured elite. The churches of the city's large and influential Christian community loom over the traffic – Maronite, Chaldean, Gregorian, Armenian Orthodox, Syrian Orthodox, Byzantine Catholic, Syrian Catholic ... the list goes on. The pavements are packed with glossy youth, sprawled over cars, packing out the ice cream parlours and juice bars, veils and black gloves having given way to skin-tight flares and platform boots. But even here there's the sense of a society that's developed far from the capitalist mainstream. There's no Coca-Cola, no MTV, or Hollywood films. There's a wide variety of mostly dated western music on sale, but the music you actually hear is all Arab. And whether it's digitalized pop, the droning of Egyptian nightclub orchestras or completely traditional, it's all imbued with the same yearning inflection and fatalistic dying fall as the Muslim call to prayer.

If I had to sum up the essence of Aleppo, it is that sound: the magnificent conversations of the muezzins – which here are live, not recorded – booming out of loudspeakers in the passageways of the old quarter, animating the shimmering heat over the city five times a day, for up to half an hour at a time. For we westerners, it represents something archetypal – the essence of the oriental other. I'd always taken it for the sound of the desert – the soul crying out amid the great solitude of sand and stars. But as our taxi weaves through the rush-hour traffic, Jalal Eddine explains that its melodic structure is derived from the rites of the Syrian Orthodox church, which are conducted in Syriac, a language close to the Aramaic spoken by Jesus.

'The philosophy of Arab music is completely Hellenistic,' he expounds. The *makams*, the melodic archetypes of oriental music, correspond to the modes of ancient Greek music defined by Pythagoras and Aristotle. 'And,' he concludes triumphantly, 'they got it all from Babylon!'

Ancient knowledge, indeed. But how am I going to find that embodied in contemporary Aleppo?

'It is around you everywhere,' he says. 'You just have to be patient.'

Outside a juice bar opposite the huge walls of the Umayyad Mosque, I found Sabri Moudallal. Eighty-two years of age, keeper of a tradition of sung poetry dating back to Moorish Andalusia, composer of some of Aleppo's most famous Sufi songs, he was listlessly flicking through his rosary, his gaunt and stubbled features as grey as his old double-breasted suit. He accepted my handshake with a weary nod, hardly bothering to fully open his eyes. The bar owner handed me a frothing mugful of carrot and banana, so dense and meaty I could manage barely half. I stood there sipping at it, wondering what to say to this old man who seemed hardly bothered to go on living.

That night, as the guests arrived for Jalal Eddine's musical soirée, there was

Moudallal, now sporting a red fez, his eyes aglitter, waving animatedly at someone in the audience. Turning and seeing nobody responding, I waved back. *Le tout Aleppo* was there – all the city's greatest musical connoisseurs: a customs man in dark glasses, a millionaire collector of Byzantine art; the Syriac bishop, portly in his tight white cassock – French expats, market traders, neighbours. The room glowed like some sumptuous Persian miniature. Then, suddenly, the musicians and the choristers – middle-aged men in white gowns – had seated themselves around the Bedouin banquette and the music had begun. Dressed in black, Jalal Eddine – looking half-priest, half-rock star manqué – led, the jangling ornamented phrases picked out over the undulating rhythm of lute and tambourine. Moudallal smiled broadly, nodding in time and the whole audience, packed around the galleries of the atrium, did likewise. After a lute improvisation of severe, mathematical brilliance, Moudallal leant forward, letting out a long note – wavering, but surprisingly powerful. As Jalal Eddine's plucked responses built up an air of jangling suspense, Moudallal explored the phrase, gesturing towards those round the banquette as he teased out the nuance of the words in exclamations, each longer, keener and more ornate than the last – the audience rocking with delight, expostulating on the greatness of God, till Moudallal conducted them suddenly into a surging anthemic chorus. The suite of songs, chants and exquisite instrumental interludes unfolded before us like a labyrinthine chain of rooms. Jalal Eddine's house, witness to centuries, seemed suddenly fully alive, and I felt I was experiencing the real life of Aleppo that had eluded me over the past days.

The following afternoon, two of the choristers returned, and as they got up to leave, Jalal Eddine gestured me to follow. The Zawiya al-Hilali, the meeting place of the Q'adri order, was square, wood-panelled, the glow from the windows in the dome the only light, and the whole room breathed with a deep rhythmic phrase – a heavy exhaling, like a locomotive shunting slowly towards speed. The sheikh, a tall, bearded figure, mythically austere in turquoise turban and long flared coat, stood in an alcove, nodding with an emphatic ritualistic movement. White-clad figures were packed along the walls, all swaying, leaning forward in a circular undulating motion, till it seemed as though the very building were moving. And all the time a voice from among the people sitting crowded on the floor kept up an insistent wailing counterpoint.

'They are just saying that there is no god but God,' whispered Jalal Eddine, as we seated ourselves at the back of the crowd.

At a nod from the sheikh – the doctor from Dortmund, or wherever it was – the rhythm picked up speed, breaking suddenly into an anthem of such ringing, exultant volume it seemed the walls would give way in a great blaze of light and noise. Then, just as suddenly, the deep chanting began again. Out in the yard, the sheikh's disciples gathered round us – bright-eyed men in their thirties with the full beards denoting religiosity – all very welcoming, but curious. What exactly did we want? In a long room with mock rococo furniture (or perhaps it was real), the sheikh sat, looking quite as dumbfounded as we were. All around the disciples crowded, watching us expectantly. 'Ask your questions now,' said Jalal Eddine, aware that we were already encroaching. Questions? My mind had gone completely blank. Was it true, I found myself blurting out – feeling, even as I was saying it, that I was violating him and everyone else there – that the sheikh had once practiced western medicine? The sheikh raised his finger, and to my astonishment spoke in English – tortuously articulated, but grammatically correct.

'I never practiced it!' His eyes grew wide. 'I only studied it! A sheikh of the Q'adri order must be familiar with all the arts and sciences of his time. I studied medicine in Berlin for six years.'

But just before he was due to qualify, his father had died, and he had returned to assume the mantle that had been passed on down the centuries. And, I asked, was there a problem in trying to reconcile the ancient Sufi knowledge with modern scientific knowledge? He smiled broadly, raising his hands. 'Why should there be a problem? Knowledge is only knowledge! Learning is only learning!'

'Damn,' I said, as we made our way up the street. 'I didn't ask about his wife.'

'Be glad that you didn't,' said Jalal Eddine.

T E Lawrence
A letter to his brother (July 21st, 1912)

Nice place Aleppo. Warm, though too hot just now, and there is scarcity of water, for the crocodiles. They line all the canals you know, and swallow the water as it comes down from the river: everything in Aleppo loves water. Even the hippopotami sit all day on the kerb with their feet cooling in the gutters, and when sunset comes they boom for very joy, till all the valley is giddy with the sound. We have nothing like that here in Jerablus, which is a country place without hippopotami: but we have frogs who croak in chorus old, old tunes that Aristophones taught them, and iguanas who sup in kings' sepulchres. And talking of sepulchres I bought such a lovely one last week: a crematory urn, a glazed jug of Bablylonian work, some Hittite terracotta horses, and bronze fibulae: one of our first finds.

T E Lawrence
From *The Seven Pillars of Wisdom (1935)*

Aleppo was a great city in Syria, but not of it, nor of Anatolia, nor of Mesopotamia. There the races, creeds, and tongues of the Ottoman Empire met and knew one another in a spirit of compromise. The clash of characteristics, which made its streets a kaleidoscope, imbued the Aleppine with a lewd thoughtfulness which corrected in him what was blatant in the Damascene. Aleppo had shared in all the civilizations which turned about it: the result seemed to be a lack of zest in its people's belief. Even so, they surpassed the rest of Syria. They fought and traded more; were more fanatical and vicious; and made most beautiful things: but all with a dearth of conviction which rendered barren their multitudinous strength.

It was typical of Aleppo that in it, while yet Mohammedan feeling ran high, more fellowship should rule between Christian and Mohammedan, Armenian, Arab, Turk, Kurd and Jew, than in perhaps any other great city of the Ottoman Empire, and that more friendliness, though little licence, should have been accorded to Europeans. Politically, the town stood aside altogether, save in Arab quarters which, like overgrown half-nomad villages scattered over with priceless medieval mosques, extended east and south of the mural crown of its great citadel. The intensity of their self-sown patriotism tinged the bulk of the citizens outside them with a colour of local consciousness which was by so much less vivid than the Beyrout-acquired unanimity of Damascus.

Eric Ormsby
Mutanabbi in Exile

Abu al-Tayyib al-Mutanabbi, the greatest of classical Arabic poets, moved from court to court in Syria, Egypt, and Iraq, earning his living as a panegyrist. He was murdered by robbers in 965.

In alien courts I melodied for bread
but now the sordid business of verse
enjoins me to this dry, northern
kingdom where disaffected ostriches
snort at sundown and the prince
idles the hours away with paradigms
in ancient grammar books.

A shabby gentility obscured my youth.
Poverty was a stench I couldn't scrub
and largesse smarted out of others' hands.
But language was immeasurable as shame
and burned in the beatific mouth of God –
He is exalted! – and now language flows
from my fingertips and from my quill
the way the spider tesselates its silk.

My heart is fringed with arrows like the sun
or the chastened, wincing surface of a blade
hammered in Damascus out of Indian steel.
My heart is like the chilly ramparts of cranes
longing southward as the winter dawns.
But my lines still rustle lovely as the slide
of rosaries of olive wood blessed by pilgrimage
or the pages, startled as acacia,
in the whispering codices of the Law.

The moon enacts its faded casuistries
and there are thorn trees twisted like beggars
by the last stones of encampments, the dry
dung of pack animals, and *thumam* grass
stuffed in the fire crevices. There I stopped,
and all my pain swept over me
in that smooth-blown place.
How could such meager anonymous shreds
summon remembrance in a spill of tears?

South of Aleppo, where the stony mesas gust
with desolation and the jackal bitch whimpers
and snuffles in an unloved earth, my longing
rang as hungry as the crows of winter.
The inkwell knows me, and the carven quill,
and the tense and crackling surfaces of parchment,
and swords and lances know me, and the strong horses,
and the night will remember me, and all empty places.

Mutanabbi Praises the Prince

The luscious reddening gold of the emir's coin

buys my encomia. I haggle in magnificence,
or then I elbow-dust his aureole.
But such praise costs. The syllables are pearl
nipped from the darkness of Bahrani seas
by clever divers, or rubies of Kashmir
pried from reluctant mines.

Let others gown the prince in obsequious fabrics
or snuggle bracelets and rings of hammered gold
over his wrists and fingers, or incense his hair
with myrrh or labdanum, or dunk his feet
in subtle unguents brought from Hadhramaut.
I garment him in the golden fragrance of praise
that gives men life forever, that will ring
in the shadowy mouths of the unborn,
his great-grandchildren's unimagined progeny,
in chains of consequence effected by the will
of the Compassionate across ungenerated time.

Mutanabbi Remembers his Father

Sometimes, half in sleep, when the dreaming mind
confuses past and present smokily,
so that dead friends and benefactors turn
and break into smile or greet you, unaware
that everything has changed forever now,
or the unmistakable pressure of a hand
consoles the shoulder of the child you were,
sometimes, then, at such half-realized
encounters, I can picture him again.
The past is knotted like the hempen length
that slides into the midnight of the well.
Each instant survives in darkness lost to us,
perhaps cherished in the mind of the Merciful
the way remembering fingers cherish heirloom pearls.

I picture a man who lurches, like a crab,
up stony alleys, who shudders like a pack mule
under punishing burdens, who sets one wary shoe

before the other as he stumbles and labors along.
Two tipping leather pails bounce on a pole
slung across his arching shoulder blades –
a water carrier, a menial, bent and thonged
to his limber crossbeam, arching like a bow
and he the dark and devastating shaft
ready to fly; or his cramped neck and arms
seem lifted like the hawk's before he stoops.

This man is lashed
to the shame that glitters in his leather buckets
and he squawls all day in his hawker's croak,
'Waw-ter! Pure waw-ter! ' A dented cup
bangs at his breastbone. He is himself all
thirst, the parched epitome of the sandy stretch
between Kufa and Samawa, where I parsed my tongue
on redolent paradigms and measured the prosody
of the subtle breezes that fluttered the tent flaps:
mutafa'ilun, mutafa'ilun, fa'ilatun! –
the way grammarians vivisect a verse –
or I lazed to the plangent amber of the oud.

That menial, that lugger of scummy drinks,
his eyes the sooty pink of a slaughter camel's lids,
his mouth cracked and cleft like a winter wadi,
his hands the paws of a Byzantine dancing bear –
that lowest of the low was my papa,
water hauler for the swells of Kinda,
who peddled the stuff of life so I could live
like a prince of Hira in my gem-sewn silks
among the purity of desert tribes whose speech
glittered with the ancient rose-quartz clarity of Adam's tongue.

Marius Kociejowski
The Master Calligrapher of Aleppo

The slight feeling of vertigo the citadel of Aleppo produces, especially at night, might just as easily be the whole of the city's past bearing down on one. History is everywhere here. There is no escaping it, not even when gossiping over tea at one of the cafés opposite. It is felt not only from above but also from beneath.

'Take care where you walk,' says the blind 11th-century poet al-Ma'arri, 'because you walk upon the dead.' Something else he said must surely have raised a few eyes in his time: 'The inhabitants of the earth are of two sorts: those with brains, but no religion, and those with religion, but no brains.' And still, cynic though he was, they love him. You can go and visit his tomb in Ma'arat al-Numan, a few miles south of Aleppo.

Across from the rising entrance bridge to the citadel, several yards to the east, is the Madrassa as-Sultaniye, which was begun by one of Saladin's sons, Sultan al-Zaher Ghazi, and completed, after his death, in about 1225, by Ghazi's son, Governor Sultan al-Aziz. Together with the citadel in its present form, the mosque stands as a fine example of Ayyubid architecture, combining boldness and grace. It is also one of the final expressions of the glorious period initiated by Saladin, which, by 1260, soon after Ghazi's death, disintegrated in family squabbles. The *mihrab* in the prayer hall is one of the finest of its type and at the rear is a modest chamber containing the cenotaphs of Ghazi, his wife, Diafa Khatoun, and their son al-Aziz. Ayyubid power ends here, in a small room, which maybe is as it should be. After all, when the great Saladin died he did not have money enough to pay for his own funeral.

Within the madrassa's thick walls one feels locked away from the world and its vicissitudes. There is one man who has made it the condition of his working existence to be at such a remove. All night long, in a small cell off the central courtyard, the calligrapher Muhammed Imad Mahhouk pushes his reed pen until the 85-year-old caretaker arrives, dragging the sun behind him. The cell is so silent all Imad can hear are the sounds of his own breathing and the squeaking upon paper of his reed pen made from the slender thorn of the Javanese palm tree, a material noted for its durability. The reed pen (in Arabic *qalam*) is often dubbed 'the ambassador of intelligence'. The two sounds merge into one: each breath Imad takes is registered in the swell of the letters he produces.

It struck me as a perfect illustration of what the monastic life must have been like in mediaeval times. Imad agrees. 'It is the same struggle,' he says. 'It all comes from the same source – it's just a different façade. This glorious spirit is for everyone, whether it comes in the name of Islam or Christianity.' When I ask him whether he is a Sufi he says that although he belongs to no one branch of Sufism he considers himself 'a Sufi with a pen'. I ask him his age and he tells me he dates back to Ugarit, when, circa 1400BC, the first alphabet was produced there. Imad, in our historical time, is about fifty. Austere, he wears designer glasses; abstemious, he stops every few minutes for a smoke; disciplined, he is ramshackle as to the comings and goings of daily existence; a master calligrapher, almost incredibly he has had no master of his own.

I began by asking him how he came to be in this sacred space.

'This small room is one of many in the mosque which, of course, is already a sacred space. This was a typical old school or madrassa where young people were taught religion and sciences. The mosque no longer has the role it once had, as a university. The rooms that once housed students are now mostly used for storage. I had connections to the head of the religious board in Aleppo, which owns land and mosques. This man admired my work and at first arranged for me to have a shop at the edge of the old souq. There were too many distractions though. I would begin to write and someone would come along and interrupt me. Isolation is essential for this kind of work. So finally I was given this room for free. This space connects me to all our history and at the same time, because it is isolated behind thick walls, it keeps me away from modern society. This chamber of energy gives me peace and it has just the right atmosphere for getting into the proper mental state. I may be in isolation but

173

I am not alone. I have no clock or watch here. I have no *time* or, rather, the only time I recognise is when I can't hold my pen anymore. My prayer mat is always next to me. Usually people pray together but because for me this space brings me even closer to the Supreme Being I prefer to pray alone. When I first enter here, I do my ablutions (*wudu*). The Qur'an must not be touched if you are unwashed. Also you must wash before prayers. I cannot start if I have not washed externally, but also I need to be internally clean, my head clear of troubles or the arguments of daily life. When I am ready, the challenge is in front of me. I know the paper's dimensions, its height and width, and yet it is almost as if I were walking into infinity. Somehow this small room gives me unlimited space in which to write. When I'm fully engaged, I do not even feel the chair beneath me. On the other hand, if I'm working on a commission and I am not interacting with the words, it can feel like a prison, as if the world has collapsed on me.'

I asked Imad what first drew him to calligraphy.

'There was no one stage or point when I decided to become a calligrapher. It was, rather, a gradual process. But to go back to the very beginnings, my father was a clerk and although he would never consider himself a calligrapher he had the most beautiful hand. My first love of calligraphy came through his writing. I was about five or six at the time. I would copy him and for me it was a fantastic game. The first beautiful thing I ever saw in my life, which I remember clearly, was the letter *wāw*, which is a circle with a tail – "و".'

There is a famous story concerning that magical letter, which may or may not be true, but as an illustration of the ascent the artist makes in his striving towards God it is not surprising the story has been kept alive in calligraphic circles. What Imad told me was clearly one of several variants of the story but clinging to just one detail, which is uniquely his, I shall try to reconstruct it here from several sources. In 1258, the Mongols invaded Baghdad, slew most of the populace, and destroyed much of the city including its magnificent library, *Bayt al-Hikma* or 'The House of Wisdom', which contained some of the greatest treasures of Islamic culture. They threw the books in the Tigris, so many of them that for a whole week the water was tainted with ink. It was even said that at one point in the river the volumes lay so thick the horses of the Mongols could cross over them. Meanwhile, the city in flames, the greatest calligrapher of his time, Yaqut al-Musta'simi, hid himself away in a minaret and all he did there was to practice, in Imad's telling, the letter *wāw*. Another source says he wrote out Qur'anic verses on a piece of linen. What is indisputable is that he survived the carnage. The image of Yaqut writing at the top of a minaret, just that little bit closer to God, appears in several miniatures.

'You can spend months on a single letter,' Imad continued, 'exploring all its dimensions. I spent five or six months going around the letter *nūn* – "ن". I once heard of an imam who asked this calligrapher, "Are you going to see your lover *nūn*?" It is a delicate process. Sometimes when you stretch a letter, curve it just a bit more, you end up somewhere else, in another dimension altogether. If you want to see the beauty in calligraphy you need to come close to the letters to see how good a piece of work it is. You can *see* the calligrapher's breath, where it has been transferred to the ink, where it collects in one place or is shifted to another. You can tell how many times he held his breath before finishing a word or even a single letter. You will be able to see that he started here, went all the way and then stopped, and, in order to master the shape, went back with the finest point of the pen to produce those dark edges.'

It is almost unthinkable for a calligrapher of any standing to have *not* had the guidance of a master. One need only glance at the biographies of the great calligraphers to see that they are invariably part of a long chain of learning. As students they had to practice *taklid* or imitation and it is only after completing those studies that they would enter the ranks of the professionals or masters. Calligraphy in addition to being a spiritual exercise, an emulation of the Divine, is also a precise science of geometric forms and rhythms. I asked Imad how it was he was able to make his way alone.

'Any answer to this takes me back to the 1990s, when I first went to Istanbul. It is often said the Qur'an came to the Prophet in Mecca, that it is most beautifully recited in Cairo and most beautifully written in Istanbul. Istanbul, for calligraphers, is the Mecca. It is where they all go. One of the living legends of the art is the master Hasan Çelebi, a student of Hamid Aytaç who was the greatest calligrapher of modern times, the last of the Ottoman line. When I went there my calligraphy wasn't as developed as it is now, and the techniques I employed were not those I'd use now. I had doubt in my abilities. I wasn't sure about the way I moved my pen, or even where to start and finish. Anyway I showed my work to the master Çelebi and he said to me, "What you do comes of its own accord, but at least you are doing it the right way." At same time I met another master, Nihat Çetim, and when he saw my work he said to me, "You have chosen to learn the hard way. You are like a wild herb that grows out of a rock in a harsh environment. Yes, it is a herb … yes, it is green … but in a very wild way." Actually his analogy gave me a kind of confidence. Also it provided me with a fresh perspective. The majority of calligraphers who learn directly from masters tend to block themselves. They stay in the same cast and will never escape it. If their master says a letter should be of such and such a length they will continue to make it so, but because I was in the wilderness I copied everybody. This is how I learnt, by copying every style. I'd copy even bad calligraphy. This made me flexible. When you do restoration, for example, you have to be able to read the other man's work and know what's bad and what's good in it and to write in exactly the same spirit as that in which he wrote. You enter another dimension, even with a bad calligrapher, and you discover things you never knew about or experienced. You can't adopt another man's style without first changing the way you hold your pen. It is like getting out of your own town and going somewhere else and then coming back to safe ground. I could see the beauty in each master's work, but at the same time I was able to make my own way. When I went to Istanbul I entered a competition they have once every three years, which is open to calligraphers from all over the world. I wanted to prove myself. I completed the piece in a day and a half, which is nothing, and got one of the main prizes. After this, I lost interest. I never went back to Istanbul. It is almost like saying I didn't need this anymore.'

'Are you considered a master now?'

'Very few people know I exist! My aim was never to achieve that role. For me, it is a natural process. It is like prayer. It is something I do.'

Salah al-Ali in his essay *Islamic Calligraphy: Sacred and Secular Writings* writes: 'The calligrapher's work lies in search of the absolute; his aim is to penetrate the sense of truth in an infinite movement so as to go beyond the existing world and thus achieve union with God.' What is produced on paper, he concludes, is as unique as the personality of whoever holds the reed. When speaking to Imad it is immediately clear that for him the notions of calligraphy as an art and as a form of religious devotion are inextricable. The only way he can express his special love for God, he says, is through calligraphy. What happens, I ask him, when calligraphy becomes a profession?

'The calligrapher will lose his soul, he will become as a tool. What he produces will not be art anymore. There are so-called calligraphers who write out people's names. They do not even deserve to hold a pen. One can distinguish between an artist and a craftsman. The craftsman might produce fantastic workmanship but it is not necessarily art because the love – the soul – has been lost. There has to be a balance and there have to be rules, and although calligraphy is not all that open there is freedom. A good artist will balance those two things, freedom and discipline, and still produce something new. He will go into unknown territory without disturbing the rules. Calligraphy, ultimately, is the expression of a state of mind.'

This, naturally enough, brought us to the question of spiritual revelation.

'It is quite rare, but it has happened to me several times, that when writing the Qur'an, especially a really fantastic passage, suddenly I feel this weightlessness. I'm floating. I become united with the words, or, rather, I come to the paper and see myself copying out what is already there. It's as if I am moved by a kind of fate, with the text already there, in a certain shape. My privilege is in being the first one to see it being written. There are phrases in the Qur'an, the hadith, and elsewhere which are so poetic and intense, so full of music, for example the traditional saying we have that relates to the Prophet:

"You are the stranger of all the strangers.'"

'It has been said that calligraphy is "the geometry of the soul". Here you are, in this very special space, where you establish a relationship between *al-qalam* "the greater, divine pen" and your own. Given that inspiration passes through the body, to what extent, then, is the physical important?'

'The soul is physically realised through calligraphy. The key to this state is the human body which is the transmitter between God and the paper. So, yes, it is a physical act and holding the reed in your hand is absolutely essential to the process, but the true nature of this relationship becomes evident on paper. It is my alibi. It is my witness. It is comparatively easy to write a single line, but to do several pages in the same style, so as to maintain a harmonious whole, this is the big challenge. There is, of course, an endless struggle between body and spirit. The spirit wants to break through the physical frame, and to expand, to reach out and to fly out of its trap, but it always hits the walls of this body and brings one down. When I'm working and get thirsty the glass of water may be just two metres away, but I won't leave my pen and paper just in order to make this body of mine shut up. I might grab a biscuit to keep me going because I don't want my body to take over. "It is not your time, it is *my* time,' the soul says to it. "It is spirit time, so let me fly. I'm doing *this* now, so don't bring me down with silly needs."'

Seyyed Hossein Nasr, in his *Islamic Art and Spirituality* draws attention to the relationship between the reed as a writing implement and as a musical instrument (*ney*). 'The song of the reed,' he writes, 'is the sonoral counterpart of the letters and words of the calligrapher.' The great mystical poet Rumi invited his audience to listen to the song of the reed as it laments its separation from the reed bed. My raising the subject with Imad hit upon a happy coincidence.

'One of my friends is a great musician, and my plan is to put on a show with him playing the *ney* while I write. One will please the eye, the other the ear. The pen and the *ney* are made from the same material and in fact the word *ney* means reed. In some parts of Egypt the colloquial word for *ney* is *qassaba*, which is also the word for the throat. So there is this complex relationship whereby all these things will fit together to create a special state – the ney is "seen" and the pen is "heard".'

'Would you consider yourself as defending a dying art? How do you see yourself in the tradition?'

'I do not see it as a dying art because the inspiration is much stronger. The Qur'an is the main source and its strength is such that it will inspire me or someone else. There is a line in it where Allah says, "Indeed We have sent down the Qur'an, and indeed We Ourselves surely are its Guardians" [*Al-Hijr*, 15:9]. The shape of the book will never change because it is protected. It is not for anyone to alter. I am merely an instrument for bringing those words to light. The beauty of calligraphy is what enabled me see the Qur'an. It is what taught me how to pray, what brought me closer to God. As long as it is there, it will not be the end of calligraphy. On the other hand, life is moving so fast people do not have patience anymore and that shifts them away from such kinds of activities. There are many ways now to produce work of almost the same quality, even on computer, but it is never the same. Calligraphy is a long and complicated process, which can't be mastered in a short time. You need to have the right background, the right inspiration.'

'When you use the computer, as I believe you sometimes do, does this not go against the tradition?'

'I get cross with myself for using it, but this is merely a stage, an exploration of all the territories. I want to know everything and be everywhere. The computer is useful for technical matters – small projects, medallions, postcards, or for scanning and printing work I've already done. It could never be instrumental in creating a mental or spiritual state. Anyone can use the computer but there will never be the same quality, the same interaction. Calligraphy is calligraphy, it's sacred, whereas I might use the computer to design a pattern for a border or a background design and so rather than redo the same border a hundred times I'll do it on the computer.'

There is a striking historical analogy here, which dates from the so-called "Tulip Period" of Ottoman rule. When Ibrahim Müteferrika, a Transylvanian convert to Islam, introduced the first printing press with moveable Arabic type to Istanbul on December 14, 1727 the calligraphers, illuminators and scribes, fearful for their future, demonstrated in the streets, carrying with them a coffin filled with the implements of their trade. When the mock funeral procession arrived at the Sultanahmet Mosque, where a prayer for the dead was said, Sultan Ahmed III who had allowed for the establishment of the printing house asked which of the masters had died to which the response was, 'It is not the master but the mastery that has died.' Although Müteferrika's printing venture amounted to only seventeen titles, all of a non-religious nature, this marked a turning-point in the history of calligraphy. It was, one might argue, the day the 'music for the eyes' began to die. Alternatively the advent of printing may have freed calligraphers from the drudgery of having to do things of no great artistic worth. Imad would concur with this, saying that the new technology has distinguished the real calligrapher from the one who merely writes or works on the computer. Now that things are set, he argues, calligraphy has acquired a still more prestigious status.

'So how do you see the role of the calligrapher in the modern world?'

'It has become even more important in dark and difficult times. The main thing is that I be honest about what I do. Unfortunately, in today's world, it is not enough. You need publicity … you need to be in contact with people … you need media coverage, marketing, to put these things in front of everyone. I'm incapable of this.'

Imad has produced two major works to date, the first of which is an astonishing 10.65-metre scroll, which took him a year and a half to complete, and which contains selected passages from the Qur'an including *Al-Ilkhas* ("Fidelity"), the 112th sura in which Allah's absolute unity is proclaimed. It is written in different calligraphic styles, ranging from the classical to the modern, all produced in miniature, and is embellished with gold. Among the scripts employed is the miniscule *al-ghubari*, which translates as 'dust-like', and is used mostly in the borders. Imad smiled at the memory of his having made it to the end without any mistakes.

'I was so nervous doing the last twelve centimetres, which is in the *Nasta'liq* or Farsi style, so-named because it comes from Iran, and because I was in such a state it took me a whole week to write.'

'You said you managed to complete the scroll without making any mistakes, but aren't you supposed to leave an imperfection somewhere?'

'Yes, in our Islamic tradition we believe perfection comes only from God and that human beings are not capable of it. If you look at the geometric designs in a Persian carpet everything down to the smallest details is perfect, there are no mistakes, geometrically at least, but look closer and you will see the maker has intentionally left something out. After I finished the scroll I didn't feel able to carry on. I was ready to break all my pens and start on something much better, which means what I had just done was not perfect. At the beginning I was very ambitious, I put everything into it, but by the end I realised there was still so much to learn and that I would have to start all over again. It is an ever-evolving process. Another thing, and I'm talking now from the viewpoint of the observer, is that most people, because they have not had the chance to enjoy and appreciate the classical tradition, are easily impressed by phantasmagoria. Only when they have seen the right things will they see the real treasure. What you have now are people who don't have any basic knowledge or practice in real calligraphy producing things that may look impressive to those who don't know anything about how these things need to evolve. Anything new must come of real evolution. I am not after any bubble of fame.'

Also Imad completed a magnificent Qur'an in thirty sections, with only five lines to each page, its total of 15,000 lines adding up to 3000 pages. The Qur'an also serves as the basis for a new project upon which he is working, which he reckons will take him fifteen months to complete. The identity of the person or the organisation who commissioned it remains a mystery. It will be, he tells me, the realisation of a dream project.

'I would like to think there is nothing called "calligraphy" and that there is nothing set in stone. There is only the calligrapher. As much as I appreciate the classical forms I would like to present something of my own, which is not like the script of *x* or *y* who came before, but which is my own style. What I'm doing now is inspired by a school of calligraphy that is almost forgotten, the *muhakak*, which dates mainly from the Abbasid period, but which started during the Umayyad period. The Abbasids developed it into its known shape and it was taken over, and then forgotten, by the Ottomans and then the Persians. It is the most glorious writing, with a balance between the very simple and the very complex unlike, say, the Ottoman scripts which are so complicated they become a challenge in themselves. I would like to bring this back to paper but with something of my own style. I will do something different with the *rā'* and the *wāw* and the *'alif* making them longer so as to give more elegance in the balance. I have written out the Qur'an before and the idea I had then was for it to be published but then there was some kind of problem. When I finished my first Qur'an, I had a vision of an even more beautiful script, this being the one I have just described. What I was really after is this commission, the best of the best. There were others who might have been given it, but in the end God rescued me. What is important is that whoever does this it will be impressive. An idiot will see the beauty in it. Whether he would be able to distinguish it from other works doesn't matter as this will be left for scholars to evaluate. This is a commission from God and that's the way it will be realised.'

'To what extent do you feel you'll be able to create something new?'

'I'm always accusing the schools of calligraphy, of which the Ottomans were the masters, of falling into a trap of abiding by rules they can't escape. They produce always same shapes. Although I do not belong to any master or school, I think I am still very conservative in my approach. This is a relative matter. What is this bringing something *new* to calligraphy? Yes, I am trying to add things but I am still tied to, and have great respect for, the old teachings, the old regulations and balances. What I create is not seen by certain other calligraphers or those contemporary artists who bring calligraphy into their work as modern. They will force the letters out of shape, which for me is almost a sacrilege. You can improvise to a certain extent but you can't play with the backbone. We have already distinguished between those people who stick to the old traditions and do not move forward and those who modernise and jump about in the air whenever they think they have created something new. I do not see myself as belonging to either group. I try to be like a musician who before playing understands everything about his instrument and knows its capacities, so that it works in the way it has been designed for. What I think of as new comes naturally with things I have learned from the classical tradition. Anything additional should come according to what the tools and those teachings will allow. You don't try to play a drum with a violin, which is what some people try to do.'

When I left Imad and stepped outside, pondering whether such a combination was possible, the moon over the citadel opposite signalled bedtime for me but for the master calligrapher of Aleppo it meant only the beginning of another night's work.

V: Saint Simeon
& the Dead Cities

THE MOST BEWILDERING thing about Saint Simeon Stylites is that although he ranked as one of the most important saints of his time, with pilgrims coming to see him from as far away as England, there is not a single biography or hagiography devoted to him. We have the three contemporary Lives, most recently published in Kalamazoo, otherwise nothing of significance. The chapter reproduced here, from my book *The Street Philosopher and the Holy Fool: A Syrian Journey,* is, in part, a reconstruction of his life from those early sources. My thesis is that he be viewed through eyes more sympathetic than those of late. I have been warned by Christians of the Orthodox persuasion not to label him as a 'holy fool' and while I am sympathetic to those pleas, it has to be said that the phrase is reserved only for those of the highest spiritual standing and that standing as high as he did, and for as long as he did, Simeon, great though he was, was more than a shade unorthodox in his penchant for high places.

The French poet, Jacques Réda, finds at Saint Simeon memories of France. William Dalrymple's *From the Holy Mountain,* is a description of a journey made in the footsteps of the Greek monks, John Moschos and his pupil Sophronius who began their travels in the spring of 587, which were described in *The Spiritual Meadow of John Moschos,* the oldest surviving manuscript of which is preserved at the Monastery of Iviron, Mount Athos. Dalrymple's book is elegiac in tone, especially in respect to the decline of Eastern Christianity, and perhaps nowhere more so than in his haunting description of one of the so-called Dead Cities, many of which are scarcely more than a few tumbled stones. The town Dalrymple finds is a rather more complete example. Such soil as there was, though not particularly rich, was perfect for the cultivation of olive trees, and, with Antioch in one direction and Aleppo in the other, neither more than a couple of day's distance by mule, the northern highlands of Syria prospered for centuries. A whole culture was built upon the olive. It lasted until the eighth century when struggles between Arab and Byzantine plunged the area into rapid decline.

Marius Kociejowski
From *The Street Philosopher and the Holy Fool (2004)*

A Likeness of Angels

> Whosoever adopts the likeness of angels, let him be a stranger
> to humans.
>
> Aphraates, *Patrologia Syriaca*

There was one more journey I had to make, which would take me to one of
the roots of holy folly, where, arguably, both Christian and pre-Islamic
traditions find a meeting place. Just how far the breeze blew the seeds sown by
one faith into the fertile ground of another is debatable. Muslims are not
particularly receptive to suggestions of Christian or even pre-Islamic
influence and Christians who actively seek a dialogue with Islam are rare. It is
impossible to ignore the fact of a shared landscape and it is harder still to
imagine the great faiths operating in complete isolation.

   If anyone can be said to be the patron saint of holy fools then arguably it
is Simeon Stylites. The base of the pillar upon which he stood for thirty-seven
years can still be seen near the village of Deir Sim'an, an hour's drive north-
west of Aleppo. The church complex, Qal'at Sim'an or Saint Simeon, which
was later built around the pillar, is one of Syria's greatest architectural
treasures.

Acanthus, the conventionalised leaf of which figures in Corinthian capitals, its
adoption inspired, according to Vitruvius, by acanthus leaves growing about a
basket of toys left in a cemetery, was given a fresh twist by the architects of
Saint Simeon. The spiked fronds skilfully carved into stone were flattened so
as to suggest the influence upon them of a strong breeze, 'the breeze itself a
pilgrim to the mysteries within,' Michael Haag writes. The blown acanthus, as
this new style was dubbed, spread rapidly throughout the Byzantine world. A
single detail bespeaks the grace of the whole. The church of Saint Simeon,
built between 476 and 491, was the greatest Byzantine structure of its time.

   What Simeon, who shunned all earthly things, whose life moved through
spheres beyond all concern for the beautiful, would have made of such
extravagance is beyond conjecture. As it is, we can barely follow that mind.
The imperial authorities at Constantinople spared no expense in the building
of the church, and in this we may suspect a strong message to those pursuing
alternative religious lines. The Monophysite heresy that allowed for no
separation between Christ's divine and human elements had already begun to
sow discord at the fringes of the Byzantine Empire. The language used by the

Monophysites was not suggestive of tolerance: 'May those who divide Christ be divided with the sword, may they be hewn in pieces, may they be burnt alive.'

Simeon pulled for the orthodox side.

The church was constructed in the shape of a cross, four basilicas meeting at an octagon at whose centre we can still see the base of the pillar upon which the saint took up residence. The earthquakes of 526 and 528 which destroyed Antioch probably brought down the roof here. The pillar was still standing at the end of the sixth century when the ecclesiastical historian, Evagrius, visited the Mandra, as the local people then called it. A couple of minor details in his account lend a curiously pagan air to the scene. Rustics, and by this we may suppose he was speaking of Bedouins, performed dances around the pillar and also repeatedly led their beasts of burden around the structure. They took literally it seems the metaphorical Mandra (from the Greek *mandra*, meaning the hovels in which sheep and goats are fed).

Simeon did not leave behind any writings, so for details of his life we are largely dependent on the written testimonies of his disciples and witnesses. There are three major accounts written by contemporaries, the first and most reliable by Theodoret, Bishop of Cyrrhus, written around 444, when Simeon was still alive and had already spent twenty-two of his thirty-seven years on his pillar. Theodoret, who, according to one tradition, may have been a student of Chrysostom's, was a historian with a historian's discipline for weighing matters, even particularly irksome ones.

> For what took place surpasses human nature, and people are accustomed to measure what is said by the yardstick of what is natural. If something were to be said which lies outside the limits of what is natural, the narrative is considered a lie by those uninitiated in divine things.

The second account, by Antonius, an intimate disciple – it was he who first approached Simeon's corpse – although disjointed and lacking the former writer's Platonic style is valuable for details others might have seen fit to exclude. There is surprisingly little of the adulatory whereas the third account, by an anonymous hand, commonly known as *The Syriac Life*, begins and ends with an over-powering smell of incense. Antonius's account is the much plainer of the two, humbler in intent, unsparing in its presentation of physical realities difficult even for his contemporaries to embrace, and seeks not to place too much emphasis on miracles. *The Syriac Life* is almost all miracle. There is not much in it that survives the acid bath of our times. Although to ignore the miracles would be akin to cutting from the *Iliad* all the battle scenes there is, in the more easily verifiable details of Simeon's life, a story far stranger than any attributed to miraculous causes. The three accounts present his early life as a shepherd, his early asceticism, his years in the monastery at Teleda, his removal to Telanissos and finally his years as a stylite, otherwise the narratives have little in common. Where they do meet, however – and, curiously, almost always at the seams of the probable – they command our fascination.

Simeon was born at the end of the fourth century, around 390, to a Christian family, in the village of Sisa near Nicopolis. A smallish but reportedly handsome youth, he tended his parents' flocks, work likely to be conducive to contemplation. According to *The Syriac Life* he would go about the fields gathering storax, a gum resin which when burned smells like frankincense. Strabo mentions its use in the worship of pagan deities. Simeon, it was said, burned the substance without understanding why he did so, and one finds elsewhere the suggestion that he unconsciously moved in the direction of the Scriptures. Such time as he had to spare was spent in the company of ascetics who advised solitude and the renunciation of bodily health and desires as vital to keeping the soul pure. After spending a couple of years as a kind of novice Simeon went, without telling his parents, to the monastery founded by Eusebonas at Teleda, not far from Antioch. There the seventeen-year-old threw himself at the feet of the abbot, Heliodorus. A good and holy man, Heliodorus entered the monastery when he was only three and, according to Theodoret, was so untouched by worldly concerns he knew neither a pig's nor a cock's shape. One suspects here a gentle joke. Theodoret who visited him frequently marvelled at the simplicity of his character and the purity of his soul.

Describing himself as low and wretched, Simeon begged Heliodorus to save a soul which although perishing desired to serve God. Heliodorus, taken aback by the intensity of the youth, asked him his name, where he came from and what his background was. The youth would not say who his parents were, and by this we may infer that in dissolving earthly bonds he had become *as dead* to them. There is a contemporary feel here. We find such reports in the newspapers of young people with odd religious leanings, who have severed all family ties, their parents struggling to break through a screen of silence. Antonius's account has Simeon's parents in tears, ceaselessly looking for him, whereas *The Syriac Life* has them already in their graves. Simeon entered the monastery where he was to spend a whole decade; at least to begin with, he was loved by his brethren, and, most vitally, he observed the rules. After a while, however, he began to move in directions that were not those of his brethren and perhaps not entirely his either. Whether divine inspiration, madness or indeed both were the spur (there is nothing in his own words to give us guidance), he began upon a course that would increasingly test the patience of the other monks. The meagre portion of bread and pulse which was his daily fare he gave away to the poor so he would go from Sunday to Sunday without sustenance, and on the seventh day consume only a few spoonfuls of soaked lentils. This did not go unnoticed by the other monks who being spiritually competitive were unable to purge themselves to such a degree. There were greater feats to come. Simeon dug a hole in the garden and stood in it up to his chest for days on end in the blistering sun. At night he would stand on a round stick so that if by chance he began to doze it would roll beneath his sagging weight, keeping him awake. The monks began to condemn more vociferously than ever those activities that put their own in the shade.

All came to a head over a length of rope.

'Behold, the new Job!' Heliodorus cried.

Maggots, this was what he had been brought to see, Simeon's bed was crawling with them. The monks gathered there agreed the boy had gone too far this time, that here perhaps was the lever by means of which he would be made to leave. Why did he go to such extremes? The stench was unbearable. Heliodorus who greatly loved Simeon was at a loss what to do. The monks had on many occasions pressed him to take measures, and because he saw in their demands something other than love his reply was always the same.

'Since he afflicts himself for God's sake, I will not be the cause of any loss to him.'

Always they spoke of the 'greater good' while never once admitting to the envy that, like scorpions at the bottom of an empty cistern, dwelled in their own breasts. This time, however, Heliodorus was deeply troubled. He had been put under severe pressure. Unless he agreed to expel Simeon the monks warned they would leave, and if that were to be the case the holy order that was entrusted to his safekeeping would collapse.

Heliodorus took Simeon by the shoulders and shook him.

'Why do you do these things? Why do you break the monastery rules? What are you, some kind of spirit come to tempt me? If you want to die, get away from this place.'

Simeon bowed to the ground in silence, tears filling his eyes. Heliodorus asked him who his parents were (if he were born of real parents that is), and from what place he came. Working himself up into a rage, he turned to the others.

'Strip him,' he shouted, 'so we can discover what this smell is.'

When they tried to do so they were unable to peel the shirt from the boy's flesh. Cloth and flesh had become as one, an integument of decay and discharge, and for three days they soaked him in warm water mixed with olive oil. When finally the shirt was removed and with it much flesh what they saw amazed them.

The missing rope.

The monks remembered Simeon a couple of weeks earlier going out to fetch water from the well and coming back, saying that the rope for lowering the bucket was gone. They begged him to keep silent about it, fearing somebody would inform the abbot. And now here was that same object, soaked with blood and infested with larvae. What had transpired, they learned, was that Simeon had taken the rope made of palm leaves, which was extremely rough even to the touch, and going into a secluded place wound it tightly around his waist so that at first it burned and then, with every movement he made, cut ever deeper into the flesh until some days later that whole part of his body was a ghastly putrescence.

'Let me be, my masters and brethren,' Simeon cried, 'Let me die as a dog, it's what I deserve for the things I've done. I'm an ocean of sins.'

Heliodorus wept to see that wound.

'You're not yet eighteen, what sins do you have?'

'The prophet David said: 'Behold, I was brought forth in iniquities, and in sin did my mother conceive me.' I have been clothed the same as everyone else.'

The abbot, much struck by Simeon's answer, immediately called for two physicians to tend to him. The operation to remove the rope was such that at one point they gave him up for dead, but finally they managed to do so and for almost two months kept Simeon under their care. When Simeon recovered the abbot summoned him.

'Look, son, you are now healthy. Go where you wish, but you must leave here.'

After leaving the monastery Simeon went to a nearby well that was dry, at whose bottom dwelled numerous scorpions and snakes. The people avoided that evil place. He lowered himself into the well and hid in a cavity in the wall. A week after Simeon's departure Heliodorus had a dream in which he saw many men clad in white, holding torches, circling the monastery. They accused him, threatening to burn the place unless Simeon, the servant of God, was handed over to them.

'Why do you persecute him?' they asked. 'Do you not know what you had in your monastery? One who will be found greater than you.'

The abbot awoke, crying out to the monks to come.

'Truly I see now that Simeon is a true servant of God!' he cried, 'I beg you, brethren, find him for me, otherwise do not bother to return here.'

A search party went almost everywhere. When Heliodorus learned that they had avoided the well he ordered them to go to that place. They prayed above the well for three hours, after which five monks holding torches lowered themselves by means of ropes. The reptiles fled from the glare.

Simeon cried out to his rescuers.

'I beseech you, brothers and servants of God, grant me a little time to die. That I cannot fulfil what I set out to do is too much for me.'

The monks took him with considerable force. The way up, they said, is not as easy as the way down. They brought him as if he were a criminal to Heliodorus who fell at Simeon's feet.

'Agree to my request and become my teacher, servant of God, teach me patience and endurance.'

Simeon stayed in the monastery for another three years, but the pressure from the monks continued until finally the abbot, fearful for the future of the monastery, promised that if Simeon did not conform to their rules he would be made to leave. Another year was spent trying to persuade him to abandon his strange practices. With Lent drawing near, Heliodorus called Simeon before him.

'You know, my son, how much I love you and how I do not want you to go from here, but I cannot change the laws laid down by our fathers. Arise, go wherever the Lord is preparing for you. I will rejoice in you.'

One night, without saying a word to anyone, Simeon left and came to Telanissos where he confined himself for three years to a small hut, living only on a diet of soaked lentils and water, and, on one occasion, fasting for forty days after which he was unable to speak or move. Gradually, he was nursed back to health on a diet of chicory and wild lettuce.

The man disturbs as much as he inspires.

We are not alone in finding certain aspects of Simeon's life repulsive. It was a problem for many of his contemporaries too, even though many ascetics indulged in similar practices. Evagrius describes their activities.

> They maintain common supplications to God throughout the day and night, to such a degree distressing themselves, so galling themselves by their severe service, as to seem, in a manner, tombless corpses ... Indeed, their own rule enjoins them to hunger and thirst, and to clothe the body only so far as necessity requires: and their mode of life is balanced by opposite scales, so accurately poised, that they are unconscious of any tendency to motion, though arising from strongly antagonist forces; for opposing principles are, in their case, mingled to such a degree, by the power of divine grace combining and again severing things that are incongruous, that life and death dwell together in them, things opposed to each other in nature and in circumstances: for where passion enters, they must be dead and entombed; where prayer to God is required, they must display vigour of body and energy of spirit, though the flower of life be past. Thus with them are the two modes of life combined, so as to be constantly living with a total renunciation of the flesh, and at the same time, mingling with the living.

Evagrius speaks always in the present tense, describing things familiar to his readers. There seems to be something in the very landscape which drove these 'fleshless athletes, bloodless wrestlers' to such extremes, many of them actually melding into the scorched wilderness, becoming 'grazers', permitting themselves only what the ground produced and that barely sufficient to sustain life. The desert was, after all, a spiritual home to those who rejected the comforts of an earthly home, a place where sleep and food seemed luxuries, where the devils one fought in the imagination took on an almost corporeal existence. Although the area we are speaking of does not, strictly speaking, fall into this geographical zone the desert was always close. There were reports of people who so completely transported themselves into the natural scene that neither panther nor lion harmed them.

We seek to understand the savagery of such a course.

> O Lord, Lord,
> Thou knowest I bore this better at the first,
> For I was strong and hale of body then;
> And tho' my teeth, which now are dropt away,
> Would chatter with the cold, and all my beard
> Was tagg'd with icy fringes in the moon,
> I drown'd the whoopings of the owl with sound
> Of pious hymns and psalms, and sometimes saw
> An angel stand and watch me, as I sang.

Edward Fitzgerald reports Tennyson reading aloud his poem on Simeon 'with grotesque Grimness, especially at such passages as 'Coughs, Aches, Stitches, etc. 'laughing aloud at times'. Simeon is for Tennyson a figure swollen up with morbid pride, whose religious enthusiasm has degenerated into a fanaticism bordering on the hallucinatory, his mind set only on a crown-bearing angel who may or may not be there. 'Who may be made a saint, if I fail here?' Although he may to some degree pity this man 'whose brain the sunshine bakes', Tennyson cuts to the bone.

As does Gibbon: 'A believing age was easily persuaded that the slightest caprice of an Egyptian or a Syrian monk had been sufficient to interrupt the eternal laws of the universe.' As did a group of monks who joined Daniel on his pilgrimage, hoping they might prove Simeon false: 'Never has such a thing happened anywhere that a man should go up and live on a pillar.' As did, although rather less eloquently, a woman from Yorkshire who, standing at the base of the pillar, remarked, 'Sounds a bloody twit to me!'

A symbol must be true to the world it addresses, and among most of his contemporaries Simeon inspired not revulsion but awe. They saw in Simeon's suffering the beauty it symbolised. A maggot that fell from his leg was picked up by an Arab who when he opened his hand again found a pearl there. Simeon took into his own body the problems of the world as they really were, not abstractions or metaphors, but pain, hunger and sickness, and enacted them in the concrete. The pilgrims who came to see him spoke his spiritual language. Simeon trimmed his body according to his soul's desire. The danger of a journey such as he made is that in more impressionable beings it may lead only to a world of illusion, where sanctity is merely a cloak for pride. Although it is true he physically made, in Theodoret's words, 'the flight of the soul towards heaven' and in doing so freed himself of the distractions of the world, he remained of the world and spoke directly to its same distractions in other people. What his witnesses were able to vouch for, and which is the basis of all Christian perfection, was his spirit of humility. As for the scowling monks who joined Daniel, who himself later became a stylite, when they saw the saint they were moved by the love he showed towards them.

The base of the pillar is all that remained after pilgrims hungry for relics chipped away the stone piece by piece. A huge boulder that sits on the base is something of a mystery, for nobody remembers where it came from. It was not there a few decades ago. When Simeon moved to the hill above Telanissos he made for himself a circular wall of unmortared stones, and wearing an iron chain twenty cubits long remained in this fashion until a cleric, Meletius, persuaded him to remove it, saying that the fetter of reason would suffice. After approximately ten years in the enclosure Simeon became a stylite, from the Greek *stylos* meaning pillar. Whether he did so because he found the people continually poking at him quite out of place with the ascetic life or because he had already made a pact with heaven is not known. There are those who argue the case for Simeon as phallobate rather than stylite, and although there are precedents in the pagan world, such as that described in Lucian's *De Dea Syria*, where a man climbs and stays on a 'phallus' for seven days, it is unlikely that Simeon rose upon such an impulse. What he did was more in keeping with the *imitatio Christi* so prevalent among ascetics, the striking of a Christ-like posture. There were three pillars, the first four cubits high (approximately three metres); this was gradually increased to eleven metres and finally eighteen metres with a platform two metres square. Simeon wore an iron collar (presumably to prevent him from falling off), and for thirty-seven years stood exposed to severe winter winds and scorching sun.

We have a reasonably clear picture of his daily activities. According to Theodoret Simeon would prostrate himself, bringing his head close to his toes, in one instance doing so 1,244 times before Theodoret's attendant lost count. Because he ate only once a week his empty stomach allowed for freer movement, and during public festivals he would stand all night with his hands raised to heaven. Twice a day he would deliver an exhortation, and after three in the afternoon sit in judgement over the cases brought before him. From around sunset on, the whole night and next day until three o'clock he spent in prayer. Theodoret supplies a vital clue to Simeon's character, saying he did all these things with unpretentiousness (and here one thinks of Gibbon's assertion

191

that monks were a foul-tempered breed) and was at all times very approachable, pleasant and charming. He spoke directly or through an interpreter to each person who addressed him. Simeon stood until his death on July 24th, 459, when he was over seventy years old.

What is beyond dispute is the incredible presence he made in his world. 'As they come from every quarter, each road is like a river,' Theodoret writes, and by the time of Simeon's death his fame had spread from Britain to the Persian empire, and among Armenians, Ethiopians, Gauls, Spaniards, Scythian nomads, sophisticates from Rome and Constantinople, and, most strikingly, among the Arabs themselves, many of whom were converted, despite the lack of a common language, and who at Simeon's death wanted to remove his corpse for burial in their own territories. The Arabs were particularly fascinated by the strange spectacle of a man on a pillar, and if, at worst, the pillar was an attention-seeking device it certainly worked upon the nomadic imagination. The Arabs were as yet without a distinct identity and it was not until the Prophet Muhammad came that they found one, but on no account should we underestimate their significant role in the development of Syriac Christianity, a matter that has been treated at length elsewhere. Christ moved among the Arab people, and it is worth noting that, according to Muslims, it will be at the minaret of Jesus at the southeast corner of the Great Mosque in Damascus that he will descend from heaven. Although Simeon may have quit human society for the company of angels, and indeed it may be that he failed in his original aim, to be alone, it was human affairs he attended to, and as such his contributions to society were concrete. Bizarre as his practices may seem to us, there was hardly anything of the fanatical in Simeon's language, if fanaticism is, as Isaac Taylor defines it, 'enthusiasm inflamed by hatred'. We are continually struck by the practicality, and, barring the miracle stories in which all kinds of ghastly retribution are made, the quick compassion of the man. He was involved in social work, spoke on behalf of slaves, in many instances securing their release, settled family disputes, sought refuge for orphans and windows, delivered the oppressed from their oppressors, had taxes remitted, unjust policies reversed and food distributed to the poor, engaged in delicate negotiations concerning ecclesiastical policy, and even took part in matters of foreign policy, mediating, for example, between the Byzantine emperor and unruly Bedouin tribes. We may ask, how did he manage to do so from such a confined space? The answer is both profound and simple: it is because people did as he told them to, such was the respect he commanded. Simeon was in possession of a quality that the Apostles had in abundance, *parresia*, a Greek word which, to give but one of its several attributes, refers to the ability to speak with the full force of one's convictions, without fear of punishment or of any human obstacle. An emperor and a beggar would be addressed in the same language. The people came hoping for a cure, divine inspiration and God's forgiveness or even in order to settle a dispute over a melon patch. Simeon was both jury and judge. As for the miracles, Theodoret writes: 'But how long shall I strive to measure the depth of the Atlantic Ocean? For just as humans cannot measure that, so what he accomplishes day after day cannot be narrated.'

Evagrius describes a posthumous miracle, or, if not exactly a miracle, then an unusual occurrence. A large and brilliant star shot along the length of the balustrade, vanishing and reappearing, whizzing back and forth several times. Apparently this, together with a bearded resemblance of Simeon's head 'flitting about here and there', occurred only at special commemorations of the saint. What are we to make of such prodigies? Evagrius was representative of an age powerfully disposed to the marvellous and in which people saw miracles even in the mundane. We may excuse that old credulity and smile, but if we mock the imagination we mock too the poetic truths to which it gives rise. Simeon would probably have winced at this blurring of religion and culture. So *what of that heavenly sphere?* Gertrude Bell who visited the site in 1905 describes 'the eye of a great star that had climbed up above the broken line of the arcade'. We may now cushion our doubts with matters of mere velocity and trajectory, and conclude that perhaps our spiritual fathers had both a weak and a strong eye. Gertrude Bell empathised with the star, finding it better to move than to remain, as Simeon did, in one place. Had she stayed longer heaven might have punished her for being a woman in a strictly male enclosure. Simeon allowed not even his own mother admittance, although when she died outside the gates of the enclosure he had her remains buried in front of the pillar so she might be always before him. It should be remembered, however, Simeon considered the small area around his pillar a monastery and not, despite the crowds that came, a place of pilgrimage. A case frequently cited of a woman who got into the enclosure being struck dead is a misreading of a miracle in which the devil comes to Simeon in various disguises, and although at times we may agree with the poet Campion that 'beauty is but a painted hell' the woman was, in this instance, a not-so-clever substitute. There is no evidence Simeon disliked women, quite the contrary in fact, if we consider how often he undid the injustices visited upon them. An honest doubter, Gertrude Bell washed her hands and face in a small pool of water gathered in the depression of the pillar's base, and looking up saw a star that to her greatly perceptive eye appeared to move.

A boy with a magnifying glass could have set the world ablaze. The heat was so intense that as far as one could see the land was scorched brown, almost black in places. Simeon had been suffering for a couple of days already from a high fever that gave much cause for concern among his disciples. They spoke in whispers between themselves, knowing full well any rumour would spread like wildfire. On the third day of his illness, by some fluke of nature (although others would say otherwise), a cool breeze blew about the pillar. The disciples remarked a sweet fragrance to which neither choice herbs nor Arabic scents could compare. As the maggot is to the pearl, so putrefaction to perfume. The crowds gathered there could not smell this for all their burning of incense. As the savour grew in intensity the disciples understood Simeon's time had come. Antonius climbed the ladder and addressed the motionless figure.

'You have not answered me, my lord.'

Antonius touched Simeon's white beard and seeing that he did not move kissed him on the mouth, then his eyes, his beard, and lifting the hem of his tunic kissed his feet too. And taking hold of Simeon's hand he placed it on his eyes, remaining there in silence for thirty minutes. When he came down and informed the other disciples a message was despatched to the patriarch of Antioch to come. Every effort was made to keep the assembled crowds in ignorance. There were too many people from the surrounding villages and also Arabs who had come fully armed ready to seize the corpse for burial in their own territories.

After four days troops and clergy finally came.

Ardabur, the military commander at Antioch, arrived with twenty-one prefects, many tribunes, six hundred Gothic soldiers, Martyrius, patriarch of Antioch and accompanying him six bishops of the province. They immediately formed circles between the pillar and the crowds already assembled there. Ardabur, son of Aspar who ruled over the eastern provinces, felt a sharp pain in his wrists. It was no worse than usual, but his coming here had the effect of condensing, as it had first done, his whole being upon a single point of anguish. Only habitude had allowed his mind to occupy a wider surface. A soldier must bear his injuries, even those inflicted during peace. Ardabur had won his rank of magister militum per Orientem *after smashing the barbarians at Thrace. And not so long ago he had fought the Arabs near Damascus, forcing them to the banquet table. A man of noble character, he spent much of his time at home in Daphne or at his villa overlooking the Bay of Sosthenium near Constantinople. As of late, according to wagging tongues (yes, the scribbling Priscus too), he revelled in the company of 'mimes and magicians and all the delights of the stage'. As though sweet music should irritate the minds of the people! As though we should not with art purge our feelings of anything harsh or disagreeable! And it was said too that he indulged in 'woman-like luxuriousness'. Ha, as though a few years of peace should weaken his hinges! What does a soldier fight for but peace? The irony was that he of all men, an Alan and an Arian too, should be sent on a mission to rescue from overzealous olive growers and gatherers of dates the corpse of a man who a few years earlier he himself might have killed with pleasure. The Antiochenes had begged him to go, and, he reflected, whom one rules one serves.*

Simeon, darling of the skies! Ardabour had pegged him for a fake. What soul was this that fed upon its own substance? Which embraced wretchedness as though only rags, blistering sun and ice could be true? What spectacle in nature is so vile as a man who'd willingly choose physical torture? As though Christ would put himself upon the cross! Yes, glorious the man who invents for himself a fresh torture, who binds himself to a stake with the bonds of pride, who begins by worshipping God with an impure love, and because he misunderstands a single phrase compounds his error until finally he looks down from on high upon whom he despises. Ah, better the scorpion lurking in the crevice than the fiery serpent suspended in mid-air. Who but an impostor or a fool would spend year after year stuck in that posture? If man's the only fool and the only wretch among creatures it is because he alone might be virtuous, happy and wise. Ardabur watched the proceedings with a jaundiced eye. This place was the cradle of his agonies. A few years ago, wishing to demonstrate that Simeon was a fake he put an arrow to the string of his bow and aimed it at the unwashed, emaciated figure. Suddenly, a skewering pain shot through his hands and he was unable to bend the bow. Then gout attacked him. A mere coincidence, of course, but those who make a study of coincidence will call their findings miracles while all they've done really is make connections between what was already there. What simile is not a miracle? The agony in his wrists and ankles would not go, and from this Ardabur suffered ever since. And now here was his soul's adversary, a small heap of rag and bone, whom Ardabur would bear home. Simeon dead! The skinny man gone. And as death makes of all men brothers, Ardabur would conduct Simeon over the rugged terrain as carefully, as gently as he would a fragile vase.

There was a screeching of birds in the cloudless skies.

Three bishops climbed up to where Simeon's body was and reciting three psalms kissed his robes. The corpse was then lowered from the pillar by means of pulleys. Only then did the assembled crowd know for sure that Simeon had died. The sound of weeping could be heard at a great distance. Although dead four days Simeon's face was fresh as if still alive. The patriarch of Antioch wanting a relic went to cut a hair from Simeon's beard but his hand withered at the attempt. The other bishops prayed for their leader and tearfully addressed the corpse.

'Nothing is missing from your limbs or clothes, and no one will take anything from your holy and venerable corpse.'

As they spoke the power in the patriarch's hand returned. Simeon's body was placed, to the accompaniment of psalms and hymns, in the leaden casket that had been brought from Antioch. That night there was much burning of incense. The journey to Antioch took five days during which time the body travelled in state, with people pouring in from the villages to pay their last respects.

At the outskirts of a village called Merope, about five miles from Antioch, the mules pulling the carriage which bore the leaden casket that contained Simeon's corpse stopped and despite the many proddings they received would not budge. They were obeying some commandment audible only to themselves. The crowd stood about in awkward silence. With such a short distance to go, why this ungodly insubordination of mules? And in the middle of a heatwave too. There was a cemetery to the right of the road and suddenly from its entrance a man dressed in rags ran at full speed towards the carriage and throwing himself upon the casket cried, 'Have pity on me, holy one of God, Simeon!' All those who knew him were amazed to hear him speak.

All the people who travelled that road knew who he was, this man whose words we remember but not his name, and taking pity on him would give him food and drink as he sat on the steps of a certain tomb that he had made his home. Other times, he would pace back and forth at the entrance to the cemetery roaring aloud, his cries so terrible people were afraid to approach him. The tomb where he had stayed day and night for these past twenty years contained the remains of a woman with whom he had fallen in love. She was another man's wife. We do not know whether she warmed to his words of love, but it was certain they had not made physical love. The young woman died, her body was placed here. So maddened with sorrow 'the hater of good might gain the soul of that man' he opened up the tombstone and did to her in death what he was not permitted to in life. Almost instantly, the wretched man went into deep shock, was struck deaf and dumb, and was no longer able to recognise anyone. He remained in this state, and, who knows, perhaps by choice, or, as someone remarked later, surely he had been reserved for heaven's mercies. At Simeon's approach the demon that had consumed the man for twenty years fled, and, with his reason restored and his tongue freed from the mental shackles, he was able once more to recognise, address and understand all the people.

The mules began to move.

On this the two accounts we have of Simeon's death and his removal to Antioch roughly agree, although there are some major differences too. Antonius explains why the man was possessed in the first place, and in doing so strikes a remarkable note of compassion. The explanation he provides suggests a tolerance we would not normally associate with the times and certainly not with a rural culture. We shudder at the lunatic's fate. We can scarcely imagine the horror of that event, the coldness of the flesh, but to label as perverse what one night entered a tortured soul would be to miss completely the tragedy of what took place. Clearly, Antonius understood this. And so too did the people of the village who quite simply let him be. Such a man were he alive today, depending on where he lived might have been either stoned to death in a public place or kept fully tranquillised on drugs in a private one. The author of *The Syriac Life* shrinks away from the cause of madness and in his account the local people fearful of being attacked by the man keep their distance. The purpose in bringing him into the narrative at all is to add one last to the many miracles that took place while Simeon was still alive. The sceptic will find more to believe in the first, in what is, in fact, the more remarkable of the two stories.

The Antiochenes, still shaken by a recent earthquake, came out by the thousands, clad in white, carrying wax tapers and lamps, to meet the corpse. They sprinkled precious spices over the people who accompanied the saint. Simeon's body was placed in a small church called Cassianus where it remained for thirty days while its final destination was being decided. The emperor Leo wanted the body brought to Constantinople, but the Antiochenes petitioned him, saying that a city without walls, such as theirs now was, needed the relics of a saint for protection from further earthquakes. After the petition was approved Ardabur had the body moved to the great church of Constantine.

After this we hear no more of the man who lived only for a woman's corpse except that he joined the procession to Antioch and spent many days in prayer in the church of Cassianus. We know Simeon's remains were seen by Evagrius, in 588, when Philippicus, brother-in-law of the emperor Maurice, requested that relics of the saint be sent to him for the protection of the Eastern armies. Evagrius describes the body as being preserved almost entire, the hair much as it was when the saint was alive, the skin of the forehead wrinkled and the greater part of his teeth present, the others having been violently removed by the faithful. The iron collar Simeon wore lay beside his head. Many others followed Simeon's example, becoming stylites, too. Simeon Stylites the Younger took to the pillar at such an early age Evagrius says 'he even cast his teeth in that situation.' It is said when Daniel became a stylite, Simeon's garment of goat's skin was bequeathed to him. A latter-day stylite was reported in the middle of the nineteenth century. There have always been men from different cultures who ascend to heaven by stages. Of Ardabur we learn that the emperor Leo suspecting him, Ardabur's brother, Patricius, and their father, Aspar, of planning a rebellion against him invited them to his palace in Constantinople. There he had them murdered by eunuchs who then hideously mutilated their bodies. A Goth called Ostrys fled with Aspar's pretty concubine.

A single image of the great church of Constantine where Simeon lay survives in the border of the great Yakto mosaic in the museum at Antakya. There is another image too, in that same border, Ardabur's private bath, which judging by its inclusion here must have been one of the most magnificent in Daphne.

A gentle breeze blew through the ruins. An Armenian from San Francisco gave me some cucumbers, small Syrian cucumbers sweeter than those we are accustomed to. We chomped at them while he spoke to me of his ambition to go everywhere connected with the Armenian people. If he was here it was because many Armenians had gone to see Simeon. There was a church in the desert, he told me, not far from Deir ez Zor, at whose centre was an open pit containing the bones of Armenians massacred by the Turks. 'You may handle them, all those thousands of bones,' he said. A group of French tourists having a picnic grimaced over a bottle of Syrian wine. I did try that wine once. A couple of Germans shouted at a boy who charged them double for beverages. As they became increasingly abusive I regretted the boy had not charged them triple. The woman from Yorkshire continued to blare through the megaphone of her ignorance. So many people from distant places, they made this an oddly secular pilgrimage. There was, despite their numbers, a tremendous sense of peace here. We may picture the wildness of the spot as it was when Simeon was alive, darkness slowly hugging the slopes, a hyena laughing in the distance.

Jaques Réda
Saint Simeon

In Lunéville, I'd climb the slopes of Méhon,
And at once my whole universe came into sight.
But it's the primal world, Bible wilderness
That encompasses the hill of Simeon.

From his wrecked column just one block remains. You
Imagine him sitting aloft like a target
For the sun's darts and God's love, riddled through.
Now the site, where an era's quiet strength reigns,

Is inhabited by poppies, butterflies, wild grasses,
And amid lit-up ruins, two or three cypresses
Dip their brushes in the sky's colourless ink.

Did I offend your soul, O pure anchorite,
When I offered, for lack of incense or honey,
Curling smoke from my last-but-one cigarette?

Translated by Jennie Feldman

William Dalrymple
From *From The Holy Mountain (1994)*

Serjilla

A series of lifts – a truck, a pick-up and finally a tractor – brought me to the ruined Byzantine town of Serjilla in time for lunch. I sat at the brow of the hill munching the sandwiches they had packed for me at the Baron, looking down over the extraordinary expanse of late antique buildings spread out across the valley below.

It was the sort of classical townscape that you normally see only in Roman and Byzantine mosaics. There were houses, a church, an inn, a set of baths, a couple of villas facing onto their own courtyards, and a scattering of farm buildings, with the pitched rooflines of still more pedimented and colonnaded buildings visible over the brow of the hill. Elsewhere such late classical towns are represented only by bald archaeological sites: tidied lines of bleached pillars, crumbling metopes and fallen architraves. But here, through a strange accident of fate, more intact domestic Byzantine buildings lay clustered at my feet in this obscure valley than survive today in all three of the greatest Byzantine metropolises – Constantinople, Antioch and Alexandria – put together.

The perfection of preservation here is extraordinary. Outside some of the houses you can still see olive presses – round basins with a stone funnel leading into a lower tub for the pressed oil – standing as if ready for this year's olive harvest. The colonnade of the inn still provides shade from the sun; the town meeting house, with its pedimented roof and tabernacled windows, still exudes an air of pompous provincial pride, as if the Byzantine gentlemen farmers who lived here were only out in the fields, overseeing their labourers, and would be back in the evening to discuss some weighty matter of village politics.

The view before me was almost exactly as it would have been when John Moschos passed through these hills on his way to Antioch at the end of the sixth century. Looking inside one villa, peering under the superbly carved entablature of a doorway, I could see in the darkness that the first-floor ceiling was still totally intact: in two thousand years, the earthquakes and upheavals that had levelled Antioch had left not one crack in this structure. Only the total absence of furniture and wooden fittings hinted at what had happened to this fine late antique townhouse; and after the perfection of the view from the top of the hill, I was almost disappointed not to find tables and chairs in the kitchens, nor plates of fruit waiting on the dressers, as they do in the mosaics at Antakya.

On the lower slope of the hillside, behind the town baths, lay an empty Byzantine sarcophagus. Its heavy granite cover was half broken off and there seemed to be no one about, so I hid my heavy rucksack inside it, out of sight under the remaining half of the covering slab, and set off across the low hills towards the neighbouring town of al-Barra.

It was a cool, bright autumn afternoon and thick clouds were racing overhead, casting quick-moving shadows over the massif. The hills were rolling and stony, and on the summits square Byzantine watchtowers rose vertically from the scree. Descending into al-Barra I found myself facing a small, square fifth-century church. It had a triple-arched portal, with each doorway surmounted by a finely carved tympanum. The doorways led into a tiny interior, only three bays long. The capitals were covered with vine-scroll interlace, each leaf raised by drilling away the stone behind it, as with an engraving; between the fronds small equal-armed Greek crosses nested like birds among the grapes and the vine tendrils.

I clambered up onto a wall and from that height saw what was invisible from the ground: that littered throughout the olive groves was another complete Byzantine ghost town, the stone skeletons of towers, vaults, and half-collapsed townhouses rising everywhere from the soft loam. At the edge of the trees, to the east, some of the largest and airiest of the villas were still inhabited. From my vantage point I could see a Syrian woman in a patterned headscarf peeping out of a late Roman window in one of the largest houses. A washing line ran from the final pillar on her colonnade to the handle of a massive Roman sarcophagus to one side; on it, children's clothes were hanging out to dry in the afternoon sun. Nearby, hens were perching on another fallen pillar which had been hollowed out to make a drinking trough. But the villagers clearly disdained to live in the slightly less grand villas that lay on the lower ground, a little deeper into the groves; after all, these houses had only four or five main rooms, which did not leave enough space for the stabling of horses, asses, goats and sheep; nor, as I discovered when I made a closer inspection, did they have any baths with hypocaust systems, so useful for keeping bantams in.

Carrying on through the trees, I began to climb over a small drystone wall that separated the land of two farmers; only when I was halfway over did I notice that the wall was made up of a pile of discarded doorjambs, carved tympana and inscribed lintels, an almost ridiculous richness of fine Byzantine sculpture piled up between the trees. Only in Syria, I thought, could a currency of this richness be so debased in value by the embarrassment of its profusion that it could be used for so humble a purpose as walling.

A little beyond this wall, across the ruins of the town's old marketplace, lay a pyramid. It rested on a squat cube of warm honey-coloured limestone. At the corners of the cube four stumpy pilasters rose to a quadrant of richly curlicued

Corinthian capitals. Bands of deeply cut acanthus ran along all four sides of the cube, the swirling leaf-patterns broken by a series of medallions. These turned out to contain the *chi-rho* monogram that Constantine turned into the symbol of his new Christian Empire. The apparently pagan pyramid was in fact a very unusual early-fifth-century Christian monument.

Inside the half-light of the tomb chamber lay five great sarcophagi. Unusually, the lids still sealed the caskets shut; the sleepers slept on undisturbed. In the centre, flanked on either side by two smaller caskets, lay the great sarcophagus of what was clearly the family patriarch: a ton of polished porphyry, unornamented but for a massive *chi-rho* monogram contained within a laurel wreath. The sheer baroque bulk of the sarcophagus some-how suggested a portly landowner, a big-bellied, bucolic figure, dangling grapes into his open mouth as he reclined on his couch.

The pyramid lay in front of the ruins of a magnificent villa, three storeys high. The way the pyramid was located in relation to the house implied that it must have been the dynastic mausoleum of the family who had lived there, not dissimilar to the arrangement – centuries later, in a very different world – at Castle Howard.

Now the villa was deserted except for a single tethered donkey belonging to one of the olive harvesters. But as I wandered around its collapsing and deserted rooms I wondered about the family that had lived here. Who had built this small palace? The provincial governor? A local landowner? A prominent senator, returning to his home town for burial after a life of politicking in the capital? The house and its adjacent tomb indicated the existence of an entire world – that of the provincial Byzantine aristocracy – which is passed over in the written sources. In the tenth century there are the writings of the misanthropist Cecaumenus, a grumpy provincial squire who advised his readers to avoid the court, lock up their daughters and keep their wives far from any visitors; but from the early Byzantine period there is relatively little to illuminate the life of the landowning class in the eastern provinces, except when such a figure forms the background for a saint's miracle story or emerges briefly from obscurity to lead a rebellion or champion some obscure heresy.

The sheer magnificent solidity of the family sarcophagi, the confidence and certainty of the workmanship and the conservative nature of the design seemed to hint at a world far removed from the nervy credulity of Theodoret's monks suspended in their cages and raised on their pillars. They also emphasised the degree of continuity between the late classical and the early Byzantine world, a continuity that is easily forgotten when reading the chroniclers' narratives of interminable palace coups, mutinous Gothic generals and collapsing frontiers.

For this ostensibly Christian monument is only barely converted from paganism, and the thinnest veneer of Christianity rests uneasily on what is unashamedly a pagan classical pyramid. Looking at the great porphyry caskets, I wondered whether the calm certainty of the mausoleum was a sham – a brave attempt to maintain classical values in a world where the surface of ancient life was being betrayed at every turn: in the new-fangled clothes that were being worn, in the beliefs that were held, in the strange chants of the Syrian monks and the prophecies of the stylites. Or did it in fact represent the reality? Did the people in these sarcophagi still lead a version of the old life of the late classical landowner: their youth spent in the law school at Beirut or the School of Libanius at Antioch; a period as a provincial official posted to Hippo or Harran; or perhaps a spell in the army on the Rhine frontier, peering over the cold battlements of Cologne or Trier to catch a glimpse of a Gothic raider padding across the ice into Roman territory; then the return to the home estate and the comforts of the richest and most civilised part of the Empire, with winters of hunting and feasting, the occasional marriage party of a neighbouring landowner or a trip to the theatre at Apamea; of afternoons wallowing in the baths at Serjilla and evenings spent reading Homer by the light of an oil lamp. Wandering through the Byzantine villa, through a succession of cool, high-ceilinged rooms, the stone still fitted perfectly, joint by joint, a classical pediment on every window frame, I felt sure that more of the ancient world had survived for longer in the Byzantine East than any of the surviving sources – including John Moschos – now indicate.

Lost in my Byzantine thoughts, I hadn't noticed that it had turned chilly. A faint yellow-gilt pallor now hung over the olive groves, and the oblique late-afternoon light threw long shadows among the trees. Worried that I had already spent too long in al-Barra, I set off at a brisk pace on the road back to Serjilla to pick up my rucksack before darkness fell. As I walked I wondered what had happened to these strange, deserted Byzantine towns. They certainly had not been burned and destroyed by raiding parties of Persians or Arabs; their marvellous preservation showed that. So what did happen?

No one is sure, but the results of a number of recent digs appear to have convinced archaeologists that the entire Levantine coast underwent some form of major economic and demographic crisis towards the end of the sixth century, a full half century *before* the Arab conquest. Plagues, political upheavals, the Persian wars and the raids of desert nomads were responsible for the gradual erosion of urban life and its replacement by a landscape of small villages and monasteries. Some of the larger secular estates and their estate villages might have survived for a while (including that, perhaps, of the entombed aristocrat of al-Barra), but in most places the ancient Levantine trading towns – places like Palmyra, Bosra and Jerash – disappeared forever, forgotten by the world until the Scottish painter David Roberts popularised their ruins, turning them into neat idylls, perfectly tailored to the tastes of nineteenth-century European romantics. While the ancient classical trading towns were falling into decay, in the countryside the ever-growing cohorts of monks and hermits were gradually settling in and taking over the abandoned forts, forums and pagan temples.

Certainly in the pages of John Moschos the three great metropolises – Antioch, Alexandria and Constantinople – still appear to be thriving: there are, for example, stories about labourers rebuilding public edifices in Antioch. But elsewhere in the eastern provinces there are only very occasional glimpses of the old classical civic life, with its theatres, schools, brothels, markets and circuses. We hear, for example, about an actor from Tarsus who cohabits with two concubines and 'performs deeds truly worthy of the demons who urged him on', implying that the Tarsus theatre was still functioning healthily. At the same time we know that the ancient trading city of Apamea still had a functioning hippodrome, for Moschos tells us how a former champion charioteer from the town went on to become a monk in Egypt, where he was later captured and enslaved by desert nomads.

Moreover, *The Spiritual Meadow* contains occasional references to merchants and trade, which implies that international commerce – the prerequisite for true urban life – had not yet completely died. At Ascalon Moschos hears about a merchant whose ship has sunk and so is thrown into prison, while his wife is forced to prostitute herself in order to pay his debts. On another occasion he tells of a gem engraver travelling by sea; he hears from his cabin boy that the crew is about to murder him for his boxes of precious gems, so he throws the entire hoard overboard.

But these stories are exceptions. Far more common are tales set against a background of small villages or remote estates, or else in the distant wilderness where hermits can live alone for years undisturbed by anyone – so much so that their deaths can go unremarked for decades. In one particularly macabre tale, a community of monks see mysterious lights at night at the top of the mountain high above their monastery. When daybreak comes they send up a party to investigate, who find that the source of the strange celestial aura is a small cave. Inside they discover an anchorite in a hair shirt. One of the monks embraces the ascetic, only to realise that he is dead. Although his body is miraculously well preserved, a note written by the dying monk indicates that he had 'departed this life' more than seventeen years previously.

The degree to which monasteries, with their mystical and other-worldly outlook, came to dominate the culture of the region is demonstrated by a set of gospels illuminated in the sixth century at the lost monastery of Beth Zagba, believed by Byzantinists to lie somewhere in the hills around Serjilla. In the illustrations of the Rabula Gospels, the angels are as real as the saints, who in turn are drawn to look like local monks: gaunt rustics caught in mid-argument, hands wildly gesticulating, their expression masked beneath thick growths of beard. In the most famous picture, of the Ascension, Christ hovers in his fiery chariot only just out of reach of the apostles. No dramatic gulf separates his divine world from that of his followers; he is the same size as them, has similar features and wears similar clothes. No barrier separates the natural from the supernatural.

Another illustration, that of Christ Enthroned, takes this immediacy even further. Christ is shown in majesty, on a golden throne studded with huge cabochon jewels. But around him, flanking him on either side, are not the expected crowd of seraphim and cherubim but a crowd of rough-robed Syrian monks. They are hooded and cowled in their sober brown sackcloth, hair grey, eyes staring, gospel books clutched to their chests as if they were clustered around the abbot in the chapter house or refectory. There is none of the chill remoteness of much late Byzantine art; here the superhuman is considered tangible and everyday, the divine imminent and directly accessible.

This sort of mystical abstraction is a world away from the practical late Roman farmers of Serjilla or the pyramid-dynasty of al-Barra. And yet if recent scholarship is correct, it seems increasingly likely that the two worlds – those of the gentrified landed estates and the isolated wild-eyed illuminator monks – coexisted side by side in these hills, and that the transition both from the pagan-classical to the Byzantine-Christian, and then, three centuries later, from the Byzantine-Christian to the medieval-Islamic, was a far more gradual process than the traditional accounts of violent change and invasion would allow.

In the Middle East, the reality of continuity has always been masked by a surface impression of cataclysm.

Returning in the dusk to Serjilla, I narrowly avoided being torn limb from limb by a pack of enormous sheepdogs. I had just rescued my pack from its sarcophagus and was returning up the hill when the beasts came howling out of the shadows, closing in on me with great leaps and bounds. With only seconds to spare, I managed to scramble up the fallen wall of a tumbledown Byzantine farmhouse, and stood there perched on a projecting gable like a stylite on his pillar. Pulling my rucksack up after me, I looked down to see three wolf-dogs growling below me, mouths open, each exhibiting a truly Baskervillian set of fangs. It was little comfort to think that sheepdogs also seem to have been a hazard of the region in Byzantine times: the unattractive anti-Semitic monastic rabble-rouser Barsauma survived an attack by dogs during his youth, which according to his biographer was understood to presage his future sainthood.

Eventually, just when I was beginning to think that I was going to have to spend the night up on my perch, the shepherd – a small fifteen-year-old boy – came up. He scattered the three dogs as easily as if they were poodles with a torrent of abuse and a hail of small pebbles. At my request he escorted me out of the ruins and onto the track before returning to his flock and the night-shelter of the old Serjilla bath house.

Quickening my pace, and mouthing prayers that I would not pass any more shepherds or their dogs, I headed back to the main road, and just managed to catch the last bus of the day before darkness fell. It was heading south.

VI: The Fertile Crescent

A FTER TRAVELLING through mostly parched landscape, suddenly one comes upon the fertile coastal crescent, which is the area for most of Syria's agricultural produce. I employ the term 'fertile crescent' in a manner somewhat looser than the geographer's, so as to include places south of Aleppo and north of Damascus. The main towns of Hama and Homs, described by T E Lawrence as 'twins disliking one another', are ghosts of their former selves. The area is visited mostly for its Crusader Castles. Robin Fedden's *Syria and Lebanon* stands as one of the finest twentieth-century books on the region. Although the last edition of his book appeared as long ago as 1965 much in it holds true. 'The curious and strange persist in Syria,' he writes, 'and the traveller will find them for himself and in the degree that he wishes.' Fedden is particularly concise in the chapter, itself a précis of an earlier book, which describes the Crusader Castles. Also included in this section is his description of the island town of Arwad. The felucca, which in his day took one there, has now been replaced by the motorboat.

Harry Charles Lukach, later Sir Harry Charles Luke (1884-1969), travelled through the Ottoman Empire during the last months of the regime of Sultan Hamid II and returned home in May 1908, when he began work on *The Fringe of the East: A Journey through Past and Present Provinces of Turkey* which was published in 1913. Luke revised the 1929 edition of Roy Elston's *Cook's Traveller's Handbook for Palestine and Syria*. Ronald Storrs, under whom Luke served as assistant governor of Jerusalem, said he had lived 'the most unwasted life of any man I have known.' What is particularly pleasing, and surely unique, in his account of Hama is that he provides a musical notation for the sound of one of the *noria* or ancient waterwheels with which one immediately identifies the place. Not much else has survived the terrible disturbances of 1982, during the course of which most of the city's ancient centre was demolished.

Homs lost its old centre through rather more peaceful means and with there being so little left for the imagination to fix upon some passages from Ibn al Fakih, Istakhri, Mukaddasi and Idrisi, pointing to old splendours will have to suffice. The old slander about the inhabitants of Homs is first mentioned in Mukaddasi.

Coming closer to Damascus, there are two Christian villages, Seidnaya, site of the famous convent, and Maalula, which is where one may still hear Aramaic, the language that Christ spoke. Mrs Delaney describes Richard Pococke (1704-65), the Church of Ireland bishop of Ossory, as 'the *dullest man* that *ever travelled*: but he is a good man.' He is not to be confused with his namesake Edward Pococke (1604-91) who was the greatest European Arabist of his age – so much more the shame, therefore, that he did not leave us his impressions of Syria. The lesser Pococke is not to be dismissed, however, for he was one of the foremost travellers of his day and his *Description of the East*, published in two volumes in 1743 and 1745, remains valuable.

The Greek Catholic church of *Mar Sarkis* (St Sergius) is on the escarpment close to Maalula. Peter McDonald whose poem records a visit to this tiny chapel is the author of three volumes of poetry, the most recent being *Pastorals* (Carcanet, 2004) and the forthcoming *The House of Clay*, which contains several poems inspired by his visit to Syria in 1998. Sergius was a Roman soldier martyred in 305, during Diocletian's reign, for refusing to sacrifice to Jupiter. The centre of his cult was Resafa, which is approximately midway between Aleppo and Deir al-Zor.

Robin Fedden
From *Syria and Lebanon (1965)*

Crusader Castles

Though it is over six and a half centuries since the last Crusaders embarked for Cyprus, the architectural imprint of the Crusades lies heavy on the Syrian littoral. Immense, and immensely solid, their castles couch on the mountain spurs, clawing the rock and the spare soil. They dominate the passes that lead from the Muslim hinterland to what was once the Frankish seaboard. Such was the liberality with which the Latins built these fortresses that some can no longer be identified. No name mentioned in the crusading chronicles will fit them; we ignore the builder, what sieges they sustained, and when they fell at last into Saracen hands. Such anonymity is inevitable when castles seem to have sprung fully armed, like the soldiers of the Jason legend, on almost every promontory and *tell*, and beside every ravine, from Edessa to the Gulf of Akaba on the Red Sea. From this multiplicity stand out in due and impressive prominence the greater castles, the best of the Crusader endeavour. As a group they constitute the fine flower of medieval military architecture and are known by their names and deeds. No anonymity here. Banias under Hermon, Beaufort, Safita, Markab, Sahyun, Krak of the Knights: these and others are famous and embody half the history of the Latin kingdom.

Both the architectural achievement of the Crusaders, and their drive and determination, are brought home in sheer weight of stone; the repeated triumph of setting up these land leviathans, often in the most inaccessible places, still astounds. It is not a matter of bulk alone; the castles impress equally in the skill of their masonry, the strategic cunning of their layout, and unexpectedly (in buildings of such severe purpose) by sudden beauty of detail. The lovely capitals and columns of the chapel doors at Markab, the Warden's Chamber at Krak with its ribbed vaulting and roses carved in stone, are an essential expression of the building sense which produced in the same castles the huge cisterns that held water for a five years' siege, and the towering south wall of the inner ward. Great strength and great delicacy: in fact, the architectural genius of twelfth- and thirteenth-century France, but doubly impressive in these hills and in such alien surroundings.

On grounds both of geographical position and function, the castles are separable into two main types. There are on the one hand the mountain castles, set to control the passes that lead from the Muslim hinterland to the sea across the Lebanon or the Jebel Alawi, and on the other the coastal castles whose duty was to watch the coast road and the ports, and to protect the littoral against the Muslim fleet centred on Egypt. Dotted up the coast from Tyre to Latakia, these maritime castles are not on the whole so large, so well-preserved, or so impressively placed, as the mountain fortresses. None the less for the traveller they have the advantage of lying on the main road and a normal progress up the coast brings him automatically to the castles at Sidon, Byblos and Tripoli. Of such coastal Crusader sites, two – Nephin and Tortosa – are particularly worth mention. The first for the intrinsic charm of its position and because it is so easily overlooked; and the second both for its architectural beauty and for the insight which it gives into ecclesiastical and civil life in the Latin kingdom.

The site of Nephin, some ten miles south of Tripoli, is hidden from the road by the houses of Enfeh village. It is a narrow peninsula of rock running out at right angles from the coast into deep water. Two great trenches carved in the solid rock to water level isolate it from the mainland. The largest of these trenches is a good hundred feet across, and it is characteristic of the thoroughness of the Franks that they should have expended so much labour to create so tiny an island fortress. The peninsula rises from blue-green water and the grass among the boulders is dotted with salty marine flowers. The local fishermen paint their boats brown and white and moor them in the lee of the island, and they come there to dry their nets. Otherwise the site is deserted and little remains of a castle whose history is almost unknown. It was presumably despoiled, as time passed, by the ancestors of these same fishermen, to supply stone for Enfeh.

Northward from Tripoli, the road to Tortosa runs through country surprisingly un-Phoenician. The strip of cultivation that is elsewhere wedged between the mountains and the coast gives way, as the Lebanese heights recede, to a dun unfruitful plain. The sandy soil looks devitalized and carries expanses of yellowish grass. Sluggish streams curl and twist through saltings to the sea and gulls stray far inland. The dead character of the landscape is somehow accentuated by infrequent flocks and their shepherds, giving, as they sometimes do, an impression of aimlessness and loss. Even the barrel-roofed huts of the pasture people, constructed of reeds, fail to break the monotony and are as colourless and unobtrusive as the plain itself. Where this country ends and the mountains – the Jebel Alawi – again approach the sea, the fishing town of Tartus stands. There, at Tortosa as the Crusaders called it, the Templars established their principal fortress. In the great banqueting hall, nearly fifty yards long, hung their standards and trophies, and there the Order met for counsel and deliberation. The castle is now sadly mutilated; modern houses and hovels have intruded without ceremony, and it is difficult to form an adequate idea of its original importance. Little even remains of the great keep from which in 1188 the Master of the Order and the Knights successfully repulsed the attacks of Saladin when the town and outer precincts of the castle had fallen. One is still shown, however, the small postern giving directly on the sea, whence after the fall of the town the last Crusaders left the soil of Tripoli and sailed to Cyprus.

Separated from the Templars' castle and standing within its own wall there existed also in Crusader times the episcopal town, centring round the cathedral shrine of our Lady of Tortosa. Of the town wall on the north and east a considerable stretch, including the North Gate, still stands; but it is the cathedral itself, preserved through a series of misadventures as storehouse, mosque and garrison, that creates the special interest of Tortosa. Tortosa was from early times an important Christian sanctuary. Its altar claimed the honour of being the first dedicated to the Virgin, and St Peter was vaguely reputed to have there celebrated mass. The earthquake which at an early date destroyed the church, but by miraculous good fortune preserved the altar intact, only served to increase the prestige of the shrine. It was thus upon a site already revered that the Franks in the twelfth and thirteenth centuries erected the present cathedral. It soon acquired reputation as a place of pilgrimage, and people from all over Europe – including Joinville the historian – came to pay homage to the Virgin of Tortosa. The exterior of the cathedral gives no impression of what is to come. It is a little heavy, almost squat in appearance, and was indeed reinforced in the thirteenth century for purposes of defence. The west front also, before which Raymond of Antioch was stabbed by two of the Assassins, though said to be remarkable, is unsatisfactory, and the disposition of the windows and their relationship to the west door cannot have been altogether pleasing even before disfigurement by the Muslims. The effect of the interior is different. One discovers with surprise and admiration a fine French church of the transition period, reminiscent of buildings to be found in Burgundy and Provence. To specify a nave carried on four arches, with side-aisles, three apses at the east end and a barrel roof, is to say nothing. It is the proportions that impress, the way in which the weight and solidity of this fortress church are translated into symmetry and grace. The effect is undoubtedly increased by the magnificent colours – a range of ambers marbled with verdigris – which the stone has acquired through time and a happy neglect.

Castles are necessary for defence, but works such as the cathedral of Tortosa suggest a settled civilization, and imply that their builders envisaged their permanency. One glimpses at Tortosa the dedicated effort to establish a permanent Frankish culture and society that was made in the quiet intervals between the alarms and excursions of two hundred years. The cathedral at Tortosa, though the greatest, is merely one of a number of ecclesiastical monuments which speak with greater intensity and pathos of the failure of this endeavour than do the sombre castles. At Tyre more than eighteen churches were built, excluding the cathedral of which the historian William of Tyre was at one time the illustrious archbishop. All these have disappeared, but elsewhere such monuments survive: among them one might mention the cathedral of St John at Beirut, now sadly mutilated and be-plastered; the church looking out to sea at Byblos with its elegant baptistery; and not least, the modest little church at Kouabba, just off the main road before one reaches Ras Chaqqa. It stands alone on a hillock among vines and olives. The chameleons on the wall-tops stare down at the intruder like gargoyles, and under a Levantine sun it is incongruously but unmistakably occidental. Few travellers visit it, yet in its simplicity and silence it evokes better than many more imposing remains the strange nature of the Latin enterprise.

Of the great mountain fortresses that guard the approaches to the coast from the hinterland, the most splendid and the most impressive is undoubtedly Krak of the Knights, and for this reason it should be visited last. Any castle after Krak is an anticlimax. One should lead up to Krak by visiting Beaufort, Markab and Sahyun, all giant Crusader castles of the first order, which have the advantage of being tolerably accessible from the coast. The best view of Beaufort is from the east. There the sprawling ruin hangs nearly a thousand feet above the Litani River, the Leontes of the Ancients, and you look straight across to it from the Merdjayoun road on the other side of the gorge. It is an impressive vantage-point. The abyss acts like a sounding-box, and in the stillness every note from the castle precipices is faithfully clear. You hear the noise of goats clambering across the scree below the castle walls before you see them, and you recognize the goat-boy's whistle, that limpid and pan-like note common to all the hillsides of the Mediterranean.

The castle belonged first to the lordship of Sayette and later to the Templars, but, in spite of the forbidding gorge, fell to the arms of both Saladin and Beibars. It is said that during the first siege the Lord of Sayette, in spite of a safe-conduct from the Saracens, was tortured in view of the castle walls in order to break the defenders' morale. Such an episode, if it occurred, is typical of many which go to prove, if proof were necessary, that chivalrous relations were rarely the rule between Crusader and Saracen. Though Saladin sometimes exercised a clemency, both humane and politic, which created a legend in Christendom (and was explained with delightful naïveté by the supposition that he must have had an English mother), he was an exception. After the fall of Safad, Beibars, in spite of his oath, massacred two thousand of the defenders. The same thing had happened earlier at Edessa, and was to recur later after the fall of Acre and of Beirut. The Franks were no better. Raymond of Chatillon's perfidy was a byword; when as a prisoner he was cut down with his own sword, it was a just end. The massacre of the tenacious Muslim garrison on the fall of Tripoli and the disgraceful and tragically ironic sack of Jerusalem, after hymns had been sung in procession about the walls, were among the exploits of Christian chivalry.

Markab lies north of Tortosa. Though the mountains tumble down to the sea, their precipitous slopes are smooth and carry turf. The rock skeleton rarely splits a skin of chalky soil, and the great mass of the castle, with its black basalt walls and towers, stands out against the sky and contrasts with the white chalk ridges it dominates. Set on a spur two or three miles inland, Markab combined the tactical position of a mountain fortress, guarding as it did the inland route to Kadmus and Masiaf, with the duty and possibility of watching the port of Banias and the coast road. Its strength was such that Saladin, even after his victory at Hattin, dared not attack it, and for a hundred and fifty years it remained in Frankish hands. Only in 1285, when the end of the Crusader occupation was in sight, did the fortress capitulate and the defenders depart with safe-conduct to Acre.

From the coast at Banias a bad, and finally precipitous, road crawls up to the castle. It was one of the strong points of the Hospitallers, and they built the finer parts of the fortifications in the thirteenth century. The water cisterns which lie under the great paved court, the chapel with its elegant doorways,

and the round keep, are particularly impressive. The last, second in size only to
that at Coucy, built in Northern France a century later and destroyed by the
Germans in the First World War, must be climbed both for the clear map-like
impression of the fortifications from the summit, and for the tremendous view
over coast, sea and mountains. From this vantage-point the size of the area
girdled by the double wall is at once apparent. Upon these walls four knights
and twenty-eight men-at-arms kept watch night and day, year in and year out.
Within them whole villages with their livestock retired for shelter, and a five
years' supply of provisions was comfortably housed. By nature fortified
perhaps more strongly than any of the great Crusader castles, Markab is posed
on the summit of a triangular spur which is joined to the main mountain ridge
by a narrow isthmus at its apex. The great works of the castle are piled up to
face this single danger-point, and the isthmus itself severed from the mountain
by a deep moat.

Sahyun is a couple of hours' drive from Markab, and the road inland from
Latakia follows the gracious valley of the Nahr el-Kebir. The landscape is unlike
the coast country. The river winds and sweeps in a wide gravel bed; watering
cattle come down to the shingle and stand knee-deep in the current. There are
solid-looking clumps of blackberry bushes, and here and there a few plane-
trees. On either side of the valley, coombs, whose streams are fringed with
dwarf poplars, run into the foot-hills. Up one of these coombs a road turns,
and climbs at last to the village of Haffeh. There a track – it is hardly more –
branches off to Sahyun and emerges in mountain country: boulders, evergreen
shrubs and tenacious dwarf oak. Sahyun does not stand out, like most of these
mountain fortresses, but grasps a rocky ridge, one among many such ridges.
After a precipitous descent into a ravine the track climbs out and up to within
a stone's throw of the castle walls. The traveller is immediately confronted by
the most remarkable feature of Sahyun: a tremendous channel, cut in solid
rock, separating the ridge on which the castle stands from the hillside behind.
This extraordinary divide, whose towering sides are haunted by that decorative
bird the black-and-scarlet wall-creeper, was spanned by a drawbridge carried
on an isolated pinnacle of rock whose hundred and ten feet still rise sheer from
the bed of the hewn channel.* There is no more astonishing testimony to the
energy and determination of the Franks. The tragedy, their tragedy, was that in
spite of such labour the castle fell to Saladin in 1188 after a bare seventy years'
occupation and was, unlike many other castles, never recaptured. Their loss
was in a sense our gain, for almost alone among the great castles Sahyun did

* Sahyun is a Frank remodelling of earlier Byzantine work; it is therefore probable that the great
rock divide was an enlargement of the artificial ditch which the Byzantines habitually set to guard
the approach to their fortresses.

not pass later into the hands of the military orders, those indefatigable building corporations which in the thirteenth century remodelled all they touched. Thus it remains a unique example of the earlier twelfth-century Crusader work and of the modifications which the Franks first introduced into the fortresses which they occupied. The long ridge on which the castle stands lies between two precipitous ravines and appears deceptively narrow. In fact Sahyun from the two-floored keep with its vaulted roofs, rising above the rock-channel, to the extreme end of the lower fortress covers a greater area than any other castle in Syria. So large is it that two hundred years after the Franks had left, a considerable town, the capital of the district, stood comfortably within the walls.

The approach to Krak announces something special. North of the Tripoli-Homs road the country grows steadily wilder, and it is in almost moorland landscape that the immense pile of Krak is first revealed on a spur of the foot-hills, jutting over a marshy snipe-frequented plain, the Boquée of the Crusaders. Fine at any time, it is perhaps most impressive in winter when clouds are hanging on the hills and the castle looms dark against the sky, and the marsh below is desolate.

T E Lawrence thought Krak 'perhaps the best preserved and most wholly admirable castle in the world'. One must agree. The solidity and the art which impress as the salient features of Crusader architecture are at Krak combined in supreme fashion. To stand on the top of the south-west tower gives the impression of being on a ship's bridge, and the kestrels, that wheel in the air above these Syrian castles, scream shrilly as gulls. Buffeted by the wind, the fortress rides above the extended landscape with the confidence and mastery of a ship. There is the same strength, together with the same beauty of design. As on a fine vessel, the precision of the scheme transcends the utilitarian and creates a work of art. The plan of the concentric walls, the disposition of the flanking towers, and the layout of the inner castle, are infinitely pleasing, but at the same time they are contrived with the exactitude and economy of a naval architect's blueprint. Yet the comparison between ship and castle ultimately fails. In its immense solidity and weight the fortress is pure mountain. And indeed the great slant wall that slopes outward beneath the south-west tower, a wall eighty feet thick, was known to the astonished Muslims as 'the Mountain'.

This creation stands, owing to the skill of its builders, time's clemency, and the faithful restoration of the French, much as it did when the Crusaders left over six hundred and fifty years ago. It is thus one of the few medieval castles that the amateur can not only 'feel', but understand. Indeed the perfection of its preservation makes Krak seem incongruously empty, and its silence out of place. These halls and passages, essentially functional architecture of the best

214

sort, should be filled with the knights and sergeants for whom they were designed; the babble of medieval French should reach one from the guard-room and the chanted Latin Mass from the twelfth-century chapel. For a hundred and fifty years without a break the Crusaders were within these walls, as many as two thousand men when the place was fully garrisoned. The Hospitallers received the castle from Raymond of Tripoli in 1142, and it was they who were responsible for remodelling it and creating the present fortress. Not long after the Order had taken over, Nur-ed-Din attempted the place and was roundly beaten under the walls. Saladin, twenty-five years later, marched on the castle, saw its strength and marched away again.

Inside the walls life continued from generation to generation, and with it continued the daily business and routine, the policy and administration, that the maintenance of an important feudal fief involved. Meetings and banquets took place in the thirteenth-century hall; great figures came and went. The King of Hungary was a visitor and left behind him, as a gift in perpetuity, the rents of many Hungarian acres. Geoffrey de Joinville died in the castle, who seemed to his brother knights the type of the true Crusader, and to Richard Cœur-de-Lion worthy, for his bravery, to quarter the arms of England with his own. He was perhaps buried in the chapel near the six Crusaders whose bodies were found some years ago. From their airy vaulted chamber in the south-west tower, the Wardens of the Castle looked down on it all and in due course succeeded one another. Their names, such as Hughes Revel, Armant de Montbrun, typify the French nature of this curious monastic community.

Elsewhere the Crusader tide began to ebb, at first slowly – the fall of Edessa as early as 1144 had been the initial sign – and then after the middle of the thirteenth century with catastrophic speed. One after another towns and castles fell: Jerusalem, the capital of the kingdom, had already gone in 1244 and Antioch fell in 1268. Soon only the coastal belt and a few strong points remained. The hinterland of Homs and Hama over which Krak had once exercised suzerainty became hostile territory, and the bastion castle, guarding the vital rift between the Lebanese and Alawi Mountains, became more and more isolated. Though the garrison could signal to the great keep-tower at Safita, whence a message might be flashed to the castle at Arima, and so to the coast,* the Saracens yearly ventured with greater impunity beneath the walls and communications grew more hazardous. No longer a bastion, Krak became a vast and lonely outpost. A letter written by the Grand Master of the Hospitallers in 1268 speaks of his financial difficulties now that most of the Kingdom of Jerusalem was in enemy hands, and, even more serious, of his reduced numbers. Whereas Krak alone had maintained a garrison of two

---

* The Crusaders had also learnt from the Muslims the use of carrier pigeons.

thousand at the beginning of the century, Krak and Markab at this date, he says, could muster only some three hundred knights between them. Three years after this letter, in 1271, the Sultan Beibars, that competent general who had started life as a slave in Damascus, brought up an army against the castle. Until Krak was taken there was no safe access to the sea. It was, as a Saracen chronicler maintained, 'a bone stuck in the very throat of the Muslims'. The castle, however, was still marvellously strong and the fighting monks who defended it, in spite of their depleted numbers, experienced and determined. Though the Saracens pierced both enceintes, they could not win the mountain-like wall and the south-west stronghold. The siege was costly and, among many others, the Sultan's squire fell in the assaults. It was at this point that Beibars devised an expedient which Christian contemporaries called treachery, but which was only one of those ruses that the morality of war approves. A letter, which the defenders took to be genuine, was conveyed into the castle. It purported to come from the Count of Tripoli and instructed the garrison to surrender. Thus after a century and a half Krak capitulated; and the knights, granted a safe-conduct provided they returned to Christendom, rode away to the coast, leaving behind them this architectural monument to their long occupation.

Before discussing various aspects of the Crusader castles, mention must be made of two fortresses of the Crusader period not primarily connected with the Crusaders: Sheizar and Masiaf. Both are accessible from Hama and, though they do not compare in size with the great castles that have been mentioned, their associations and their dramatic situation render them remarkable. Sheizar lies in the rolling plain that stretches far southward from Aleppo, having on one side the blue line of the Alawi Mountains and on the other the emptiness of the desert. It is a plain of mud villages, with conical beehive huts, where the men wear saffron robes, and the women dresses of red and blue. It is the plain where they rear the best horses in Syria, descended perhaps from the stock of the Seleucid cavalry whose stud farm was situated there, at Apamea. No vista but shows a man cantering on a horse with fine trappings; and no vista is without a bald trodden threshing floor for corn and barley, the sole wealth of the district. It is in this treeless rolling country that Sheizar stands on a bend of the Orontes River. As often in its course, the river is sunk below the level of the surrounding plain and the traveller looks down from steep escarpments to a winding cleft of green, where huge wooden water-wheels lift and parcel out the water to shady orchards and gardens. The castle stands on a long thin spur of rock whose shape acquired for it the name of the 'Cock's Comb'. Its importance lay not only in the strength of the position but in the fact that it controlled one of the major fords of the Orontes.

The ancients realized the value of the site and it is mentioned in the inscriptions of the Pharaoh Totmes III. Though fortified in very early times, the present castle dates mainly from the twelfth century when it was rebuilt after a disastrous earthquake. It is of Saracen workmanship and was one of the chief Arab fortresses. It thus affords a glimpse of what the people on the 'other side' were doing. The stronghold belonged to the princes of the Banou Munqid family, and it is closely associated with Usamah Ibn-Munqid, perhaps the most readable and entertaining of the chroniclers of the early crusading period. His memoirs not only reveal an exceptionally cultivated Muslim gentleman, but describe the chase, life in the castle, the expeditions against the nearest Frankish stronghold at Apamea, and the successful resistance which Sheizar put up on more than one occasion against the crusading armies. Today, though the entrance with its Arabic inscription and the keep to the south are still impressive, 'La Grand Césare', as the Franks called it, is in a sorry state. A stinking village squats among the ruins and emphasizes the disappearance of the arts of war and peace which were successfully cultivated at Sheizar in Usamah's lifetime. It is the old story, so often repeated in Syria, of six hundred years of haphazard neglect and destruction under Mameluke and Turkish rule. Only poverty remains.

The castle of Masiaf introduces the traveller to another factor of considerable importance in the history of the Crusades, the Assassins. They were members of a heretical Muslim sect, the Ismailis, followers of the Prophet's son-in-law Ali. Their beliefs at the time of the Crusades were also held by the Fatimid dynasty in Egypt, but fortunately for the Franks they quarrelled with their fellow heretics and adopted on the whole a policy of co-operation with the invaders. The name of Assassin they acquired from the inveterate habit, first contracted in Persia, of taking the drug *hashish*. The perfection to which they brought the use of assassination as a political weapon accounts for the sense given to the word 'assassin' in the West. The chief of the Ismailis in Syria in the middle of the twelfth century was Rashid el Din Sinan, known to the Franks as the 'Old Man of the Mountain', a title which they conferred without distinction upon his successors. Joinville describes with great picturesqueness the embassy and the gifts – including a giraffe in rock crystal and a set of chessmen – which the Old Man of the Mountain sent to St Louis. The value to the Franks of the Ismaili alliance lay largely in the fact that the latter were established in the Alawi Mountains and thus protected a sector of the Latin flank. To bulwark their mountain stronghold the Assassins built a series of castles, often on earlier Byzantine sites, of which Masiaf was, and remains, the most impressive. The castle itself is nothing – the Assassins at their best were mediocre military architects – but the position is admirable and the ruins stand on a bold rock, dramatically detached from the eastern flanks of the Alawi Mountains. The village and the surrounding country are attractive. The road from Hama winds up a small valley, whose stream, tributary to the Orontes, is overhung with azaleas; and the descendants of the Assassins, the Ismaili inhabitants of Masiaf, now turned industrious peasants, plant their lanes with pomegranate hedges. Castle and village were once a compact unit, enclosed in an encircling outer wall. Though much of the latter remains, the village ignores its stone boundary and spills pleasantly into orchards and gardens. The general air of cleanliness and well-being, of stone-built houses and mountain activity, provide a striking contrast to the rags of Sheizar, the dust and abjection of the villages of the plain.

To return to the great Crusader castles. The stranger visiting them will ask a number of teasing questions. Why were the castles built in such numbers and on such a scale? What architectural influences were predominant in their construction? How were such vast defensive works captured? And lastly, what was the society of which they were often focal points? The answers to these questions involve consideration of certain aspects of the crusading enterprise.

The twelfth and thirteenth centuries in Western Europe inaugurated the golden age of military architecture, but that in itself is not sufficient to account for the fever of Crusader building, and for the number and the vast size of their castles. The latter were brought into being by a serious problem non-existent in the West – lack of manpower. The huge Crusader army that crossed the Bosphorus had dwindled, it has been estimated, to one hundred thousand when it sat down before Antioch. On the subsequent march southward each fief and feudal principality, as it was created, drained off its complement of men, leaving an ever smaller force available for concentration against the enemy. Of the original army perhaps not more than one in twenty reached Jerusalem. When that city fell and many Crusaders sailed home, it is said that only five hundred knights remained in the southern province of the Latin kingdom. For every armed knight one must count ten, or perhaps more, foot soldiers; this amounts to a total force of something over five thousand men. But only the knights really counted. They were the decisive element in the battles of the time, and it was essentially the superiority of the mounted Crusader over the Muslim horseman that made possible the capture of the Holy Land. Time and again the charge of the Crusader knights, with their heavier armour and larger breed of charger, achieved victory against vastly greater forces. Though the disparity in numbers was exceptional, the defeat which Raymond of Toulouse, with three hundred French gentlemen, inflicted outside Tripoli on a Saracen army of many thousands exemplified the military superiority of the armed and mounted nobility who constituted the striking weapon of the Crusader force. During the twelfth and thirteenth centuries no new development in tactics challenged this superiority. Though the Muslim horse-bowmen with their skirmishing methods, light armour and small fast Arabs, could work havoc on a disorganized force, they never learnt to meet the weight of a Crusader charge.

When knights were numbered by scores every casualty counted. The reinforcements that trickled in, younger sons, adventurers, pilgrim-knights, were barely enough to make up losses. When the first properly organized reinforcement – the Second Crusade – came to hopeless grief in Asia Minor in the middle of the twelfth century, it was evident that the inadequate forces available in the Latin Kingdom could not maintain themselves without intensive fortification. Lack of manpower necessitated the Crusader castles. Even with a sizable army the country would, for two reasons, have been difficult to hold without strongpoints: first it was elongated in shape, a maritime belt stretching from the last spurs of the Taurus range to Akaba on the Red Sea; and second the Crusaders did not control the route running north and south on the desert fringe to the east of Palestine and the Lebanon. Along this route the Saracens could bring in reinforcements from Egypt, or from Baghdad via Aleppo, and thence they could continually harass the Latins. It has been said, and probably with truth, that the tactical error of not seizing Damascus, and with it this inner route, at the time of the First Crusade, in the end cost the Crusaders their kingdom. Had this hinterland been taken at once, when there was a force adequate for the enterprise, the Latin Kingdom would have had at its back three hundred miles of almost waterless desert, not easily traversed by any large armed force. In addition Egypt would have been isolated from Baghdad and the Islamic world effectively cut in two. The hinterland, however, was not taken. Later, when manpower failed, the great inland castles were built to watch it and to hold, as best they might, the long Crusader flank.

The major castles created their own problems. Their upkeep was so costly, and the charge of garrisoning so great, that the ordinary feudal lords found them difficult to maintain. Such men had other obligations whereas the supervision of these mammoth fortresses was a whole-time occupation. Further, life in the frontier castles was inevitably of a semi-monastic sort and over long periods could have little attraction for the secular knight and his retainers, who knew and appreciated the pleasures of the coast. Again, continual vigilance was necessary and continuity of command; on the death of a feudal owner, who might even leave a minor as heir, continuity was broken. These problems were solved by the creation of the military orders, the Hospitallers and Templars. The former had been established in Palestine in a civil capacity since before the Crusades, and had supervised the pilgrim traffic, supplying accommodation and, as their name suggests, creating hospitals for the sick. With the foundation of the Latin kingdom they acquired immensely increased importance. Forming themselves into a highly organized military-monastic order, responsible directly to the papacy, they acquired lands, wealth and power. The Knights Templar, an offshoot of the Hospitallers created in 1118, were a parallel organization taking their name from the Temple enclosure at Jerusalem, where their first quarters were situated.

These orders of armed monks, wearing on the surcoat that covered their mail respectively the white cross or the red, familiar from the illustrated history books of one's childhood, came to provide the backbone of resistance to the Saracens, and in due course acquired the charge of the great castles. This was a task for which they were eminently fitted. Their monastic vows suited them to the dour life, their direct responsibility to the papacy placed them above local feudal quarrels, and their character as undying corporations ensured continuity. They also possessed both the necessary wealth, acquired through vast endowments, and the necessary organization. The latter was strict. Each order was composed of three classes of men – knights; sergeants recruited from the bourgeoisie; and chaplain-clerks. Each order levied its own taxes, possessed its own diplomatic service, and ran its own marine. Such were the states within the state on which devolved the defence of the great castles. To the Hospitallers fell the monster fortresses of Krak, Markab and Banias; to the Templars, Tortosa, Safita, Chastel Rouge, Arima, and finally Beaufort. By 1166 there were only three castles in the kingdom of Jersualem which the military orders did not control.

The next question that arises is architectural. What conception of military architecture do these Crusader castles express, and what was the predominant architectural influence in their construction? The question is a specialized one, and angels tread the ground with circumspection. One theory, in extreme form, is that the Latins were initially naive in these matters, but that after seeing the Byzantine castles in Asia Minor, and as a result of prolonged contact with the Byzantines, they adopted the methods of fortification with which the Eastern Empire had been familiar since the time of Justinian; that they had in fact everything to learn and that the inspiration for their architecture came directly from Byzantium. Another theory, again expressed in extreme form, is that the inspiration of crusading architecture came directly from France and Italy. Neither of these extremes represents the truth, which probably lies somewhere between the two. Arab influence further complicates the problem, for Arab fortresses of Byzantine inspiration, such as Kasr el-Heir had gone up in Syria centuries prior to the Crusades, and Arabo-Byzantine contacts had resulted in the evolution of indigenous Arab fortification.

One thing is certain: if the Franks came in ignorance, they proved apt pupils and, whether exploiting their own knowledge or that of Byzance, they rapidly evolved a military architecture more formidable than anything that had been seen before.

Robin Fedden
From *Syria and Lebanon (1965)*

Arwad

Two hundred kilometres north of Sidon lay the island town of Arvad, northernmost of the Phoenician tetrarchy. Like Sidon it has character and atmosphere, though only vestiges of the Phoenicians remain. The town early acquired importance among the Phoenician kingdoms, and founded satellite towns on the mainland known as '*Daughters of Arvad*'. It even extended its rule for a time as far inland as Hama. When the Eighteenth Dynasty drew southern Phoenicia into the Egyptian orbit, Arvad retained its independence, but it lagged behind Tyre and Sidon in their heyday. Under the Seleucids, it again came to the fore, and, though only briefly independent, it continued to enjoy commercial importance until Roman times. It was then displaced by Antaradus, the modern Tartus.

It is from Tartus that you hire a felucca for the short crossing to Arvad, or Ruad as it has come to be called. Early in the morning there is often a misty haze on the water, distorting shapes, blurring the horizon and confounding sea and sky. At an indeterminate distance, the island of Arvad, catching the slanting sunlight, seems to float above the water. There is rarely a wind after dawn and the sea is smooth, heavy as blue oil. In spite of oars to help the flapping sail the boat hardly seems to advance. Though the mainland recedes, the unreal island with its shining quays, its suggestion of towers and palaces, floats away. The boatmen talk monotonously in an Arab patois. The stillness, the early sun and the ineffective splash of the oars, induce a drowsiness improper to the hour; in an imprecise world of haze, sun and water, following the elusive island, you nod in the stern. Looking up you find the island near. For no reason its flight has stopped, and with it the airy towers and palaces have disappeared. There awaits you simply a fishing town crowded on a little island eight hundred metres long.

However, as you soon discover, it is a fishing town of special charm and interest. The island was once a vast fortress encompassed with huge sea walls, and many of the houses on the water's edge are built into their ruins and give, by reason of the lighter stone of which they are constructed, an effect like an inlay. The façade of the town – an alternation of umber houses and darker ruins – stretches like a ribbon along the blue sea. In front, a mole protects anything up to thirty schooners at anchor. As your boat approaches, voices echo over the water, and with them the pleasant noise of hammers on timber. Ruad lives by the sea, and in the very streets they build the skeletons of schooners that enable them to run a coasting trade from Turkey to Egypt. Even the people are amphibious, and as you draw in, furling your sail, a shoal of naked brown bodies, boys and the little girls of the town, come sporting round your boat.

Along the harbour front, among the drying nets, the cafés throw out rush-work awnings in whose shade the local seafarers looking curiously unmarine in their baggy Turkish trousers, smoke their hookahs over coffee and talk of their trade. The active life of the place is on this harbour front and there are no proper streets in the warren that lies behind. The people are Sunnis, as you will guess seeing the veiled women creep down the alleys, and hopelessly poor. Wealth is in the hands of three or four families who own most of the schooners, exploit the fishermen and run the island in a degenerate feudal fashion. Yet the people retain pride and self-respect. It is a pride that history justifies, for these *Ruadis*, men of Ruad, work perhaps the oldest shipyards in the world. Few such tiny harbours played so great a role. Phoenician Arvad was, as we have seen, the centre of an important kingdom. Girdled with cyclopean walls, and deriving its water-supply from fresh springs that rise in the sea itself, it was an impregnable fortress and warehouse. In the harbour was fitted out the expedition which served with distinction against the Greeks at Salamis, and later when Alexander hellenized the coast the wealth of the merchants splendidly adorned the town. Over a thousand years later, Ruad was the last stronghold of the Latin Kingdom and held out, garrisoned by the Templars, for eleven years after Acre had fallen. Lastly – and their part in this adventure the *Ruadis* have not forgotten – the island was seized from the Turks in 1914 by a single French vessel and for four years remained an isolated Allied outpost on the Turkish flank, whence the *Ruadi* sailors smuggled supplies to the starving population on the mainland.

This history has left little to show. Atmosphere and the harbour must help imagination to eke out the past, together with the remains of the Phoenician walls, and oddly enough, a liquor shop which also does duty as tobacconist and chemist. The shop lies just off the harbour. The owner, who knows French, enquires curiously of the world, but his interests, as one soon finds out, are strictly subordinate to business. He is a merchant, and the chaffering Phoenician blood runs in his veins. After you have bought his great yellow sponges, fresh as the divers bring them from the sea, he produces a bag: odds and ends found in the ruins, blurred intaglios, and a few Phoenician coins. Coins stamped with the gods of Arvad: he lays them out on the palm of his hand, knowing you want them. He is informative, he talks discursively of old things; yet all the time he is testing your temper, silently bartering, probing for a price. When you finally buy, you have paid too much. How could it be otherwise? A man of Arvad handling Phoenician coin.

It was such counter-cunning that amassed the wealth to build the great sea walls. Hewn in megalithic blocks, their remains indicate how formidable the *enceinte* must once have been, and on the west at one point they still rise nearly forty feet sheer from the sea. The scale of the ruins leaves no doubt as to the importance of the place or the energy of the builders. Of later date, there is a Crusader castle, subsequently taken over and rebuilt, as was most of the town, by the Muslims. Over the gateway is the Lusignan coat of arms – the Lion and the Palm – adapted with malicious Saracen humour, or so the legend goes, by the addition of a chain firmly securing the royal beast to the palm over which he had presumed to rule. The Saracens were at liberty to record their victory, but the Muslim occupation meant the end of Ruad's history.

On the mainland facing their island, the people of Arvad founded one of their earliest settlements now known as Amrit and marked by a series of ruins scattered across a mile and a half of ground. It seems queer country to have chosen. Salty, barren land, where a sluggish river twists out to the sea, it is good only for light grazing, and breeds only malarial mosquitoes. It has, however, the charm of desolation and eerie grandeur in its strange ruins. There are three main things to see. First, as you come up the coast road, appears, some way to the left, a sombre mausoleum. A great black cube, raised in cyclopean blocks and called by the Arabs for some reason the Tower of the Snails, it stands today in a marshy pool. You approach it across barren undulating ground, the haunt of lizards, and covered with tall yellow-flowered thistles. In the evening the shepherd who pastures in the area leaves with his flock for an inland village, and as the sun sets and the crickets abruptly fall silent, the place is lonely. In the quiet you become aware of the sinister hum of mosquitoes. A pair of Kitlitz plovers, that probably breed somewhere near, run with mincing steps along the edge of the dark pool. They are the only life. No one knows who built the giant Phoenician cube or for whom its two funerary chambers were prepared, or when the pyramid which crowned it came crashing down, where it still lies, in the pool below. The city that surrounded it has gone, but the savage black structure gains by its isolation and, as the light weakens, dominates the wastes.

Harry Charles Lukach
From *The Fringe of the East (c. 1907)*

Hama

You see nothing of Hama until you are close upon it, for the reason that it is concealed in a declivity made by the beds of the Orontes, the new and the old.

Part of the town lies along the former, part in the latter; and the whole completely encircles, as with a moat, the *tell* which rises in the middle.

The usual Arabic name for the river Orontes is Al-'Urunt. In Hama, however, and its neighbourhood it is called El-'Asi, the Rebel; and three reasons are given why this invidious designation has been bestowed upon it. The first is that, unlike most rivers of Syria, it flows from the south to the north; the second, that in so doing, it abandoned the lands of Islam for those of Antioch, in the old time the country of the Infidels, the Greeks; the third, that it refuses to do as other rivers and freely water the meadows on its borders, but insists on being raised by water-wheels before it will consent to irrigate the fields.

If the latter is the true cause, then Hama owes much to its river's rebelliousness. For the water-wheels, the *na'uras*, are to Hama what her canals are to Venice, or its towers to San Gimignano; and to few places is it given to possess so charming a distinguishing feature. By day and by night the town is pervaded by the presence of the *na'ura*. All along the curving river side you see these high, narrow, graceful wheels, which attain, sometimes, a diameter of as much as sixty feet, slowly lifting the river water in their buckets and pouring it into lofty aqueducts; and where you cannot see them, you hear the beautiful noises which they make as they revolve. From the bridge by the serai no less than five are visible; and when, after dark, the citizens have returned to their houses and are preparing for sleep, they are lulled, in whatever part of Hama they may be, by the lovely discords of their drone. Each *na'ura* has its name: there is the Hamidîyeh, the Derwishîyeh, the Jisrîyeh, and so forth; and each, as it creaks lazily on its axis, sings its own particular song. Their music is mournful and deep, deep as the organ tones of a sixty-four-foot pipe, mournful as the wailing of the double-bass; and although they blend wonderfully well, the ear can pick out, after a little practice, the different parts of the great choir's everlasting chant. This is the tune of the Jisrîyeh wheel, the one by the *serai* bridge:

and this the reiterated groan of another, easily distinguishable in the general *mêlée* of sound by its persistent and plaintive melody:

Now booming, now moaning, now pleading, now despondent, as though they know well that theirs is the labour of Sisyphus, the *na'uras* accomplish their never-ending circuits, delightful to eye and ear. Long after I had left Hama, there came back to me at times, while at others I undoubtedly missed, their curiously haunting, curiously soothing, curiously sad refrain, imprisoned beneath no other roof than 'that inverted Bowl we call the Sky,' and marred by none of the imperfections which the best of human performers are not always able to avoid.

But Hama, even without its *na'uras*, would be an attractive town. While Homs is built of unrelieved black, Hama goes one better; black and white are its colours, basalt and limestone its materials. Either they lie in alternate layers, as in Siena and Orvieto, or else the black picks out patterns on the white, like no other place that I have seen. Not only dwelling-houses, but square towers and round minarets, of which there are in plenty, do honour to the treatment, which is seen at its best, perhaps, in the Great Mosque. Golden limestone and dull volcanic black, alternating effectively in the paving of the court and in the tower, throw into greater relief the dazzling whitewash of the mosque itself and the age-worn grey of the beautiful *qubbet* outside it. In the mosque and its accessories are many traces of their Byzantine origin. The large wooden *minbar*, or pulpit, is supported on Byzantine columns; other columns and capitals are embedded in the walls; others stand at random by the fountain of the court; on the most delicate of all is borne the *qubbet*. With a foreground such as the court affords, and the five-domed mosque in the background, you have as pretty a sight as you could wish to see. But if you care to cross the Orontes to the Derwishîyeh quarter, the quarter of the dervishes, you may see yet a prettier one. On a slight eminence above the right bank of the river, facing the *tell* now bare of all traces of its castle, is a plain little mosque, unadorned within save by a stone dado round three sides of the wall, engraved with texts from the Qoran. The fourth side is latticed and open to the river; and in the middle, dividing the lattice, is the pillar which gives to the place its name of the Serpent Mosque. This pillar is composed of four smaller pillars, each of which, again, is subdivided into four double strands, intertwined and interlacing, and more bewildering in their spirals than the snakes of Medusa's head. In the courtyard, by the small and crumbling minaret, is the tomb of the geographer-prince, 'Abu'l Fidâ, who reigned in Hama, as El-Melek el-Muayyad, from 1310 to 1331, and gave to his city, before it relapsed into a placid provincialism from which it has never issued since, one last epoch of distinction. And below, the Orontes flows swiftly by, growing wider as it approaches the centre of the town; but crossed on the left, where it is still narrow, by a quaint old bridge crowded with tumbling little booths and houses, for all the world like the Ponte Vecchio of an oriental Florence.

Ibn al Fakih, Istakhri, Mukaddasi and Idrisi
From *Palestine Under the Moslems*

Homs: Selected Passages

'Of the wonders of Hims,' says Ibn al Fakih, 'is an image which stands over the gate of the Jami' Mosque, facing the church. This is of white stone, and the upper part of the image is in the form of a man, the lower being in the form of a scorpion. If a scorpion stings a man, let him take clay and press it on the image, and then dissolve the clay in water and drink it. It will still the pain, and immediately he will recover. They say this image is a talisman specially made against scorpions.'

'Hims,' writes Istakhri, 'is the capital of the province of the same name. The city lies in a fertile plain; it enjoys an excellent climate, and its soil is one of the best in Syria. Its people are extremely handsome. There are neither scorpions nor snakes in Hims, and should one enter the place, it dies. Water, trees, and arable fields are seen everywhere, and most of the village lands are watered by the rains (not artificially irrigated). There is here a church, half of which is used as a Mosque, while the other half belongs to the Christians, and they have here their chapel and altar. This church of theirs is one of the largest in Syria. The Greeks have invaded this country during our own days (tenth century), and ruined many of its lands and villages. The desolation is gaining everywhere, since these incursions of the Infidels began, and though the people are seeking to return to their old homes, the Badawin Arabs eat up their crops, and plunder their land, time after time. Nearly all the streets and markets of Hims are flagged or paved with stones.'

Mukaddasi, writing in 985, says of Emessa:
'There is no larger city than this in Syria. There is a citadel high above the town, which you perceive from afar off. Most of the drinking-water is obtained from the rainfall, but there is also a river. When the Muslims conquered this place they seized the church, and turned the half of it into a Mosque. In the market-place near by is a cupola, on top of which is seen the figure of a man in brass, standing upon a fish, and the same is turned by the four winds. About this figure they relate many stories, but these are unworthy of credence. This town has suffered great misfortunes, and is indeed threatened with ruin. Its men are witless. The other towns of these parts are also falling into decay, though prices are moderate, and such of them as are on the coast are well provided with ramparts.

'There is at Hims a talisman – it is the wind-vane, and it serves against scorpions. For whosoever takes clay and presses it thereon, by Allah's permission, will obtain a cure for their sting; and the cure is effected by the impact of the figure on the vane, not by the clay alone.'

In 1099 Hims was captured by the Crusaders. Idrisi reports in 1154:
'Hims, the capital of the Province of the same name, is a fine town standing in a plain. It is populous, and much frequented by travellers who come here for its products and rarities of all kinds. Its markets are always open. The ways of the people are pleasant; living with them is easy, and their manners are agreeable. The women are beautiful, and are celebrated for their fine skins. The drinking water is brought to the city by an aqueduct from a village near Jusiyyah, about a day's march from the city in the direction of Damascus. The river Urunt (Orontes), called also Al Maklub, flows by the gate (of Hims), and there are gardens one after another along it, belonging to the city, with trees and many water channels. They bring the fruit from these gardens into the town. Since the beginning of Islam this has been of all cities that which has produced most grapes; but now these gardens are for the most part laid waste. The soil is excellent for the tilling and raising of crops; and the climate is more equable than that of any other town of Syria. There is here (in Hims) a talisman which prevents the entrance of any serpent or scorpion, and should one enter through the gate of the city it immediately dies. For on the summit of a high dome which is in the middle of the city, is an idol of brass in the figure of a man, riding, and it turns with every wind that blows. In the wall of the Dome is a stone on which is the figure of a scorpion, and when a man is stung or bitten, he lays on this stone some clay, and then puts the clay on the bite and immediately he becomes healed. All the streets and lanes of the city are paved with blocks of hard stone. The agriculture of the province is extremely productive, and the cultivated ground needs but very little rain or irrigation. There is a large Mosque here, it is one of the largest of all the cities of Syria.'

Translated by Guy le Strange

Richard Pococke
From *A Description of the East (1745)*

Maloula & Seynaida

There is a way which goes up the plain for about four leagues to the north, and then turns up the mountain to the north west; and at the end of three leagues there is a village called Malouca, built on the side of a steep high hill, over a narrow valley; opposite to it, on the side of the other hill, is the Greek convent of St Thecla; it is a large grott open to the south, in which they have built a small chapel; and at the east end of the grott there is another, in which the place is shewn where St Thecla suffered martyrdom; She was the disciple of St Paul, according to the

227

legends, and fled to this place from her infidel father; her picture is in the niche where, they say, her body lies. There is a Greek inscription on it, signifying, that she was the first martyr of her sex, and contemporary with the apostles. At one corner of the grott there is a basin, which receives a clear water that drops from the rock; and, they say, that it is miraculous both in its source and effects; on each side of the mountain, at the end of this vale, there is a narrow opening in the rock, by which there are two passages up to the top of the hill, a small rivulet runs through the northern one, which rises on the mountain. From this source a channel is cut into the side of the perpendicular rock, which, without doubt, was designed to carry the water to the convent, and to the higher parts of the town. Near the entrance into the other passage, between the mountain, there is a plentiful spring that flows out of a grott, to which there is a narrow passage; they say, it rises in five springs; and have some history concerning it, that relates to St Thecla's flying to it to hide herself; at which time, they say, a fountain rose there. On top of the mountain, between these two passages, is the convent of St Sergius; it is ill built and uninhabited, but there is a tolerable church belonging to it. In the perpendicular parts of the rock before mentioned, where there are several sepulchres for single bodies in a very particular manner; a semicircular niche being cut into the rock, and the bottom of it hollowed into a sort of a grave to receive a body; these are in several stories one over another. There seem also to be some grotts cut into the cliffs, that are now inaccessible; and on the top of the mountain, about the convent of St Sergius, there are a great number of fine square grottos cut out of the rock, in many of them there are broad solid seats, like sophas, cut out at the further end; they have also several niches in them, as if they were designed for domestic uses; others, which are level, and about six feet high, have holes cut in the rock round the side of the room at the ceiling, as if horses were to be tied to them. I saw one cut out very regularly with a well in it, about ten feet deep, which had channels to it from all parts of the grot; so that I concluded the use of it was to make wine; I found several cut in the same form in a rough manner, which are now actually used as wine vats. It is difficult to say what was the original use of these grots, which are cut all down the gentle descent of the mountain westward to a sort of a vale which is between two summits of the mountain; the situation does not seem proper for any city; and I should rather think it was formerly a town of stone-cutters, who might supply some neighbouring cities with this fine stone, and in cutting it might form these grots; and as I observed in relation to the grottos about Jerusalem, they were made so, as that the stone which they took out, might be of use for building; these grottos indeed might be inhabited both by the workers in stone, and by those people to whom the vineyards and lands belonged. In the town of Malouca there are two churches, one of the Greeks, the other of the Roman Greeks, there being several here of that communion: There is only one monk in the convent, who lives in a cell built below the grot. After the feast of Holy Cross, the Greeks from Damsacus come out to this convent, and to that of St Moses, some leagues to the north, and likewise to Sidonaia, and spend a fortnight or three weeks in a sort of religious revelling. Making an excursion to St Thecla from Sidonaia, we dined at Touaney, in a house appointed for the entertainment of strangers, there being four of them, who take it in their turns, the people of the village supplying them with provisions in an equal proportion. Here we saw the horses of a party of about forty Arabs, who were encamped not far off; they go about to take tribute of the villages under their protection, which may be about ten, and a man sent with any one by the Sheik of these villages, is a protection against them: These Arabs were of Arabia Felix, the Amadei being of Arabia Petraea: The Janizary seemed to be much afraid, talked often of the heat of the weather, and would not move until he knew they were gone, and which way they went. In the plain on the left, near the entrance into the vale towards St Thecla, there is a village called Einatirieh, which some years past was inhabited by Christians, who on a discontent turned Mahometans; some say, because the bishop refused to permit them to eat milk in Lent; and others, because he would not suffer an excommunicated body to be buried: To the right, further to the south, is Jobaidin. From St Thecla we went southward again in a plain between two chains of mountains; about two leagues from it, we passed by the ruined convent of St Joseph on the mountains to the west; and about four leagues from that convent, we arrived at a village called Marah, where there is a Greek parochial church of the Roman communion, and a Greek convent, which had in it only one lay brother, who lives there to entertain those who come to see a chapel, which is about two miles to the east, near the top of the mountain; it is built, as they say, at the grot of Elisha, where Elijah came to anoint him to be his successor, as he was commanded by God, when he ordered him to go towards the wilderness of Damascus; and on the outside of it there was a passage, which is now stopped up, that led to some other grots, the entrance to which I was also shewn. The Greeks pretend, that it is the place where the prophet was anointed, and that it is dangerous to go to it; which seems to be a piece of policy to hinder the Mahometans from taking possession of the place, and turning it into a mosque; it commands a fine view of the whole plain of Damascus, and of the city itself, and in that respect is a very delightful retirement.

From this place we went about a league to the west to Sydonaia, a village situated on the south part of a rocky hill, on top of which there is a famous Greek nunnery, founded by the emperor Justinian; who endowed it with lands that brought in a considerable revenue, for which they pay rent to the grand signor; he also gave the convent three hundred Georgian slaves for vassals; whose descendants are the people of the village, and are of the Roman Greek church: The convent has the appearance of a castle, with high walls round it; the buildings within are irregular; towards the bottom of the hill there is a building where strangers are lodged; the church remains according to the old model, though it has been ruined and repaired; it consists of five naves, divided by four rows of pillars, and has a portico before it. Behind the high altar they have what they call a miraculous picture of the virgin Mary, which, they say, was painted by St Luke, but it is not to be seen. The convent is governed by an abbess, whose office continues during life; she is put in by the patriarch, and nominates the nuns who are about twenty in number; these nunneries are more like hospitals than convents, the members of them being mostly old women, and are employed in working, especially in the managing of silk worms; and the abbess shewed me her hands, and observed to me, that they were callous with work; she eat with us both above in the convent, and below in the apartment for strangers; the women seldom take the vow in less than seven years, and often remain many years at liberty; they may see and converse with men, and go any where even to distant places with leave. A great part of the revenue of the convent arises from their vineyards, which produce an excellent strong red wine: They have two chaplains to the convent, one is a monk, who lives in the convent, the other is married, and resides in the town. Near the town there is a small building called the convent of St George, a Roman Greek priest belongs to it, who lives in the town; and south of it is the ruined convent of St Christopher, to which there is a good church; and there are seven or eight more ruined churches and chapels here. Those of St John, St Saba, and St Barabara, are on the north side, have three naves, with an altar at the end of each after the Syrian style; and I saw in them several Doric capitals, and remains of fresco paintings; near them is the chapel of the transfiguration; and in two little grots, on the side of the hill, are altars to St Thecla and St Eleazer: To the east are the small chapels of St Sergius and St Christopher, and likewise an entire chapel of St Peter and St Paul, which appears to be a building of great antiquity; it is a very solid work, and is thirty-two feet six inches square; there is an ascent all round on the outside of the three steps; the cornish, door case, and a sort of a basement above the steps, are proofs that the architecture is antient, it may be, before Christ; within, it is in form of a Greek cross, and there is a stair case to the top of it. There is a Roman Greek church here, called St Sophia, in which are two rows of slender pillars with Corinthian capitals, which seem to have belonged to some antient building on that spot; adjoining to it there is a long chapel, now in ruins, dedicated to St Elias, in which there are remains of several fresco paintings. On the high mountain to the north was the convent of St Thomas; the church, which is entire, very much resembles in its architecture the beautiful church of Abel, but is rather plainer; the convent, which was built of large hewn stone, is entirely destroyed: There are several spacious grots near it, particularly an extraordinary one, called the grot of the council; and from the manner of it one may conjecture, that it might have served as a chapter-house, and also as a library for their churchbooks, and other manuscripts; it is fifty-five feet long, twenty broad, and ten high; there are two seats and a shelf round the grotto, and four square pillars in the room; there is likewise an apartment at the further end, and on each side; and all is cut out of the rock. About two hours to the north, on the very highest summit of the mountains, is the convent of St Serphent (Sergius) the way to it is somewhat difficult and dangerous; they say the church is of the same kind of building as that of St Thomas; the convent is inhabited only by one monk. These two convents, as well as the nunnery, are said to have been built by Justinian. On the north side of the hill, under the convent of Sidonaia, there is a sepulchral grot about twenty-two feet square; over the front of it there are three niches with semicircular tops, and a scollop-shell cut in the arch; the cornishes of them are supported by two round Corinthian pillars; in each of the niches are two statues of a man and woman in alto-relievo, the heads of which are broke off; the drapery of them is very fine; those on the right seemed to be women, and the other to be men; the drapery of the former coming down to the foot; but the latter only within eight inches of it; under each of them there is an imperfect Greek inscription containing the name of the man and woman.

Peter McDonald
Mar Sarkis

I sampled the priest's home-brew
and his tapes of the Lord's prayer
recited in strong Aramaic
(the original, for all I knew)
before trying out the stairs
cut in rock, and the tiny door

so low that I had to stoop
into candle- and mosaic-
light, then stop
for twenty minutes, half an hour,
in front of Bacchus and Sergius;
there on the stone floor,

watched by those two imperious
big-eyed, mounted soldiers
whose haloes had worn through,
I said words like a foreigner:
I bent double in grief
and prayed for your life.

VII: The Haroun

ARMADUKE PICKTHALL (1875-1936) is best remembered for his English version of the Qur'an; also he also wrote a number of novels, several of them deplorable, and a couple of which stand as the very best to have been directly influenced by the Middle East. While E M Forster gives Pickthall credit where credit is due, describing him as 'the only contemporary English novelist who understands the Nearer East', he goes on to suggest that ultimately the encounter may have been a failure and that he 'abandons his Salute to the Orient before it has been completed.' A devout Anglican for half of his life, Pickthall for the second half of his life was a devout Muslim and served as acting imam at the London mosque. *Saïd the Fisherman*, his best novel, contains a vivid description of the massacre of the Christians in Damascus in 1860, written, one suspects, with a convert's enthusiasm bordering on glee. *Tigers* is taken from *Oriental Encounters, Palestine and Syria* (1894-5-6) and while there is no certainty that the piece is set in the Djebel Druse the scene it describes is suggestive of that landscape.

The poem that follows is, in part, a response to Pickthall's piece. It also has its roots in a conversation I had with my friend Subhi in Damascus, who informs me that in Arabic there are sixty-seven words for 'lion'; I assume, perhaps wrongly, that there must be almost as many for 'tiger'.

Barnaby Rogerson, as well as being a travel writer specialising mostly on North Africa, published his biography of the Prophet Muhammad in 2003 (Little, Brown) and, most recently, from the same publisher, *The Heirs of the Prophet Muhammad*. Among the many books he has edited is *Marrakesh* (Eland, 2006). His take on the archaeological wonder that is Bosra is to divide it into the corporeal and the imagined, both of which has its own historical name and neither of which is the less true.

Dame Freya Stark (1893-1993) was one of the greatest twentieth-century travellers. She may not accept Bosra was the scene of the great event that Barnaby Rogerson describes, although, in truth, his belief is to be preferred over her doubt, but she paints a vivid enough picture of what she sees. There is insufficient space here to list her many achievements and publications but her early literary successes were such that 'Although short and plain in appearance, Stark now had the resources to indulge a taste for *haute couture* and flamboyant hats', according to her entry in the *Dictionary of National Biography*, authored by Peter H Hansen.

Marmaduke Pickthall
From *Oriental Encounters (c.1895)*

Tigers

The fellahin who came to gossip in the winter evenings round our lamp and stove assured us there were tigers in the neighbouring mountain. We, of course, did not accept the statement literally, but our English friend possessed the killing instinct, and held that any feline creatures which could masquerade in popular report as tigers would afford him better sport than he had yet enjoyed in Syria. So when the settled weather came we went to look for them.

For my part I take pleasure in long expeditions with a gun, though nothing in the way of slaughter come of them. My lack of keenness at the proper moment has been the scorn and the despair of native guides and hunters. Once, in Egypt, at the inundation of the Nile, I had been rowed for miles by eager men, and had lain out an hour upon an islet among reeds, only to forget to fire when my adherents whispered as the duck flew over, because the sun was rising and the desert hills were blushing like the rose against a starry sky. I had chased a solitary partridge a whole day among the rocks of En-gedi without the slightest prospect of success; and in the Jordan valley I had endured great hardships in pursuit of wild boar without seeing one. It was the lurking in wild places at unusual hours which pleased me, not the matching of my strength and skill against the might of beasts. I have always been averse to every sort of competition. This I explain that all may know that, though I sallied forth with glee in search of savage creatures, it was not to kill them.

We set out from our village on a fine spring morning, attended by Rashid, my servant, and a famous hunter of the district named Muhammad, also two mules, which carried all things necessary for our camping out, and were in charge of my friend's cook, Amin by name. We rode into the mountains, making for the central range of barren heights, which had the hue and something of the contour of a lion's back. At length we reached a village at the foot of this commanding range, and asked for tigers. We were told that they were farther on. A man came with us to a point of vantage whence he was able to point out the very place – a crag in the far distance floating in a haze of heat. After riding for a day and a half we came right under it, and at a village near its base renewed inquiry. 'Oh,' we were told, 'the tigers are much farther on. You see that eminence?' Again a mountain afar off was indicated. At the next village we encamped, for night drew near. The people came out to inspect us, and we asked them for the tigers.

'Alas!' they cried. 'It is not here that you must seek them. By Allah, you are going in the wrong direction. Behold that distant peak!'

And they pointed to the place from which we had originally started.

Our English friend was much annoyed, Rashid and the shikari and the cook laughed heartily. No one, however, was for going back. Upon the following day our friend destroyed a jackal and two conies, which consoled him somewhat in the dearth of tigers, and we rode forward resolutely, asking our question at each village as we went along. Everywhere we were assured that there were really tigers in the mountain, and from some of the villages young sportsmen who owned guns insisted upon joining our excursion, which showed that they themselves believed such game existed. But their adherence, though it gave us hope, was tiresome, for they smoked our cigarettes and ate our food.

At last, towards sunset on the seventh evening of our expedition, we saw a wretched-looking village on the heights with no trees near it, and only meagre strips of cultivation on little terraces, like ledges, of the slope below.

Our friend had just been telling me that he was weary of this wild-goose chase, with all the rascals upon earth adhering to us. He did not now believe that there were tigers in the mountain, nor did I. And we had quite agreed to start for home upon the morrow, when the people of that miserable village galloped down to greet us with delighted shouts, as if they had been waiting for us all their lives.

'What is your will?' inquired the elders of the place, obsequiously.

'Tigers,' was our reply. 'Say, O old man, are there any tigers in your neighbourhood?'

The old man flung up both his hands to heaven, and his face became transfigured as in ecstasy. He shouted: 'Is it tigers you desire? This, then, is the place where you will dwell content. Tigers? I should think so! Tigers everywhere!'

The elders pointed confidently to the heights, and men and women – even children – told us: 'Aye, by Allah! Hundreds – thousands of them; not just one or two. As many as the most capacious man could possibly devour in forty years.'

'It looks as if we'd happened right at last,' our friend said, smiling for the first time in three days.

We pitched our tent upon the village threshing-floor, the only flat place, except roofs of houses, within sight. The village elders dined with us, and stayed till nearly midnight, telling us about the tigers and the way to catch them. Some of the stories they related were incredible, but not much more so than is usual in that kind of narrative. It seemed unnecessary for one old man to warn us gravely on no account to take them by their tails.

'For snakes it is the proper way,' he said sagaciously, 'since snakes can only double half their length. But tigers double their whole length, and they object to it. To every creature its own proper treatment.'

But there was no doubt of the sincerity of our instructors, nor of their eagerness to be of use to us in any way. Next morning, when we started out, the headman came with us some distance, on purpose to instruct the guide he had assigned to us, a stupid-looking youth, who seemed afraid. He told him: 'Try first over there among the boulders, and when you have exhausted that resort, go down to the ravine, and thence beat upwards to the mountain-top. Please God, your Honours will return with half a hundred of those tigers which devour our crops.'

Thus sped with hope, we set out in good spirits, expecting not a bag of fifty tigers, to speak truly, but the final settlement of a dispute which had long raged among us, as to what those famous tigers really were. Rashid would have it they were leopards, I said lynxes, and our English friend, in moments of depression, thought of polecats. But, though we scoured the mountain all that day, advancing with the utmost caution and in open order, as our guide enjoined, we saw no creature of the feline tribe. Lizards, basking motionless upon the rocks, slid off like lightning when aware of our approach. Two splendid eagles from an eyrie on the crags above hovered and wheeled, observing us, their shadows like two moving spots of ink upon the mountain-side. A drowsy owl was put up from a cave, and one of our adherents swore he heard a partridge calling. No other living creature larger than a beetle did we come across that day.

Returning to the camp at evening, out of temper, we were met by all the village, headed by the sheykh, who loudly hoped that we had had good sport, and brought home many tigers to provide a feast. When he heard that we had not so much as seen a single one he fell upon the luckless youth who had been told off to conduct us, and would have slain him, I believe, had we not intervened.

'Didst seek in all the haunts whereof I told thee? Well I know thou didst not, since they saw no tiger! Behold our faces blackened through thy sloth and folly, O abandoned beast!'

Restrained by force by two of our adherents, the sheykh spat venomously at the weeping guide, who swore by Allah that he had obeyed instructions to the letter.

Our English friend was much too angry to talk Arabic. He bade me tell the sheykh he was a liar, and that the country was as bare of tigers as his soul of truth. Some of our fellah adherents seconded my speech. The sheykh appeared amazed and greatly horrified.

'There are tigers,' he assured us, 'naturally! All that you desire.'

'Then go and find them for us!' said our friend, vindictively.

'Upon my head,' replied the complaisant old man, laying his right hand on his turban reverently. 'To hear is to obey.'

We regarded this reply as mere politeness, the affair as ended. What was our surprise next morning to see the sheykh and all the able men, accompanied by many children, set off up the mountain armed with staves and scimitars, and all the antique armament the village boasted! It had been our purpose to depart that day, but we remained to watch the outcome of that wondrous hunting.

The villagers spread out and 'beat' the mountain. All day long we heard their shouts far off among the upper heights. If any tiger had been there they must assuredly have roused him. But they returned at evening empty-handed, and as truly crestfallen as if they had indeed expected to bring home a bag of fifty tigers. One man presented me with a dead owl – the same, I think, which we had startled on the day before, as if to show that their display had not been quite in vain.

'No tigers!' sighed the sheykh, as though his heart were broken. 'What can have caused them all to go away? Unhappy day!' A lamentable wail went up from the whole crowd. 'A grievous disappointment, but the world is thus. But,' he added, with a sudden brightening, 'if your Honours will but condescend to stay a week or two, no doubt they will return.'

Marius Kociejowski
Tiger Music

'You see that eminence?
You shall have your heart's fill of them there.'
The village elder, almost blind, pointed to a crag floating
in distant haze.

Thus sped with hope,
Our guns cocked, although it never was our purpose to kill,
we went looking for tigers.

If what the *fellahin* said was true,
if there was nothing they could not, in their language,
describe,
We met not a soul who knew all the words, the more than
fifty or so,
That speak the many shades of tigerness between one
which dozes
And another that lunges,
the different music they make.

All day we watched for movement in the stone.
We saw lizards which at our approach slid off like lightning
    into crevices.
A couple of eagles from an eyrie
                        on the crag above
Wheeled and hovered, their shadows like two
Spots of ink moving upon the mountain-side.
We watched for tigers but saw none, although we did see
A gazelle, its gashed throat jewelled with flies.
Whiteness pooling his eyes, the village elder
                  was confused or so he appeared.
'What could have made them go away?' he asked. 'Once,
    I saw tigers everywhere.'

               All night we fought among ourselves.
One man said leopards dwelled here, while another lynxes.
Anything but tigers, such was the consensus of all but one.
The old boy stuck to his guns, of course, warned us
Of the dangers that come of grabbing tigers by the tail.
'A snake doubles back upon half its length,' he said,
    'whereas a tiger goes it whole.'
Our dragoman, scoffing at him, said this was
A country as bare of tigers as his soul of truth.
'So why, then,' the other replied, 'if indeed there are none,
Should our language have fifty or more words for the many
    moods they strike?'
                  We drank our bitter coffee,
And discussing what provisions we should take,
Said tomorrow perhaps would see the settlement of our
    dispute,
As to what those famous tigers really were.

Barnaby Rogerson
Busra, Bostra and Bosra (2006)

I know a woman who offers up her necklace of stories, a string of ancient stones mixed with worn glass trading beads, to her children. I have watched them finger the different colours and feel the shapes that have come warmed from their mother's neck, before carefully choosing one bead, which then unleashes its own tale. I have also heard of another story-teller who used to carry an old purse filled with beach-pebbles. She would dip into this and feel her way around before deciding which story, out of her great stock of tales, was to be told. The listeners were forbidden to touch the purse and were seldom trusted with the sight of so much as a single stone. The dramatic nature of these two story-tellers, with their tactile, silent introductions, has never failed to awaken my admiration while the symbolism of two different story-telling traditions allows me to keep my memories of Busra, Bostra and Bosra together and apart.

It was under the compulsion of a great story that I found myself travelling to Busra. I have imagined Busra for years, for it is an essential and mysterious part of the life of the Prophet. Muhammad worked on the caravans throughout his manhood. Indeed it appears that a good part of his childhood was spent in an apprenticeship on these routes, criss-crossing their way through the awful wildernesses of ancient Arabia. Muhammad was trained in these duties and skills by his paternal uncle Abu Talib who had sole charge of the boy, for by the age of eight Muhammad had been thrice orphaned. His father Abdullah died before he was born, his mother Amina died before his eyes on the ten-day desert journey from Mecca to Medina when he was but six years old, and then his next of kin, his kindly old grandfather Abdul Muttallib, died just two years later.

It was in the company of his uncle Abu Talib that Muhammad travelled with the trading caravans radiating out from Mecca: to the harbours along the Red Sea, south to the highlands of the Yemen and north up the forty-day road that led to the cities of Syria and the ports of Palestine.

It was on one such Syrian-bound journey that the caravan reached Busra. Here dwelled an ancient Christian monk named Bahira, a great scholar and a recluse, who came out of his hermit's cell and invited the whole caravan of Meccan merchants to dinner. The cell that Bahira occupied had always been inhabited by monks who had passed down holy books and knowledge to each other from generation to generation. While meditating in his cell Bahira had experienced a vision of this Meccan caravan in which the forces of nature, from the clouds to a passing thorn tree, had bowed down in honour of the presence of a holy man hidden somewhere amongst the veiled camel-riding merchants.

The men of Mecca were not a little surprised, for they had often passed this way and the old monk had never proved himself the slightest bit friendly before. They asked the old monk, what has happened to you today that you should be so friendly? Bahira replied that, 'You are right in what you say, but you are now my guests and I wish to honour you and give you food so that you may eat.' With this gnomic reply, the men of Mecca had to be content, though they were delighted to accept his unexpected hospitality. They corralled the pack animals under a tree, hobbled the riding camels and left the youngest of their number to keep watch over the piles of baggage.

Bahira for his part, greeted each and every one of his guests with great attention, but he could not find anything the least bit inspiring or unusual about this collection of Bedouin traders. Without revealing his disappointment, Bahira asked one of the elders if they had not, by chance, left someone behind. This man of Mecca immediately stood up and chastised himself for his rudeness at leaving young Muhammad behind, and went back to the pile of baggage, embraced the lonely boy and led him to join the circle of men who were happily filling themselves on Bahira's hospitality. Bahira waited until they had all eaten their fill and then began to carefully question the young Muhammad about his dreams, his daily habits and thoughts. Later, when the opportunity presented itself, Bahira looked at the back of this young man from Mecca and saw a mark between his shoulders, which the old monk knew was the seal of prophecy in the very place that he had seen it described in some old books of his.

When the caravan was about to depart, Bahira took Abu Talib aside and told him to keep a special watch over Muhammad, 'for if others see and get to know about him what I know, they will do him evil for a great future lies before this nephew of yours.'

I love this tale for many things; for the way it honours the humble apprentice before all others, for the way it hints at secret prophecies known only to cell-dwelling hermit-monks, for the way it hints that Muhammad learned many things on his journeys across ancient Arabia as a young man, but most especially for the way it places the young Muhammad as a happy guest in the company of a Christian sage. In this tale, the monotheistic faiths of the ancient world seem to touch and acknowledge each other, in the same way that the infant Jesus is recognized by a wise old seer of the Jewish temple who greets him with the words of the Magnificat. It is also a tale set in a very intimate landscape, a place where there is a tree beneath which to pile up the baggage, a monk's cell known to have been occupied for centuries by learned ascetics and a sense of a wide and visible horizon. For years I had pictured Busra as a tiny oasis, a small watering station on the caravan trail, empty apart from a lone desert-dwelling hermit who watched over his secrets and his small, walled garden shaded by a dozen palm trees. This illusion was helped by the many wonderful variants in the westernised spelling of the Arabic language, and so I had never made the connection between Busra, the intimate little oasis of my imagination and the well-known ruins of Bostra.

Bostra is a brooding, magnificent site. Not beautiful, for the landscape is too flat and the building stone too dark, harsh and volcanic to fit into any of our patterns of antique elegance. It is vast and still partially inhabited by villagers who use its historic mosques while excavations continue to unearth an extraordinary heritage of impressive domestic buildings. The place that summons it all up, in scale and power, is the superbly preserved Roman theatre, wrapped up in a further layer of dense stone – to become a forbidding medieval fortress.

It very soon becomes clear that Bostra was no way-station of the caravan trail but the great central urban metropolis of late-Roman and Byzantine Syria. It was protected by a great circuit of black city walls which abutted a barracks known to have housed an entire legion. Well policed Roman roads run off in every direction from Bostra, towards the other great cities of the region: Damascus, Palmyra, Petra, Gaza, Aqaba and Antioch, for Bostra was the administrative spider in control of a rich and varied province. By the time the young Muhammad passed through the city in the 570s or 580s, Bostra had been ruling the region for five hundred years, the lineal heir to both the Nabatean and Palmyrene cultures of Arabia.

The archbishop of Bostra ruled over a diocese with thirty-three junior bishops, not to mention the schismatic representatives of the vigorous Jacobite and Nestorian churches whose missionaries were working amongst nations that had never been ruled by Rome. The domed cathedral of Bostra is one of the lost masterpieces of antiquity, and although it only survives at foundation level, there is enough on the ground with which to build castles in the air. It must have been one of the most impressive and revolutionary buildings of the ancient world, the inspiration for both Justinian's St Sergius and St Bacchus and the Ayia Sophia in Constantinople, not to mention the Dome of the Rock in Jerusalem. It was raised in 512 and dedicated by Julianos, Archbishop of Bostra, in honour of the Christian martyrs of Arabia: Sergius, Bacchus and Leontius. Its vast high dome was punctured by fifty windows and yet a bigger, older cathedral has just been discovered nearby that connects with a vast administrative courtyard-palace. The longer you stay looking at Bostra the bigger and more architecturally impressive it grows.

It was only when the local guides (all equipped with impressive but bogus bunches of keys which they jangle like a curator) pointed out to me the Basilica of Bahira that I made the connection. Bursa, Bostra and Bosra are *all* the same, Bosra being the Arabic name for Latin Bostra. And what a disappointment that the church should be so empty of any sign of devotion. I don't quite know what I was expecting, but I suppose I was at least half hoping for a small domed chamber thrown over a blackened cave dense with the smoke of centuries of devotion – like Saydnaya with its hidden icon of the Virgin - but with a lively inter-faith conference hall attached. The Basilica of Bahira does not flatter any belief system. It is impossible to place a lone scholar hermit in this massive stone barn. If anything this sturdily built hall from the fourth century with its gallery of high windows, is filled with the spirit of centuries of hard fact-finding labours by Bostra's civic clerks and taxation officials. I looked elsewhere of course, and found places of genuine spirit and delight: archways, underground shaded-shopping vaults, baths complexes, lovely street markets and vast irrigation tanks, austere minarets not to mention the august, columned interior of Omar's mosque – a noble hall whose doors open both into the world of antiquity and medieval Islam. At dusk, filled with shadows and the call to prayer, the small ancient mosques of al Naka and al Khidr came closest to my hidden expectations for Busra. But I have to confess that the impressive ruins of Bostra were impossible to square with my understanding of the story of Muhammad and Bahira.

Thinking later about my disappointment, I promised myself that I would come back and look again for Bahira's cave on the far edges of this impressive power-house city of late antiquity. I realised that the dusty caravans from Mecca would never have penetrated the walls of the metropolis. They would have stayed out amongst the stables, orchards and vegetable gardens that were scattered like so many suburbs around the edge of greater Bostra. However I also realised the attraction of the cumulative evidence of the beauty of the city, the well-ordered magnificence of its great avenues and entrance arches, not to mention its skyline of domed cathedrals, its court of clerks to the governor, its staff officers humming around the commander of the legion and the junior bishops bobbing around the archbishop. A simple spiritual tale had been overshadowed by my instinctive delight for the physical evidence of the gorgeousness of late-imperial architecture and my pleasure in the smooth running of a sophisticated Byzantine city.

There are two sorts of history. One history analyses power, and the endless story of its rewards and how it is lost and won. The other story tells the history of human spirituality. They can occupy the same time but will record completely different landscapes. While one records a brilliant city on the edge of the desert, glittering with domed buildings and triumphal arches, the other focuses on the memory of an evening meal, a gift of hospitality and the generosity of an old man blessing a neglected apprentice.

Freya Stark
From *Letters from Syria*

To her Mother   Transjordania, May 19th, 1928

Darling B,

Our only experience of a night among the Moslems was rather awful. We never thought there were so many varieties of biting things, and longed for the morning; and we slept in the harem with two ladies whose mattress was close to ours, so that we could not fling Keating's about too openly.

Bosra is a wonderful old town; a Roman provincial capital with the straight road running to its ancient gate and ruins on either hand. There are great parts of it uninhabited on either side of the old pavement. The city gate is ruined, but on the way down to it one goes by a perfect arch still standing, lovely in proportion. That also is cracked right across. A little off the main road is the Christian church, which became a mosque: we sat among the columns, their marble yellow and rose-coloured in the evening light, and the make of the old stone roof shewing very clearly. The little tower was also roofed with stone. None of this building is younger than the fifth century.

We found another little gem of a mosque, also a converted church it must have been. The stone slabs of its doors are intact and the stone trellis windows. An old tree and temple columns stand beside it, and a square stone tower; and here Muhammed, in his youthful travelling, is said to have first learnt about Christianity from an old monk in Bosra – a doubtful story.

But the castle is the best of all. It is a mass of huge square buildings with a fosse round, and a bridge, and the Saracens built it round the Roman theatre. We have become familiar with garrisons now. We never hesitated to go up and say that we wished to look over their citadel, which is armed to the teeth, like Salhad. The two officers we applied to themselves conducted us, after calling an Algerian trooper with a lamp. The whole centre of the theatre is filled in and three great halls built in it; one above the other, the lowest not yet explored and none of them lighted (except perhaps the top one). We climbed down by the theatre steps and along the subterranean passages which once ran round the tiers of seats. Here and there some marble columns gleam under the lamp, walled in the rough stone. The old porticoes were turned by the Arabs to defence. In the heart of the place is a dark damp mosque built by Saladin, with an inscription; and there are Arabic lines running round the outer walls too. The Algerians look well with their baggy light uniforms and turbaned heads under the old walls and arches. We saw them riding through the streets of the town, a splash of colour, on high medieval saddles, with the black-bearded Moslems scowling at them from their doors.

As we came away I stopped to look at a stone built into the wall of a house. It gave the name of the third legion. The French Intelligence officer beside me told me that this was the Gallic Legion. He said it as if the French had been settled here ever since. A terribly dangerous thing is history.

They have a curious ornament over many of the Bosra gateways: a kind of small parapet built out of mud and straw, and little flags stuck into it, ostrich feathers and long streamers of any old stuff. All I could discover about them is that they are put up when a boy is born in the house.

We got home quite late and sat down to wait for supper. It is the stranger host's duty to put himself about for his guests, and our twelve days have taught us to take this for granted. But after the respect and friendliness of the Druses, we felt our female inferiority rather acutely among the Moslems, for we sat with the women on the far side of the coffee hearth and the men came dropping in, heavily bearded and fierce to look at, and never spoke to us; and when the coffee was ready they all drank first, and then sent only the little son of the house in his long blue gown and bare feet to carry us the cups. The women, dressed in blue like the Bedouins or the Christians of Leja, sat with us unveiled.

There was a sensation, however, before we reached the coffee stage. The door was flung open and two native soldiers strode in. All sprang to their feet except Venetia and I. They came up and asked us to spend the evening with the Commandant in the fortress. The Arabs, all standing in a circle, waited for our reply. It was already late, and it meant going right across the dark town with two rough-looking soldiers, and insulting our host by leaving his coffee untasted; and all to see uninteresting Frenchmen. We excused ourselves politely. The soldiers looked with stupefaction. You might have heard a pin drop in the room. After a prodigious pause, one of them exclaimed: 'You are women; and tired: the Commandant will pardon you'; then they turned on their heels and left.

Silence followed. The assembly settled back to continue the interrupted evening; but we felt it was a moral victory, and that our audience was pleased. Presently the lady of the house murmured that we were quite right not to 'venture at night among the French soldiers,' which view of the question had not struck us. As no British ladies are remembered to have stayed here before, I hope we may have established a national reputation for propriety!

We were taken to sleep in the harem. The Sheikh's young wife was having her hands tattooed; they were caked over with wet earth and tied up in rags, and she and her friend lay on a mattress close beside us. The mother-in-law locked us in with a big key which she afterwards threw in through the window. Half-way through the night we could bear it no longer, and thought we would risk the wickedness of the Moslems rather than suffocation. We consulted with the ladies, and unlocked the door (with some trepidation because of mother-in-law): we flung it wide and were able to breathe.

This morning our host gave us the most friendly send-off. Our humiliation was due to our sex and not personal. He told us that the greatest pleasure we could ever give him was to come and stay again, and pressed my hand over and over: and I feel sure it is because of what we said to the soldiers. We sat for a while watching the mounted troops out in the open manœuvring: wild galloping squares and circles, the dust flying, the sun catching the red and white as they turned.

There is a railway line at Bosra, and we said good-bye to Najm at the station; to Najm and 'Arif and our three little donkeys. A sad parting. Najm will travel slowly home by Damascus.

Your own FREYA.

VII: Travellers, Old and New

TWO TRAVELLERS, one early seventeenth-century and the other twentieth-century, are focussed upon here. Scholar and teacher, Gerald MacLean, travels in the footsteps of William Biddulph, a name that not often arises. MacLean is a member of The Great Anatolian Ride, a group of Ottoman historians, botanists and equestrian experts planning to ride from Istanbul to the Iranian border along routes documented by early travellers; they will be in search of rare Anatolian horse breeds. Among his publications is *The Rise of Oriental Travel: English Visitors to the Ottoman Empire, 1580-1720* (Macmillan).

Philippa Scott's memoir of Robert Tewdwr Moss, author of *Cleopatra's Wedding Present*, is the first such piece of its kind and serves to redress some of the errors and magnifications raised by the popular image. There could not be a happier conjunction of names because not only were the two close friends but also, aesthetically, they were bound by what Philippa Scott describes as 'a Silk Road of the mind and spirit' and, she continues, 'those of us who have always felt ourselves to be outsiders, observers, and somewhat out of place, are travellers on this alternative Silk Road, always looking for something that might perhaps be in the next caravanserai, the next country, the next experience, the next passion.' She is author of *The Book of Silk* (Thames and Hudson), a monumental work that has been translated into several languages.

Gerald MacLean
Strolling in Seventeenth-Century Syria (2006)

We were following in the footsteps of William Biddulph, the English clergyman who recorded his overland journey from Aleppo to Jerusalem made in the signal year of 1600. Four centuries later, I wrote a book about early English travellers to Ottoman lands, Biddulph among them. In May 2003, armed with his book, *The Travels of certaine Englishmen*, which he published in 1609 after his return to England, Donna Landry and I set out on a bus from Antakya (ancient Antioch) for Aleppo, our aim being to retrace his journey to Damascus and beyond.

For many Europeans, travelling in eastern climes has often seemed like a journey into the past. This was certainly Biddulph's view. Sent out to minister to the spiritual needs of English merchants living in Aleppo, he was among the first of many Englishmen to write about his Levantine travels and discover he was journeying into places little changed from biblical times. In his *Travels*, Biddulph frequently translates his experiences through the lens of biblical history. Wandering in desert places and 'having the ground to our bed, a stone to our pillow ... and the skie to our covering,' he sees himself as an Old Testament prophet. He also insists he is no Catholic pilgrim superstitiously seeking special grace; solid Protestant that he was, he was interested only in visiting the historical sites where his profession had its roots.

Biddulph's account is otherwise entirely original, and provides the first detailed record of a route that would be travelled regularly for more than a century by later generations of Aleppine chaplains and merchants, several of whom wrote about it, most famously 'the chaste, the accurate and the pious' Henry Maundrell, whose *A Journey from Aleppo to Jerusalem in 1697* was first published in 1703 and reprinted regularly during the eighteenth and nineteenth centuries. Not all who set out from England survived the dangers of climate and disease. For some, the voyage itself proved fatal: at the fever-stricken harbours of Tripoli or Scanderun new arrivals regularly sickened and died before they could reach Aleppo. But for those who survived, life in the ancient city afforded ample opportunities for further travel. During the plague season, many adopted the annual ritual of journeying to Jerusalem. And so it was that, on March 9th, 1600, Biddulph with a group of English merchants set off on the overland route via Damascus, a journey taking them twenty days on horseback across upland deserts and through dry valleys of volcanic rock.

Biddulph complains about tolls along the way, and notes how not all travellers got through unscathed. For his part, he likes wearing his clerical robes because he enjoys the respect and prestige they give him, but he is no foolish provoker of hostility and is always ready to pay when the toll-collectors are especially fierce. When his group meet 'many Turks and Arabs, with maces of Iron and other weapons' who stop them to demand 'Caphar or tole money,' Biddulph and his compatriots pay up without hesitation. Soon after, the Protestant chaplain takes evident delight telling of a 'Caravan of Christians, who came after us' who refused to pay and were 'shrewdly beaten with their iron mases.' Biddulph gloats for a moment because there was a Jesuit among this group 'who escaped not without stripes ... rejoiced, and counted it meritorious, in that he suffered such misery in so holy a voyage.' 'But I know,' Biddulph continues, 'had it not beene more for love of his purse than for love of Christ, he might have escaped without stripes, yea with these kinde speeches, Marhabbah Janum, that is, Welcome my friend or sweet-heart.'

Despite the sprawl of new and uniform sandstone buildings that greets you, arriving in old Aleppo felt magical. In 1763 Charles Perry observes: 'Its Houses in common are large, built with a handsome Sort of Stone, and in a good Taste. Some of its Streets are spacious and handsome, (a Rarity in this Country) and are well paved with flag Stones.' The inner city has changed little since Biddulph first wandered among the holy sites four centuries ago. On arrival, the English clergyman was 'extreamly sick,' as was so often the case with new arrivals from England. A few years before his arrival, Fynes Moryson reported from Aleppo 'the aire was so hot, as me thought I supped hot broth, when I drew it in; but it is very subtile, so as the Christians comming hither from Scanderona ... continually fall sicke, and often die.' But Biddulph survived and, by late July, had fully recovered.

In Biddulph's time, the English merchants in Aleppo, together with the French and Dutch, lived in a splendid Ottoman khan built in 1574, a rectangular two-storey building with stabling and warehousing arranged around a central courtyard. We had read that the Khan al-Gümrük, or 'Customs House' as it has been known since the late eighteenth century, is still one of the finest khans inside the Aleppo souk, and were eager to see it for ourselves. But first we needed somewhere to stay, so set off from the bus stop with directions for the legendary Baron's Hotel. On the way we passed the New Ommayad Hotel that, claiming only two stars, looked like the sort of place that might serve nicely if the Baron's were full. Turning onto Baron Street we are instantly overcome by the noise of pneumatic hammers and the noxious fumes of what must be the first attempt to replace a drainage system already laid down when the Baron's was being built. Towering in front of the hotel terrace, a huge crane was gradually depositing a section of concrete pipe that looked large enough to channel the Euphrates. As the crane driver eased the gears, the engine roared and farted a giant plume of blue-grey diesel smoke straight into the hotel entrance. We turned back to the New Ommayad where we were welcomed effusively by Omar, a history student eager to use his fluent English, who escorted us to a decent room at the back, complete with fridge, full bathroom, *klima* and television.

We set off in quest of the Khan al-Gümrük. The souk itself was easy to find, but even for those accustomed to the Grand Bazaar in Istanbul, with its serpentine passageways packed with shopkeepers eagerly jostling to pull you in to inspect their wares, the Aleppo souk proved so amazingly vast, narrow, and crowded, yet so orderly, relaxed, even peaceful, that we were initially distracted from our project. The narrow corridors were jammed solid with covered women and extended family groups going about their daily shopping among the butchers, grocers, apothecaries, sellers of coffee, spices, tea, tobacco, buttons, scarves, jewellery, shoes, wedding dresses, bolts of cloth, nails, aluminium cookware and electric light bulbs. Every so often the crowd miraculously parted to allow an earnest young boy clapping bare heels to a donkey bearing sacks of who-knows-what to pass. But how would we find the Khan al-Gümrük? Summoning my best Turkish, I asked an old man, resplendent in a white *jallabiya*, who was sitting outside a stall selling rope. Gently and firmly he took hold of my right forearm and lifted it until I was pointing along a passageway. He then shook it while counting in time to ten, first in Turkish, then in Arabic, then in French: the Khan al-Gümrük was ten metres down the passage to the right. We followed these directions and there it was: a quiet gateway off to one side with vertical metal bars set in the ground to prevent vehicles going in. The doors were solid, with metal straps and great iron studs; it was not at all difficult to imagine Biddulph passing through them, dressed in full clerical regalia of the time.

Entering through the high-domed gateway, we found ourselves in a courtyard full of wholesale textile merchants dealing in brocades and synthetic fabrics, many of them bearing labels from factories in Korea. At the centre of the courtyard was a domed *mescit*, or prayer hall, with lean-to stalls on three sides, while on the fourth, next to the entrance, a tea-vendor had set up shop. The khan followed the familiar Ottoman pattern for such places: stabling and warehousing on the lower floor, accommodation above. Climbing to the gallery that runs around the upper floor, we found that the rooms where Biddulph and other European merchants once lived were now offices or additional warehouse space. The gallery ceiling was made up of decorated wooden beams that looked every bit as original as the massive doors at the main entrance. Biddulph says nothing about everyday life here, other than that he was 'kindly entertained' on his arrival and that, in 1600, it was still known as the Khan Burgol. A century and a half later, however, the Scottish merchant Alexander Drummond would observe how 'our consul has by far the best apartments; yet they so much resemble the cells of a convent, that I could not help fancying myself immured while I tarried in town' – a sentiment the English chaplain might very well have approved when in one of his more pious moods.

Curiously, Biddulph writes nothing about any of the ancient sites of Aleppo, not even the great medieval Citadel. We headed there anyway. Pausing for tea in one of the stalls outside the entrance, we fell into conversation with Mohammad. 'I am a licensed guide,' he explained, 'and the guard is my cousin.

You will not pay him for entry. And you will not pay me, but every time you must correct my English. There are no tourists in Halep now, and tomorrow I must go to Dubai and become a waiter in a hotel. So you see, today is special. You are my last guests here and must have much pleasure!' True to his word, Mohammad not only saved us the entry fee, but also took the custodian's great bunch of antique iron keys and showed us places that we would otherwise have missed. 'Here are dungeons where they were keeping bad men' Afterwards, we strolled back through the souk and drank more tea outside the medieval al-Maliki hamam. 'This,' Mohammad explained, 'is where your Englishman was washing, but it is not so good as al-Nasri hamam. Tonight you must eat where I told you, and tomorrow you must go to al-Nasri and see how beautiful it is, better than before.' We ate that evening at the Sissi House, just as Mohammad had suggested, and were surprised to find ourselves drinking a clear and robust red wine curiously named after the local ascetic, St Simeon Stylites. Later, we found ourselves being drawn irresistibly up the stairs and into the bar at the Baron's for a nightcap.

The bar was empty. There really were no tourists in Aleppo. The barman could not have been more pleased to see us and greeted us effusively. 'Ah! English! Good! Please sit and I will bring you arak! You must drink only arak tonight!' Which we did with great pleasure, recognising at once the subtle but indescribable differences from the more familiar Turkish rakı that had become a favourite over the years. When asked where we were staying, the barman burst into laughter and I remembered the strange and distant look that had briefly overtaken Mohammad's face earlier in the day when we had answered the same question. 'But you must stay here! We have so many splendid rooms, and the Ommayad! Well, there are too many Natashas there! Very many! Come, and I will show you why you must stay here!' So we dutifully followed on the grand tour, visiting Agatha Christie's and T E Lawrence's rooms, and admired the grand suite where Hafez al-Assad had regularly stayed. 'Tomorrow you will come here and have your choice! How much are you paying at the Ommayad? You will have the best room here for the same price! I will arrange everything!' It really was impossible to refuse. After all, several of the suites at the back of the hotel, including Lawrence's, had recently been restored and were well away from the road works. Promising to return the next day, we drank some more arak before stumbling our way back to the Ommayad. Omar was delighted to see us and ushered us directly to the lift, making sure we avoided the passage leading to the restaurant from which we could hear some lively music and girlish laughter. We collapsed into bed, amused to have found that we had booked into a knocking shop. Next morning, we checked into Lawrence's old room.

When Biddulph set off from Aleppo on his jaunt to Jerusalem, his group stopped for the first night at Khan Touman, barely ten miles beyond the city walls, and spent the evening carousing with friends who returned to the city before nightfall. Next day the travellers reached 'Saracoope' and followed a route that is still the main road to Damascus, passing through the ancient towns of Maarat en-Numan, Hama, and Homs. Biddulph's description of the route was clearly the basis for the rather schematic map designed to accompany Thomas Fuller's *Pisgah Sight of Palestine* (1650), a comprehensive though inaccurate historical geography of the biblical Near East. In a fascinating dialogue that ends the text, Fuller confesses that this map is less accurate than the others provided in this work. From a purported memory of reading Biddulph, one Philologius challenges Aletheaus, the authorial persona:

> You make Marra the next modern stage South of Aleppo: whereas there be many moe[sic] miles and intermediate lodging-places (namedly Cane-Toman, and Saracoop) betwixt them. Aleth. I confess no less, but am sorry your memory is so short, that I must so often inculcate the same rule unto you: That places situate on the Um-Stroke (such the location of Aleppo in our Map) are not in their exact position, whilst we only make a long arm to reach them confusedly into our description, though otherwise they be at greater distance, than the scale of miles will admit.

The *Oxford English Dictionary* tells us that this is the only known instance of 'um-stroke,' the edge or circumference of a map, so the passage is particularly resonant since we never made it to Khan Touman or to Saracoop because the driver, convinced that we were mad and should really be visiting Ebla, refused to stop in either place. '*La! maafish!*' he insisted, blithely passing by the signpost marking the turn to Khan Touman and then driving directly through the sprawl of poorly equipped workshops and black-tented communities lining the road through Saracoop. He did take us to Maarat, the limit of our trip that day, where Biddulph and his party stayed overnight at the Murat Pasha Khan, a fine stone building now housing a museum that features some spectacular Roman mosaics. The khan reminded Biddulph of 'Leaden-Hall in London, or rather the Exchange in London,' and he explained how Murat Pasha's endowment provided 'of his own cost ... Bread, Pilaw, and Mutton' which – in a moment of particular mean spirits – the party of English travellers refused, 'scorning relief from Turkes without money.' When the rather surly guard firmly instructed us not to take photographs, not to sit down anywhere, and not to eat or drink anything while inside the khan, the improbable thought briefly crossed my mind that we had inherited the backlash of that scornful Protestant self-reliance of centuries before. Driving back to Aleppo, we wondered what the generous Murat Pasha would have made of the present regime.

On the trip to Damascus, we discovered that Fuller's map both exaggerates the distances separating the khans between Homs and Damascus, and misrepresents the relative size of the communities surrounding them. After Homs, which the biblically sensitive Biddulph notes 'is said to have been the City where Job dwelt,' he stopped for three more nights before reaching Damascus: in 'an old Castle' in Hisyah, in 'a poore village called Nebecke, or (as they pronounce it) Nebhkeh, where we lodged in an old Cane,' and then the next day in 'Cotifey' (Qutaifah) 'where we lodged in a very stately new Cane, built by Synan Bashaw.' We stopped to photograph the Sinan Pasha Khan and mosque and found Biddulph's description to be entirely accurate – except that we were in An'nabk. In Qutaifah we were told by several local people that there was no khan in their town, only the Khan al-Arus some kilometres away, so I concluded that Biddulph, or his editor, had confused the two towns. Months later, back in the British Library, I found two eighteenth-century travellers who reported overnight stops at a khan in Qutaifah. John Green's *A Journey from Aleppo to Damascus* (1736), based on an anonymous manuscript, follows Biddulph's route exactly while adding further details such as the existence of the 'Khan al Arus, that is the Bride's Castle or Inn,' situated outside Qutaifah, a simple, single storey structure which we found still being used by local herdsmen for bringing in their mixed flocks of sheep and goats at night. Green's source described the Sinan Pasha Khan as 'the most beautiful Khan of the whole Country,' and agreed with Biddulph that it was in Qutaifah, adding: 'In this Khan Travellers are furnished gratis with meat for themselves, and Provender for their Cattle, at the Founder's Charge.' A decade later, Richard Pococke disputed this claim in *Observations on Palaestine or the Holy Land, Syria, Mesopotamia, Cyprus, and Candia* (1745). Pococke reports staying 'in a very fine kane, which has a portico round it' in 'Kteiphe,' but notes that 'in the account of the journey from Aleppo to Damascus, in which it is said that the kane was built by Sinam[sic] Pasha, but I heard nothing that travellers were supplied with provisions gratis.' Now, as readers familiar with Alexander Drummond's *Travels* (1754) will know, even the highly respected Orientalist Richard Pococke regularly made things up, or borrowed dubious evidence from previously published sources. The khan he describes in 'Kteiphe' is certainly not the Sinan Pasha Khan we visited in An'nebk, nor can it be the khan described in Green's manuscript. So questions remain: were we simply misinformed? Was there once a khan in Qutaifah of which neither trace nor memory remains? And why did Biddulph and the author of Green's manuscript not know where they were?

For his part, Biddulph characteristically believes the Bible even when it conflicts with the assertions of local residents. Arriving in Damascus, his group lodge inside the walled-city at the 'Cane Nebbe, that is, the Cane of the

Prophet; but by the Turkes, Cane Haramin,' where, the accommodation being so cheap, 'we hired three chambers for our mony.' Next, he reaches for his Bible, using it to interpret everything he sees: 'Damascus is a most ancient City, and as Esay spake of it in his time, The head of Aram is Damascus: *Isa.7.8.* so Damascus is the chiefest City of Syria to this day.' While in Damascus, their Greek guide 'shewed us first a stately Muskia, or Turkish Church,' but thanks to his Bible, Biddulph reports that the Ummayad Mosque had been 'erected in the place where the Temple of Rymon stood, mentioned *2.King.5.*' He fails to mention the nearby red-domed tomb of Salah ed-Din, the Kurdish military leader who famously united Muslim nations against the Crusaders.

Like later British visitors to Damascus, Biddulph and company sought out sites famous from biblical history, beginning with the underground house where Ananias 'lived in secret for feare of the Jews.' Biddulph registers frustration that 'many Christians comming thither to see that place, with a coale write their names on the wall, and there are so many names there already, that there is scarce roome for any other to set his name.' Today, no trace remains of those seventeenth-century signatures scrawled in charcoal in the house of Ananias. The walls are now damp and crumble to the touch.

Armed with police permits, we set out the next day for Quneitra. Like Biddulph, we took the road that passes through Daraya, where Saul of Tarsus fell off his horse and became Paul. In Biddulph's day, enthusiastic pilgrims 'of sundry Nations,' would pass through town on their knees, a practice that would soon create traffic problems today. A proper Protestant Englishman, Biddulph stayed on his horse and rode contemptuously past the pilgrims prostrating themselves and grovelling through town. We stayed in our taxi and admired the carefully watered tree-lined streets and noticed where a large number of skilled furniture makers had set up small workshops.

Between Damascus and Quneitra, the countryside for miles around offers a splendid model of well-managed and sustainable arable usage. The cooler climate and rough but fertile soils easily support an important late season cash-crop of fruits and olives for the Damascus market without chemical fertilizers: instead, small boys skilfully herd mixed flocks of fat sheep and sleek goats that manage the weed growth and provide organic nourishment. Patches of dark volcanic soil are locally famed for distinctive varieties of garlic and onion. As we entered Sa'ass'a, a small group of magnificent bullocks were being moved along the shaded river. It was now late May, sunny but still cool. The snow capped peaks of Mount Hermon promised to trickle slowly and keep these lands wet throughout the longest summer.

The ancient market town of Quneitra has seen many changes since Biddulph's visit. When Biddulph arrived after two days of 'tedious travell,' he found 'the place pleasant at our coming thither' and his group 'walked about to solace ourselves in beholding the greene pastures and running rivers nere unto it, and in viewing the order of sundry Nations there assembled together from sundry places.' Green pastures do remain; but now they are only distantly visible across the Israeli border since those running rivers have been diverted to feed directly into the Lake of Galilee. From afar they appear so radiantly green, striking the eye with such an intensive emerald glow, that we could not help recalling farms in the Netherlands, watery and richly over fertilized. Yes, one can make the 'desert' green, but perhaps most remarkable was the golden swathe of dried grassland making up the no-go area, now a wilderness of wildflowers and grasses providing home to hosts of bird and insect life.

More strikingly, the people are all gone now. The entire population moved to Sa'ass'a and the outlying area in 1972 after Israeli bulldozers destroyed their city. Wherever you look the collapsed roofs of shops and houses are slowly growing back into the land. The Greek church and a minaret still stand from before, and the small museum of prehistoric, Roman, and Byzantine finds is worth the visit. The cloistered market where Biddulph once strolled has disappeared. Commerce has taken up residence in the shops stretching back up the road between Khanl'sheeh and Sa'ass'a where, if one were so inclined, one still might take pleasure from 'viewing the order of sundry Nations there assembled together.' Four centuries after Biddulph's visit, we found that Quneitra had become rather less than spectral, a ghost town without any ghosts. Our trip there had been not so much a journey into the distant past, to the way things used to be, but a grim reminder that what some consider historical progress requires the destruction of what went before.

A fuller account of this piece can be found in *Strolling in Syria with William Biddulph*, *Criticism* 46:3 (Summer 2004): 415-40.

Philippa Scott
Remembering Robert Tewdwr Moss (2006)

I remember clearly that summer when we first met and became friends. At the time Robert was working on a women's magazine, and freelancing for whoever would commission an article. While researching a story on lace curtains for the *Telegraph* magazine, Robert met a textile dealer who referred him to me, and he telephoned to make an appointment. We sat in the garden sipping chilled white wine, picking at olives and a bowl of pistachios. It was 1988, the year that Chaos had kittens, Robert picked up a tiny cat, his long slender fingers gently traced round its pansy face. 'I love cat's mouths, the way they are drawn'. Chaos, *sans* kittens, settled on my lap to pose for the photograph – we shared a page with Eartha Kitt. 'Tewdwr Moss' was an invention; at the time there was another journalist, Robert Moss. Robert used other *noms de plume* too. When he interviewed me in 1995 for the *Evening Standard*, the article was filed under the byline 'Oliver Llewellyn'.

I recognized familiar aspects in his obituaries, but these were glimpses of his public persona, not the gentle, kind, dear friend with whom I shared paupers' picnics, made cat-worshipping sojourns to unmystical blocks of high rise flats, or plotted frankly ridiculous 'money-making' projects destined to save us from penury and attendant evils. One of these unlikely life-rafts was to be a history of 'Blind Date', and as Robert was finishing *Cleopatra's Wedding Present* we were already gathering source material for this, which we imagined to be the next project, a joint effort. Our agent, Simon Trewin, told me later that he could conceive of no more inappropriate combination than pairing Robert and me, with Cilla's popular show. True, it was an extremely low point when we thought of it, a case of drowning desperados clutching at the most fragile of straws, but we embraced the surreal nature of the challenge. Robert relished the fantasy of being Mr Perfect Date.

Which brings me to the inevitable mention of sex. Look up Robert Tewdwr Moss on the internet, and you will find *Cleopatra's Wedding Present* is not only acclaimed as modern travel literature ('a new Chatwin'), but Robert himself is acclaimed as an icon of gay literature! I can see him smiling; 'Well I never, Heavens. What d'you know, what do you know'. The book tells of homosexual encounters and a love affair, but Robert is not to be so easily or conveniently pigeon-holed, for his consummated loves were not only male; his taste was for the exotic individual, and one of his greatest loves was a beautiful young Persian woman. They had been close since both were students at SOAS, and when Robert and I first became friends, he was deeply in love with her; they looked, in fact like a couple, might even have been brother and sister. He fantasised about married life with her, and children, and longed for all of this, but knew too that his attraction to young men was too strong to resist, and would lead them both to inevitable heartbreak. They agreed to resume their original platonic friendship. Robert then suffered torments of jealousy and dreams of heightened anxiety when his love eventually found another, serious relationship. By absenting himself, by journeying to Syria, by immersing himself in adventures and research for his book, Robert also sought to smother the unbearable jealousy he was going through.

Anxious not to damage a precious friendship, he created geographic and emotional space. Of course he wanted to expand his career from journalism into writing books, it was a natural and inevitable progression of his writing life, but the timing of his Syrian journeys was also a time of immense inner turmoil. He wanted to go somewhere east, asked me whether I could find him a place as tutor in an Indian royal family, considered various options, and finally was drawn to Syria. He had some knowledge of Arabic, had studied its history, was fascinated by travel literature and the descriptions left by earlier writers. Syria was not back-packer terrain, no holiday hordes swarmed its ancient sites, redolent with such evocative names – Zenobia, Palmyra, Aleppo, Damascus – the palaces and fortress castles of the first Muslim dynasties beckoned, the lure of a Street called Straight. Who could resist the temptations of Cleopatra's wedding present? Syria retained its mystery, beckoned him. Fate whispered in his ear. He made a first trip, returned to London, and after the usual – discuss with agent, write proposal, rewrite, discuss, rewrite, write sample chapters, discuss rewrite discuss and so forth – his agent Simon Trewin sold Robert's proposal to Fourth Estate. With an advance to help defray the expenses of a longer trip, Robert gave up the day job, and returned to Syria.

In his obituary Philip Hoare likened Robert to '... some ghost of the *fin de siècle* past... clad in velvet and brocade, surreptitiously passing on a morsel of gossip here, imparting some arcane piece of knowledge there...' John Walsh in *The Independent's* obituary described Robert, who worked on *The Indie* for a time, as 'cooing over my shoulder in a waft of parma violet'. Coo yes, he did a good coo, very dove-like and just a touch nasal, though I remember Robert describing his own voice as 'the plummy tones of a vicar's wife' – fruity, slightly arch, slightly camp. Waft, yes, wafted wonderfully, in a plum velvet jacket, brocade waistcoat and ruffled white shirt. His shoulders stooped slightly, the way tall people do from habitually bending down to speak to shorties like me, and clad in velvet, his shoulders echoed the folded wings of some elegant bird. Shortly before his first trip to Syria, he swooped into my flat to display his newly pierced ear, and an array of jewelled studs destined to glitter there. The earring suited his dark beauty, lending him the air of a pirate, or a raffish dandy.

But parma violet, oh no, quite wrong. Robert's bag was the spicy scent of clove carnations. He wore Malmaison from Floris, until he discovered the ultimate carnation scent in the perfume souk in Damascus. Or was it Aleppo? He telephoned me, delighted; 'Something from Ottoman times, d'you think?' he mused. We discussed meeting up in Syria, then again in Istanbul, but his ill health in Syria – typhoid – put an end to those plans.

In 1990 I rented a cottage in County Cork, and on April 1st, All Fool's Day, drove off, car laden with manuscript, books, computer, five cats and a dog. I had tumbled into an ill-starred romance, and during the course of my madness, when the object of my obsession was being tossed around the Pacific on his wretched raft, Robert, always ready to offer an understanding ear and comforting shoulder, but also with a journalist's natural relish for other people's dramas, came to stay. Typical Robert, he chatted to his neighbours on the plane over and by the time the plane landed, they were old friends. 'I've invited them to come and visit tomorrow' he said. 'Hope that's okay. You'll really like them, they're lovely.' His new friends were Fred Astaire's daughter Ava and her husband, and indeed, as he said, lovely people. And with cats. Of course.

Robert's visit coincided with the Courtmacsherry Shrimp Festival, which he hoped would provide a newspaper story to underwrite his travel, to which end we attempted Quiz night at the local pub and entered the Shrimp Spitting Contest. 'A good full mouthful of whisky, gives the shrimps wings y'know.' No matter whether the alcoholic fumes helped propel the (live) shrimps further along the pavement, we fell for it, suckers to the last. What can I say? We were total amateurs at shrimp spitting, and after our feeble, dribbling first and last attempt, retired from the sport. 'Nah, it'll never make Olympic status.'

In time, I slunk back to London. That year, Robert had interviewed Jean Gimpel, and inspired by his Sunday afternoon salons, began his own afternoon gatherings, tea parties brimming with old friends and new acquaintances – crazed countesses, mad hatters and delightful dormice – there was no telling who you might meet there.

Our last outing and adventure together was that autumn before Robert's death. We went to Cornwall. Robert was researching a story for *Tatler*, I took the train and he met me with a hired car. Interspersed with 'work' Robert with his Welsh blood, me with my Scots/Irish, visited Celtic springs hopefully dabbling water on ourselves for good Celtic magic and wish fulfilment. In Portelliot he surprised me with a tiny model cat 'fortune-teller', Mystic Mog, scrying her crystal ball. She still sits on my shelf.

When we returned to London, Robert asked me for the telephone number of a tarot reader and went to have his cards read. We arranged to go to see a film – *The Secret of Roan Innish* – seal people mystery and magic, set in Ireland – and afterwards Robert told me, elated, that the cards predicted success for the book he was just completing and acclaim for him as a writer. The cards were right.

But the cards did not predict his death a week later. The tarot reader was aghast when she, like the rest of us listed in Robert's address book and diary, was called to Paddington Green Police Station for questioning and finger printing. The police at Paddington Green deal with terrorism, and the energy field around these men conveys a sense of giants, at least ten or fifteen feet tall, far more than their already towering physical presence. Nobody in their right mind messes with those men. No surprise, then, that they tracked the killers, arrested them within a matter of days. One was caught as he packed his bag ready to flee, a one-way aeroplane ticket to Sweden clutched in his hand. For the cover of his book, Robert wanted a photograph of a beautiful youth at the entrance to a souk, and one day with this in his mind, his attention was drawn to a young man coming out of a public telephone booth on the corner of the street where he lived. They struck up conversation. The young man was a young Muslim convert who lived in the nearby council flats, and he took to calling in on Robert: 'Please can I come by for a cup of tea, to watch you writing your book about Syria?' One evening, he called to say that his friend would like to meet Robert, and could they both call round. That same evening Robert entertained them with tea and jaffa cakes, and then they beat him, broke his aquiline nose, tied him up with his dressing gown cord, and left him face down to smother in his own blood. Robert was strong, fit, regularly worked out at a gym, and not easily overpowered, but his killers had surprise on their side, and they were two against one.

Had Robert confided to the youth that his book included a gay love affair in Syria? Or was it a horrible act of brutality with no purpose or reasoning behind it, other than the theft of a computer, the ransacking of a flat for money (little hope of that). Neither man was Syrian, and though both were Muslim, neither was Arab. Inevitably people wondered, was the killing somehow connected with Syria, with Robert's adventures there, with his book. But his book was still unpublished, unread, unfinished even – the final draft had been completed that very day. It seems somehow even worse that his death was fuelled by ignorance, ill-chance, ugly enviousness, such a terrible, tragic waste, and that it should happen in his home, when his flatmates just happened to be out and elsewhere.

I left for India while the trial was still on-going, and when I returned some months later, Fourth Estate, who had commissioned the book, had pulled out. Robert's laptop with his final draft was never recovered, and Robin Baird-Smith of Duckworth's took all the working papers and existing drafts, and assigned a brilliant script doctor to edit the book, which Duckworth's then published. I have read it and re-read it, and I hear Robert's voice throughout the pages. Whatever final tweaks he may have planned, the book that was born is very definitely Robert's book, true to his intentions, and throughout its pages, cats thread their way, subtle but insistent, as is only proper and right, for he adored cats and was an ardent supporter of the Cat Protection League. His own he adopted as feral kittens from a housing estate. He named them Wayne and Sharon, AKA 'Miss Love'. A photograph taken for the 'author's portrait' of the book jacket shows Robert almost in profile, sitting on the steps of his flat, with Wayne, the tabby, next to him. I would like to think the great cat goddess Bastet looked over his shoulder, purring, as he wrote his book. I would like to think that Sekhmet's wrathful feline energy helped the police find and bring to justice Robert's killers.

Our last conversation was when I dropped him home after the film. He said that although *Tatler* had not yet paid him, he could reimburse me for my train fare to Cornwall. I said not to worry, wait until *Tatler* paid. No no, he said, he had the cash, and he would rather do this now.

'And besides, you just never know, do you.'

Those last words still haunt me, in my head I hear them, and wonder.

Robert's birthday was late December, an early Capricorn, and he was thirty-four when he was killed. It happened one August Bank Holiday weekend ten years ago, just before Portobello Carnival. The last thing I felt like that day was answering the telephone, and the wretched thing kept ringing. I refused to answer. At the end of the day I switched on the six o'clock news. 'West London travel writer murdered,' said the newscaster. The phone rang again, this time I picked it up. It was Robert's beautiful Persian girlfriend, who had been trying to contact me all day so that I did not have to hear the horrible news via public airways.

Cats were a recurring theme in Robert's life, and it seems right and fitting that as I wrote this remembrance, the last of Chaos's kittens warmed his old bones on my lap, and then slipped away from life. Robert's gentle empathy with faded beauties, yesterday's roses, women with exotic pasts, was like that of a courteous troubadour; they could not help but fall in love with him, and he gently responded with thoughtful little attentions which engendered impossible fantasies, but also revived sad hearts and lost spirit. He had had a wonderful, almost magical gift for friendship, a genuine liking for and curiosity about people irrespective of age or sex, and an endearing openness, which made him attractive to all. This blessing was ultimately his tragedy.

Epilogue:
Syrians in Two Worlds

Peter Clark

O
N MY FIRST VISIT to Syria, in 1962, I travelled by bus from Homs to Palmyra and sat next to the headmaster of the secondary school in Tadmor, the modern town to the east of the classical site. He invited me to visit the school. I took up the invitation and the next morning the headmaster put me into the hands of the teacher of English, Ibrahim Abd al-Nour, a bachelor aged about thirty, a few years older than myself. We spent the evening visiting friends, and playing table tennis and chess. After a brief correspondence we lost touch.

Thirty years later I was back in Syria, reopening the British Council. I had fond memories of my first visit and of my evening in Tadmor, and wanted to find Ibrahim. I made enquiries wherever I went, and a senior army officer friend suggested we get the security services to trace him. I resisted that idea, imagining the alarm of an elderly teacher suddenly being interrogated about a friendship with some foreigner thirty years earlier.

The Principal of the University in Homs helped me to track Ibrahim down. One of the students at the university – studying English – was called Abeer Ibrahim Abd al-Nour. To her consternation she found herself summoned to the Principal's office. We met and I asked whether her father had taught English in Palmyra thirty years earlier. She thought so. She told me her father was retired and living in his home village, a Christian village, Fairouza, a few miles east of Homs. Abeer's initial wariness of me melted and later in the day we went in my car to the village and called on her father. On the way Abeer puzzled me by her talking of diamonds growing in the fields. It was only later that she corrected herself – 'Almonds, not diamonds.'

Ibrahim was shorter and stouter than my memory of him, but there was the same round rubicund face and we greeted each other with a spontaneous bear-hug. His English was precise with strange nineteenth-century English turns of phrase, the result of reading much Thackeray and Dickens. His memory of that evening in Palmyra was as clear as mine. Ibrahim was now married with four children – three sons and a daughter, more or less the same family set-up as my

263

own. The eldest son was in the United States, and Abeer was engaged to an American, called George.

Over the next few months I got to know the family and the village better. Abeer's fiancé, George, did have American citizenship but he had actually been born in Fairouza. Abeer, on graduation would be joining him there, in Burbank, on the northern outskirts of Los Angeles, where George ran a liquor store. The eldest brother was also in Burbank. Indeed I gradually learned that there were hundreds of people who had migrated in the last decade or so from Fairouza to Burbank, creating a curious informal twinning arrangement. 'People from the next village, Zaidan', Ibrahim told me, 'go to Jacksonville Florida, but we go to Burbank California.'

The next summer George came over and I met him in Fairouza. George had a cheery Californian accent and a big grin. He and Abeer married in the village and they went off to Burbank. The following year Ibrahim died but I continued to call on the family in Fairouza. I also exchanged Christmas greetings with George and Abir.

I left Syria in 1997 and in the summer of 2000 I was in Los Angeles and phoned George's liquor store. My wife and I were invited to spend a day with Abeer and George, and their two young children, Linda and Ibrahim. I took for Abeer a packet of almonds. They lived in a house, one of six, around a shared courtyard. Three of the houses were occupied by people originally from Fairouza, one by Abeer's closest friend from their primary school days.

We ate a meze and a Syrian stew, followed by sweetmeats from Damascus. A video was playing all the time, the record of their recent summer trip to Fairouza. They had taken the children back to be baptised by the village priest. The video included scenes of a late night party in the Fairouza community centre. People were dancing into the night. The women looked exhausted. Had they been up from dawn, chopping tomatoes and parsley for the tabbouleh?

'Every night there is a party,' said George. 'People go back there from Burbank looking for brides and bridegrooms for the young men and women.'

'But how many people from Fairouza are there here in Burbank?' I asked.

'About two thousand.'

'And what work do people from Fairouza do?'

'Mostly the liquor trade. The first migrant in the early 1960s became involved in selling liquor. There are now about two hundred liquor stores in the northern Los Angeles area, either owned or managed by people from Fairouza. We sell everything, and also araq that is produced in Fairouza and exported here.'

We talked on. The children spoke only Arabic, but they would quickly learn English at school. Abeer and George saw themselves as having come to live in Burbank for good, although they did maintain their links with the home village.

'I have some land in Fairouza,' said George.

'Who looks after that?'

'My mother and my sister.'

The Syrian President, Hafez al-Assad, had died earlier that year, and George and Abir had been to the Syrian Consulate-General in Los Angeles to cast their votes for the Syrian presidential election, voting for Bashar, the late President's son. Taking advantage of their US citizenship they were also preparing in the autumn to vote for George W Bush, another son of another former President. Until the second Bush, most Arab Americans voted Republican. The Republican Party was more representative of non-European, and especially Arab immigrant, culture – suspicion of and distance from Federal government authority, shared family values and belief in and practice of private enterprise.

The Lebanese in the World: A Century of Emigration, edited by Albert Hourani and Nadim Shehadi, published by the Centre for Lebanese Studies in association with I B Tauris of London in 1992, deals primarily with Lebanese migration. But the reader is able to place the Fairouz/Burbank phenomenon into a broader context. Migration from Greater Syria to Europe and the Americas and elsewhere has persisted since the early nineteenth century. It was not – as local myth maintains – the consequence of Ottoman oppression. Life steadily improved for Syrians in the latter years of the Ottoman Empire. The explanation can rather be found in rising expectations and increased opportunities following faster and cheaper steam-driven shipping. Often the pioneer from one village would settle in one place in the new country, and others from the village or the area would follow. Druze and Syrians from the south of the country migrated to Venezuela. People from the small town of Yabrud, eighty kilometres south west of Fairouza migrated to Argentina. The latter included the parents of former President Carlos Menem, who exchanged their Islam for Christianity and modified their family name of Abd al-Munim. Southern Lebanese went to West Africa and people from Homs went to Sao Paolo. Occasionally one village may buck the trend. People from Bishmizzine in northern Lebanon migrated in all directions.

The pattern of Syrian/Lebanese migration is similar to other waves of immigration – organised by no government and the result of individual initiative on a huge scale – such as Poles, Greek and Italian to the United States in the nineteenth and twentieth centuries, and from South Asia to West Europe in the late twentieth. The migrants become citizens of the adopted countries and, to a greater or lesser extent, become assimilated in the new country. The first generation are traders and the second generation become professionals. But contacts are maintained with their places of origin, in the form of marriage partners, language, food and values. A minority return to their home country. Many Syrians returned from South America to the region south and west of Homs, bringing back some customs such as mate tea, sucked through a metal filter.

Syria now has a Ministry for Expatriates, headed by Dr Bouthaina Shaaban, who has a PhD from the University of Warwick for a thesis on Chartist poetry. She has also taught at university level in the United States. The establishment of the Ministry follows the example of Lebanon. Some Syrian expatriates have become extremely rich – in South America, but also in Europe and, to a lesser extent in the United States. The new Ministry is keen to attract investment from those who still feel Syrian. The communities of expatriates are also seen as possible allies in presenting Syria in a favourable light.

My accidental but cherished friendship, now well over forty years old, with Ibrahim and his family revealed on an individual scale something that has been happening to Syrians (and others) on a massive scale, to the enrichment of the societies of both worlds.

Additional Biographies

Marius Kociejowski, poet, essayist and travel writer, lives in London. He has published three collections of poetry, *Coast* (Greville Press), *Doctor Honoris Causa*, and *Music's Bride* (both Anvil Press). Most recently, he published *The Street Philosopher and the Holy: A Syrian Journey* (Sutton Publishing) and is currently working on a second book, *The Pigeon Wars of Damascus*.

Ross Burns is the author of *Monuments of Syria* (I B Tauris, and New York University Press, 1992; reissued in paperback 1999), the most complete handbook to Syria's archaeological and historical sites. He has also recently published *Damascus: A History* (Routledge, 2005), the first work in English to relate the city's story from its ancient beginnings to 1919. A graduate in history and archaeology from the University of Sydney, he first got to know Syria in the 1980s when he served as Australian Ambassador. He recently retired from the Australian Foreign Service. Though he held a number of assignments in the Middle East, Europe, Africa as well as Asia, his time in Syria provided the perfect combination of a stimulating work environment and a chance to explore thoroughly the country's rich past.

Peter Clark has been visiting Syria since 1962. From 1992 to 1997 he was British Cultural Attaché, a period that was professionally satisfying and personally enriching. He is now an independent writer, one of the foremost translators of modern Arabic literature and tourism consultant. From Syria, he has translated two novels by Ulfat Idilbi, a play by Sadallah Wannus and stories by Abd al-Salam al-Ujaili and Nadia Ghazzi. Also he is the author of *Marmaduke Pickthall: British Muslim* and *Thesiger's Return* and a contributing editor to *Banipal*. He devises and takes tour groups to Syria. 'I want to see Damascus before George Bush comes here,' is how one tourist put it.

Bibliography

Anonymous *Rambles in the Deserts of Syria and among the Turkomans and Bedaweens* (John Murray 1864)

Beawes, William. 'The Diary of William Beawes' in *The Desert Route to India: being the Journals of four travellers.* Ed Douglas Carruthers (Hakluyt Society 1929)

Bell, Gertrude. *The Arabian Diaries: 1913-1914.* Ed Rosemary O'Brien (Syracuse, University Press 2000)

Burton, Isabel. *The Inner Life of Syria, Palestine & the Holy Land, from my private journal* (Henry S King 1875)

Cleveland, Catherine Lucy. *The Life and Letters of Lady Hester Stanhope* (John Murray 1914)

Dalrymple, William. *From the Holy Mountain: A Journey in the Shadow of Byzantium* (HarperCollins 1997)

Deonna, Laurence. *Syrians: A Travelogue 1992-1994.* Trans Christopher Snow (Passeggiata Press, Pueblo 1996)

Doughty, C M. *Arabia Deserta* (Cambridge University Press 1888)

Fedden, Robin. *Syria and Lebanon* (John Murray 1965, 3rd edition)

Flecker, James Elroy. *The Golden Journey to Samarkand* (Max Goschen 1913)

Gibbon, Edward. *The Decline and Fall of the Roman Empire* (W Strahan and T Cadell 1776-1788)

Ibn Battuta. *The Travels of Ibn Battuta.* Trans Sir Hamilton Gibb and C F Beckingham (Hakluyt Society 1958)

Kociejowski, Marius. *The Street Philosopher and the Holy Fool: A Syrian Journey* (Sutton Publishing 2004)

Kociejowski, Marius. *Music's Bride* (Anvil Press Poetry 1999)

Lamartine, Alphonse de. *A Pilgrimage to the Holy Land, comprising recollections, sketches, etc, made during a tour in the East in 1832-3* (Richard Bentley 1835)

Lawrence, T E. *The Letters of T E Lawrence.* Ed David Garnett (Jonathan Cape 1938)

Lawrence, T E. *The Seven Pillars of Wisdom* (Jonathan Cape 1935)

Le Strange, Guy. *Palestine Under the Moslems, translated from the Works of Mediaeval Arabian Geographers* (Palestine Exploration 1890)

Lukach, Harry Charles. *The Fringe of the East: A Journey through Past and Present Provinces of Turkey* (Macmillan 1913)

Mukaddasi. *Description of Syria, including Palestine.* Trans Guy le Strange (Palestine Pilgrim's Text Society 1892)

Nasir-I-Khursrau. *Diary of a Journey through Syria and Palestine* (Palestine Pilgrim's Text Society 1897)

Ormsby, Eric. *For a Modest God: New and Selected Poems* (Grove Press, New York 1997)

Paton, Andrew Archibald. *The Modern Syrians; or, Native Society in Damascus, Aleppo, and the Mountains of the Druses, from notes made in those parts during the years 1841, 2, 3, by an Oriental Student* (Longman, Brown, Green and Longmans 1844)

Pickthall, Marmaduke. *Oriental Encounters: Palestine and Syria (1894-5-6).* (W Collins 1918)

Pococke, Richard. *A Description of the East and some other countries* (J & R Kanpton 1743-5)

Raswan, Carl R. *The Black Tents of Arabia: My Life among the Bedouins* (Kegan Paul 2000)

Russell, Alexander and Patrick. *The Natural History of Aleppo* (G G & J Robinson 1794, 2nd edition, revised and enlarged)

Sandys, George. *A Relation of a Journey Begun An. Dom. 1610* (W Barrett 1615)

Stark, Freya. *Letters from Syria* (John Murray 1942)

Teixeira, Pedro. *The Travels of Pedro Teixeira.* Trans William F Sinclair (Hakluyt Society 1902)

Thubron, Colin. *Mirror to Damascus* (Heinemann 1967)

Valle, Pietro della. *The Travels of Pietro della Valle into East India and Arabia Deserta.* Trans G Havers (John Martin and James Allestry 1665)

Varthema, Lodovico de. *The Navigation and Voyages of Lewis Wertomanus, in the yeere of Our Lorde 1503.* Trans Richard Eden (1576)

Volney, C F. *Travels through Syria and Egypt in the years 1783, 1784 and 1785.* (G G J and J Robinson 1788, 2nd edition)

Volney, C F. *The Ruins: or, A Survey of the Revolutions of Empires* (Edwards Brown 1878)

Wood, Robert. *The Ruins of Palmyra* (Published for the author 1753)

ELAND

61 Exmouth Market, London EC1R 4QL
Fax: 020 7833 4434
Email: info@travelbooks.co.uk

Eland was started in 1982 to revive great travel books
that had fallen out of print. Although the list has diversified
into biography and fiction, it is united by a quest to define the
spirit of place. These are books for travellers, and for readers who aspire to
explore the world but who are also content to travel in their own minds.

Eland books open out our understanding of other
cultures, interpret the unknown and reveal different environments
as well as celebrating the humour and occasional horrors of travel. We take
immense trouble to select only the most readable
books and therefore many readers collect the entire series.

All our books are printed on fine, pliable, cream-coloured paper.
Most are still gathered in sections by our printer and sewn as well
as glued, almost unheard of for a paperback book these days.
This gives larger margins in the gutter, as well as
making the books stronger.

You will find a very brief description of all our books on the
following pages. Extracts from each and every one of them can be
read on our website, at www.travelbooks.co.uk. If you would
like a free copy of our catalogue, please fax, email
or write to us (details above).

ELAND

'One of the very best travel lists' WILLIAM DALRYMPLE

Memoirs of a Bengal Civilian
JOHN BEAMES
*Sketches of nineteenth-century India
painted with the richness of Dickens*

Jigsaw
SYBILLE BEDFORD
*An intensely remembered autobiographical
novel about an inter-war childhood*

A Visit to Don Otavio
SYBILLE BEDFORD
*The hell of travel and the Eden of arrival
in post-war Mexico*

Journey into the Mind's Eye
LESLEY BLANCH
*An obsessive love affair with Russia and
one particular Russian*

Japanese Chronicles
NICOLAS BOUVIER
*Three decades of intimate experiences
throughout Japan*

The Way of the World
NICOLAS BOUVIER
Two men in a car from Serbia to Afghanistan

Persia: through writers' eyes
ED. DAVID BLOW
*Guidebooks for the mind: a selection
of the best travel writing on Iran*

The Devil Drives
FAWN BRODIE
*Biography of Sir Richard Burton,
explorer, linguist and pornographer*

Turkish Letters
OGIER DE BUSBECQ
*Eyewitness history at its best:
Istanbul during the reign of Suleyman
the Magnificent*

My Early Life
WINSTON CHURCHILL
*From North-West Frontier to Boer War
by the age of twenty-five*

Sicily: through writers' eyes
ED. HORATIO CLARE
*Guidebooks for the mind: a selection
of the best travel writing on Sicily*

A Square of Sky
JANINA DAVID
*A Jewish childhood in the Warsaw
ghetto and hiding from the Nazis*

Chantemesle
ROBIN FEDDEN
*A lyrical evocation of childhood
in Normandy*

Croatia: through writers' eyes
ED. FRANKOPAN, GOODING & LAVINGTON
*Guidebooks for the mind: a selection
of the best travel writing on Croatia*

Viva Mexico!
CHARLES FLANDRAU
A traveller's account of life in Mexico

Travels with Myself and Another
MARTHA GELLHORN
*Five journeys from hell by a great
war correspondent*

The Weather in Africa
MARTHA GELLHORN
*Three novellas set amongst the
white settlers of East Africa*

The Last Leopard
DAVID GILMOUR
*The biography of Giuseppe di Lampedusa,
author of* The Leopard

Walled Gardens
ANNABEL GOFF
An Anglo-Irish childhood

Africa Dances
GEOFFREY GORER
*The magic of indigenous culture
and the banality of colonisation*

Ask Sir James
MICHAELA REID
The life of Sir James Reid,
personal physician to Queen Victoria

A Funny Old Quist
EVAN ROGERS
A gamekeeper's passionate evocation
of a now-vanished English rural lifestyle

Meetings with Remarkable Muslims
ED. ROGERSON & BARING
A collection of contemporary travel
writing that celebrates cultural difference
and the Islamic world

Marrakesh: through writers' eyes
ED. ROGERSON & LAVINGTON
Guidebooks for the mind: a selection
of the best travel writing on Marrakesh

Turkish Aegean: through writers' eyes
ED. RUPERT SCOTT
Guidebooks for the mind: a selection
of the best travel writing on Turkey

Valse des Fleurs
SACHEVERELL SITWELL
A day in St Petersburg in 1868

Living Poor
MORITZ THOMSEN
An American's encounter with
poverty in Ecuador

Hermit of Peking
HUGH TREVOR-ROPER
The hidden life of the scholar
Sir Edmund Backhouse

The Law
ROGER VAILLAND
The harsh game of life played in
the taverns of southern Italy

Bangkok
ALEC WAUGH
The story of a city

The Road to Nab End
WILLIAM WOODRUFF
The best selling story of poverty and
survival in a Lancashire mill town

The Village in the Jungle
LEONARD WOOLF
A dark novel of native villagers struggling
to survive in colonial Ceylon

Death's Other Kingdom
GAMEL WOOLSEY
The tragic arrival of civil war in an
Andalucian village in 1936

The Ginger Tree
OSWALD WYND
A Scotswoman's love and survival
in early twentieth-century Japan

Poetry of Place series

London: Poetry of Place
ED. BARING & ROGERSON
A poetry collection like the city itself, full of
grief, irony and delight

Andalus: Poetry of Place
ED. TED GORTON
Moorish songs of love and wine

Venice: Poetry of Place
ED. HETTY MEYRIC HUGHES
Eavesdrop on the first remembered glimpses
of the city, and meditations on her history

Desert Air: Poetry of Place
ED. MUNRO & ROGERSON
On Arabia, deserts and the Orient of
the imagination

Istanbul: Poetry of Place
ED. ATES ORGA
Poetry from her long history, from paupers to
sultans, natives and visitors alike

The Ruins of Time
ED. ANTHONY THWAITE
Sized to fit any purse or pocket, this is just the
book to complement a picnic amongst the
ruins of time

SYRIANA
Travel & Tourism

Syria's leading tour operator for small groups.

With four decades of experience, Syriana offers a fast, professional service with creative and thoughtful itineraries and immaculate attention to detail.

SYRIANA TRAVEL & TOURISM
Ahmad Mareiwd 036 St.
Damascus – Syria
P.O. Box: 7814
Tel: ++963-11-3313612 / 3315381
Fax: ++963-11-3315430
E-mail: tours@syriana.com
Website: www.Syriana.com